I0385146

RICH, FREE, AND MISERABLE

Praise for *Rich, Free, and Miserable*

"John Brueggemann's sociology of everyday experience shows how the power of the market is stealing our neighborhoods, our families, our time, our lives. I was reading it on the plane from Fargo to Los Angeles, and it was so fascinating that my seat partner surreptitiously read it as I did. And then he started talking about how it makes sense of his own life. This is a great conversation-starter." —**Glen Harold Stassen**, Fuller Theological Seminary; author of *Kingdom Ethics: Following Jesus in Contemporary Context*

"A highly accessible account of what Brueggemann calls the Death Zone—the grim moral universe of an America where markets have overwhelmed government and civil society. A Durkheimian critique that, despite the unsparing assessment of the moral crisis, points to the hopeful possibility of American renewal." —**Charles Derber**, Boston College; author of *Greed to Green*

"The conversational and open-ended approach the author engages in is excellent. The biggest questions and conundrums of our day are tacked head-on. Grounded in important issues and questions, and up-to-date in current social science research, this book addresses the core questions of our time in a well-balanced, nonpartisan tone." —**Vincent Roscigno**, Ohio State University; author of *The Face of Discrimination*

RICH, FREE, AND MISERABLE

The Failure of Success in America

John Brueggemann

Rowman & Littlefield Publishers, Inc.
Lanham • Boulder • New York • Toronto • Plymouth, UK

Published by Rowman & Littlefield Publishers, Inc.
A wholly owned subsidiary of The Rowman & Littlefield Publishing Group, Inc.
4501 Forbes Boulevard, Suite 200, Lanham, Maryland 20706
http://www.rowmanlittlefield.com

Estover Road, Plymouth PL6 7PY, United Kingdom

Copyright © 2010 by Rowman & Littlefield Publishers, Inc.

All rights reserved. No part of this book may be reproduced in any form or by any electronic or mechanical means, including information storage and retrieval systems, without written permission from the publisher, except by a reviewer who may quote passages in a review.

British Library Cataloguing in Publication Information Available

Library of Congress Cataloging-in-Publication Data

Brueggemann, John, 1965–
  Rich, free, and miserable : the failure of success in America / John Brueggemann.
    p. cm.
  Includes bibliographical references and index.
  ISBN 978-1-4422-0093-7 (cloth : alk. paper)—ISBN 978-1-4422-0095-1 (electronic)
  1. United States—Moral conditions. 2. United States—Social conditions—21st century. 3. United States—Economic conditions—21st century. 4. United States—Civilization—21st century. I. Title.
  HN90.M6B783 2010
  306.0973'09051—dc22   2010011252

∞™ The paper used in this publication meets the minimum requirements of American National Standard for Information Sciences—Permanence of Paper for Printed Library Materials, ANSI/NISO Z39.48-1992.

Printed in the United States of America

For Peter, Anabelle,
Emilia, and Christina

CONTENTS

ACKNOWLEDGMENTS

This work would not have been possible without the assistance and encouragement of many generous people. It is my pleasure to thank them here. Sarah Stanton of Rowman and Littlefield saw promise in this project and helped make it happen.

Colleagues and administrators at Skidmore College have cultivated a vibrant intellectual environment in which scholarly research is fostered and acknowledged. For me, this has been manifest in a Skidmore College Faculty Development Grant and an Andrew W. Mellon Foundation Grant to Support Faculty Research. I am especially appreciative of the support of Beau Breslin, Phillip Glotzbach, Chuck Joseph, and Susan Kress. I also want to thank the Quadracci family for endowing the Quadracci Chair in Social Responsibility.

Linda Santagato provided endless clerical support with energy, competence, and good will, which is much appreciated. I have very much enjoyed working with Peter Brownell, Tiana Olewnik, and Sarah Rosenblatt, each of whom provided valuable research assistance, substantive input, and inspiration. I owe all of them thanks.

I have benefited from years of mentoring from and collegial discourse with numerous faculty at Skidmore. I owe a debt of gratitude to members of the departments of sociology, anthropology, and social work in general. For substantive input and encouragement related to this project in particular I want to thank Caroline D'Abate, Sue Bender, Kate Berheide, Pat Fehling, Bill Fox, David Karp, Mary Lynn, Mehmet Odekon, Rik Scarce, Linda Simon, Denise Smith, Sheldon Solomon, Susan Walzer, Joanna Zangrando, and Jon Zibell.

Three friends at Skidmore read the manuscript several times and worked through the ideas in my argument over and over. Special thanks to Jennifer Delton, Dan Nathan, and Pat Oles.

I am fortunate to have received suggestions from a number of other scholars and friends, who guided me to relevant readings, examples, and ideas. They include Robert Bellah, Cliff Brown, Charles Derber, Richard DuBose, Arlie Hochschild, Howard Kimeldorf, Andrew Lindner, Michael McQuarrie, Douglas Meyer, Joya Misra, Vincent Roscigno, Rick Rosenfeld, Barry Schwartz, Anne Stassen, Glen Stassen, Alan Wolfe, and Jon Woodring.

Several family members, including Lorraine McHugh, Belle Miller McMaster, and Patrick D. Miller Jr., listened patiently and responded thoughtfully as I shared ideas about this project. The same is true of the most important teachers in my life, my parents, Mary Miller Brueggemann and Walter Brueggemann. Beyond giving me life, they have shaped this project in countless direct and indirect ways, for which I am indescribably thankful.

Throughout this project, I have maintained the conviction that ideas matter and the hope that our work in the academy will have relevance to people outside of it. This moral commitment has become an urgent passion as the lives of my children—Emilia, Anabelle, and Peter—unfold before me. For their inspiration and for their presence I feel enormous gratitude.

Finally, I want to recognize the persistent contributions and support of my truest collaborator and best friend. Thank you, Christina.

1

INTRODUCTION

Americans rush to work, gliding past stop signs, talking and texting on the phone, incrementally compromising public safety because our busy schedules feel more important. Once we get there, we stay, longer and longer, while simultaneously regretting the neglect of our loved ones. As a result, many of us have no network of social support, a trend that has worsened significantly over the last two decades. And despite this commitment to hard work and all the resources it yields—the highest gross domestic product (GDP) in the world—most Americans report not being able to afford what they need. Widespread dietary choices now known and recognized to be unhealthy contribute to substantial physiological ailments. And our consumption patterns create many other problems. The central claim of this book is that this mess is the result of a moral crisis brought about by market culture. The logic of the market—that everything is for sale and we should strive to get as much as we can—has pushed beyond the economic sphere into other parts of our lives. The most important consequence is a deteriorating capacity for meaningful relationships.

THE DEATH ZONE

On May 15, 2006, on the slopes of Mount Everest, some forty people noticed a mountaineer named David Sharp was in serious trouble and walked right past him before he died. When you climb Mount Everest, according to Sharp's mother, "Your only responsibility is to save yourself—not to try to save anyone else."[1] About one out of ten people who have ever tried to climb Everest have died along the way and most of their corpses are still there. For those few who make it to the top, the payoff is unimaginably rewarding. In pursuing that goal, people act in ways they would never behave elsewhere. Attempting the summit entails putting your own life, limbs, and ethical standards at risk.[2] The entire 30,000-foot mountain is unforgiving, but the most perilous part is the spare terrain above 26,250 feet, the "Death Zone," where human (and most other) life is unsustainable. The air is thin, the soil is infertile, and the weather is incredibly volatile. If you try to climb a few more hundred feet when it is time to turn around, or stop to help someone, the danger to your own life could be greatly exacerbated.

There is nothing like Mount Everest. Singularly demanding and dangerous, it is literally the defining pinnacle of human achievement. But symbolically Mount Everest has many analogues in social life. Why do it? To prove that I can! The possible triumph of standing at the top calls to us relentlessly. The risk, the thrill, the deeply personal achievement, as well as the bond shared with few others who have endeavored and succeeded in the same way are all interconnected. Pushing past the boundary and exploring your own limits are social norms deeply enmeshed in modern society. More broadly, this "Everest psychology" of voluntarily taking on chancy, expensive challenges that have no tangible, socially valuable payoff is prevalent throughout our society. Perhaps it is the removal of firm social constraints and the irony of progress in modern life, but the need to be the best or find a new frontier is manifest in countless ways every day. Most glaringly, we encounter this mind-set in big-time sports, Hollywood film, popular music, and wherever else celebrity is recognized. It is also alive in information technology, fashion design, financial trading, and many other industries. For people in each context their ambition, effort, and daring yield big returns—if they win.

Several aspects of the Death Zone make it a useful metaphor for various other settings in modern society. I am talking about unforgiving conditions in which sacrificing one's own interests for another is extremely costly, and split-second decisions have vital consequences. To reach our goals in such circumstances, we must be utterly committed, disciplined, and focused. To get "there," we need to block out distractions along the way, even worthy ones like taking care of someone in need. Such a thin line separates winners from losers that we dare not gamble being on the wrong side by attending to anything but the highest priorities. We cannot afford to indulge the golden rule.

The market is such a place. For many, the risk and allure inspire total devotion. And for anyone who wants to be in the game tomorrow there is no space for altruism. Insofar as the values of the market are built into other parts of our lives, we may be captive to the Everest psychology. There are of course millions of ways kindness and generosity are expressed every day to our family members, neighbors, and people we do not know at all. But the market culture of our society is becoming a Death Zone within which our old commitments are eroding and human decency is thinning.

The frenzied pursuit of the next big achievement blinds us to this shift. We see the "Everest psychology" manifest in our daily attempts to not just keep up with but beat out the Joneses. If I can just get in to the right school, find the right mate, land the right job, buy the right house. The elusive summit is always within sight but just out of reach. I may recognize the man in distress sitting along the path as I walk by, throw my garbage on the ground, or know the hour is too late and I should turn around and return to a safe altitude. That is, I may keep long hours at work with some awareness that I do not need the money or other rewards and my family does need me. I may grasp that my burning ambition and narrow focus are costing me friends, health, balance, and perspective. In the mythology of the market, nevertheless, I must proceed to the peak. Higher. Better. More. The compulsion to stay on the mountain—both literally and figuratively—can overwhelm good judgment. For instance, it was just this kind of risky behavior that helped bring about the recent economic recession, as Richard Posner notes. "Even if you know you're riding a bubble and are scared to be doing so, it is difficult to climb off without paying a big price."[3]

In some sense, the most important expression of "Everest psychology" is not in the behavior of extraordinary overachievers at the top of their field—because they are so few—but in the daily choices of ordinary people—because they are so many. Neither their decisions nor the consequences are so dramatic as the dangers of mountain climbing, but failure in their efforts to produce, achieve, and accomplish is to be avoided at all costs. I am thinking along the lines of the obsessed professional so engrossed in her work she cedes her role as mother to the nanny; the father always too frantic with his children's schedules to spend time with a lonely aunt; the neighbors so busy working to pay off debt accrued through extravagant indulgences they do not have time for a visit to the hospital after someone they know is in a car accident; the family whose primary activities revolve around shopping; the executive who compromises every important relationship in his life due to complete devotion to his ambitious career goals; or the public servant who surrenders his integrity by way of lucrative graft.

In addition to all the costs of such endeavors, the real price is in fact inevitable failure because, unlike the real Everest, there is no peak. We never arrive at a place of completion and joy. As Gertrude Stein lamented in not finding her childhood home, "there is no there there." While we have much to be grateful for, the goals of market logic are in some fundamental way elusive. The market teaches us there is never enough. If that is where we seek comfort and security, sooner or later we are painfully enlightened. Ambitious careers always come with risk. Material comforts can only satisfy some needs. And the modern self is greatly overburdened and consequently fragile. For the vast majority of us, we simply cannot survive the Death Zone intact. This book is about the sociological forces that promote this sort of Everest psychology and compel us to enter the Death Zone of market culture.

CONFUSION AT THE TOP

The great irony of this psychology is that we have, in a different, broader sense, already reached the summit and do not even realize it. For middle- and upper-class Americans, this should be the best time and place to be alive in human history. Having developed a remarkable level of security, comfort, and ease, we have the extraordinary luxury of thinking beyond here and now. With all the lessons of what has transpired before us, we have at our fingertips more cumulative knowledge than previous generations ever dreamed possible. And the recent history in American society is one of amazing progress.

The standard of living in the United States is the envy of the world—even, or perhaps especially, in the midst of an economic crisis, at least comparatively speaking. Lifespan has been extended substantially. Crime rates are down. Our ability to understand and influence natural forces through the marvels of science exceeds what most people expected even a few decades ago. The means of sharing information in particular are wondrous. We nurture a rich and noble heritage of government "by the people" in a political system that has won over most of the world as the best available. We give more support and charity to other peoples than any other country. While frightening to contemplate, even the new threats of international violence have not penetrated the daily lives of most Americans in any demonstrable way. All in all, a very promising picture.

And yet, something is not right. Uncomfortable questions persist. Is this all? Is this the society, the life, so many have labored, fought and died for? The American Dream is in trouble. Maybe it always has been. But at a time when so many things have been going well, the basic premise of imminent improvement in our lives and those of our children seems to be in question. The level of frustration, anxiety, and fear so common among our people feels more substantive than the usual questions challenging each generation. With the promise of all these assets in our favor, how did this happen?

The main answer is not economic recession—as devastating as that is to so many Americans—but rather a moral crisis. Some of it is small stuff, like increasing rudeness, too much television, or not enough healthy food. Some of it is grave like the abuse of children, the decline in community, and corruption in government. Much of popular culture—from Hollywood, TV, pop music, or big-time sports—is so vulgar, cynical, or just inane that any notion that it would contribute to our collective well-being is simply passé. Headlines are taken up by the likes of Jeffrey Skilling, Jack Abramoff, Duke Cunningham, and Bernie Madoff. We see appalling images of the New Orleans Superdome and shoppers on "Black Friday" after Thanksgiving, and hear scandalous courtroom proceedings involving entertainers, professional athletes, or other famous people. But these big stories obscure the more mundane symptoms of this crisis that affect and implicate ordinary people in direct and immediate ways. And the main problems are not simply a matter of a bad economy or a bad presidency.

To acknowledge that many of us are repeatedly making bad choices is to recognize a breakdown of morality. To understand such choices, though, requires the fundamental insight of sociology, that each individual's biography must be understood in the context of society's history. People make decisions in the context of certain perceived choices, which are determined by broader forces, and in so doing participate in those forces. In pondering how such forces will shape the biographies of my three young children, Emilia, Anabelle, and Peter, the intellectual topic of a sociologist becomes the urgent concern of a parent. What hopes will they nurture? What challenges will they face? What dreams will they realize? With such questions constantly on my mind, I have become preoccupied with the moral disorder of our time and found the dominant discourse among commentators associated with the Left and the Right to be largely unhelpful.

Few Americans think of themselves as immoral or bad, but many are stuck making unappealing decisions among choices they regard as problematic, with real costs to themselves and others. And many more feel intense pressure in managing their lives, which include some burdens that are largely distinctive to this time and place. Overworked parents, overscheduled kids, unhealthy personal choices, fears of the dangers in public spaces, and weakening commitment to community are all interconnected pieces in this story. For individuals the effects include anxiety, exhaustion, anger, depression, obesity, addiction, debt, rudeness, and violence, each of which has obtained startling levels of incidence.

From a broader perspective, confidence in core institutions is thinning. Moral authority has waned in government and religion. The social functions historically served by key institutions such as the media, organized labor, and academia are increasingly viewed with skepticism. Each of the issues in this litany is in fact complex and may be framed in terms other than morality. Indeed, moral choices are always shaped by forces that are not moral, whether psychological, economic, political, or technological, for instance.

The reason our current crisis can be characterized as moral, though, is that it involves consequential choices made by many people, including powerful leaders of major institutions as well as countless individuals of no special standing. Just as such choices have led to this situation, different choices could lead to its amelioration. In other words, the trouble we are facing does not require the resolution of unanswered questions like the cure for cancer or the confrontation of some maniacal tyrant. Rather, this set of problems can be resolved through reprioritizing principles and reorganizing current resources, through different choices.

Such reconfiguration, however, would require profound unsettling of how we live and committed engagement with the possibilities for serving the greater good. At the moment, not enough people are setting aside short-term self-interest for our common life. Through laziness, narcissism, and willful ignorance, some of us are failing to make the hard choices that serve the long-term well-being of others and, to a large extent, our own selves. For many of us with the best intentions, the confusing cultural circumstances in which we live make us uncertain of what the right choices are. The loss of moral grammar has rendered us incoherent in attempting to script our lives with some meaningful order.

Morality is a notoriously difficult concept to pin down. That said, the ongoing struggle to clarify moral guideposts is healthy for society, and healthy society is good for individuals. This basic premise has been clear to sociologists since Émile Durkheim illuminated the topic more than a century ago.[4] In recent decades, however, we have become distinctly unintelligible in articulating such lessons. As indeterminate as it often is, moral reasoning is a vital, useful endeavor that could and should be productively renewed in public discourse.

More of us should wrestle with the question of what our society—our family and neighborhood as well as our coworkers and fellow citizens in general—needs from us. What standards of decency, integrity, and accountability must I observe and protect? Durkheim showed that the payoff for thinking in terms of sacrifice, compromise, generosity, and social solidarity in general, at least in modern society, is a much more psychologically vibrant setting for individuals. In effect, the healthier my community is, the healthier I will be.[5]

The focus of this inquiry is on those Americans who have been able to take advantage of the unique strengths of our society, the "middle class," or more accurately, middle classes. Those who know real poverty are entangled with some of these issues but also face other challenges. The rich have a different story as well. Most among the truly rich have inherited the bulk of their wealth. They too are connected to these problems, but their motivations and pressures are also distinctive.

I am especially interested in those who have purportedly been able to succeed themselves, what might be thought of as the roughly three-quarters of the population who are winners of the American Dream.[6] Their fate is tied to the particular opportunities and burdens distinctive to our society. They comprise the vast majority of the electorate and in some meaningful way define the core of the American experience. Within this group is a diverse set of people with vastly varying experiences and backgrounds. While the sources and implications of this moral failure are numerous and complex, though, there are broad effects comprehensive enough to affect most Americans. Some individuals or categories may contribute disproportionately to the problems and some may suffer inordinately, but the big picture is one that few can escape fully.[7]

Some might think that the problems of affluent people who work unnecessarily hard and consume too much reflect a previous era before the recent economic crisis, or a narrow segment of our population, that is, the truly rich. Certainly, part of the goal here is to understand and report on the experience of middle-class Americans during the last few decades. However, this is not just a matter of chronicling history.

First of all, our economy will in all likelihood stabilize eventually and much in American life will return to the way it was before the recession began. Second, the problems underlying our current moral crisis are largely still in place. It appears that most Americans have not abruptly altered their consumption or work habits in any profound way. The economic crisis guarantees that we will seriously rethink some things, but how intensive that reflection is and how substantive our response is remains to be seen.

THE ARGUMENT

In this book, I seek to bear witness to this mess—an important project in its own right since, as with all cultural problems, this moral crisis is sort of hidden in plain view. We breathe in and contribute to this atmosphere without even knowing it. The key to addressing this problem is to see it clearly and understand how it developed in the first place.

There once was in our republic a balance of institutional forces consisting of the state, the market, and civil society.[8] At first, the market and civil society acted in concert to contain the exertion of government authority. Over time, the market's influence grew, shaping government to serve its interests and nudging civil society to the side. The key development was the relative weakening of noneconomic social institutions, which accelerated decisively in the second half of the twentieth century.

Three forces converged in the 1960s to decisively destabilize this balance, enhance the market's leverage and weaken that of civil society, which has led to the moral collapse unfolding now. The most fundamental factor was the logic of the market itself, which is inherently expansive. Through its many agents—policymakers, boards of directors, executive managers, stockholders, advertisers—the market always seeks to spread its influence. Whether it is the experience of outdoor adventurers, the adoption of babies, or emotional nurturing, the market fosters the buying and selling of all kinds of things once considered genuinely priceless. In some sense, all of us who participate in production and consumption are involved in such agency and therefore in such expansion.

The second factor was the gap between our nation's stated ideals of equality and democracy and the reality of injustice and exclusion, which has been a contradiction since the founding of this country. This inconsistency became more conspicuous after World War II, and led to heightened tension during the rigid assertion of authority during the 1950s and the unrest that followed.

The third factor, which was activated to some extent by that tension, was the diminished credibility of authority produced by the turmoil of the sixties. The protest movements confronted normative expectations of "success" and even at times the idea of anyone being in charge. The notion of institutional moral authority would thereafter remain a problematic, precarious ideal, more often interrogated than not and never taken for granted again.

The influence of countervailing institutions in government and civil society has since deteriorated. This is true of a large range of organizations, voluntary associations, and small groups. The most serious effects related to the spread of market logic, though, involve just a few major institutions, including religion, organized labor, media, education, and government, each of which has a special character that has at times enabled it to serve this valuable counterbalancing function relative to the capitalist economy. During different periods, each compelled people to think about and commit to other values beyond narrow self-interest. These institutions cultivated moral habits among a wide range of people that provided balance and leverage in economic life. Because of the three factors that converged during the 1960s, as described above, and due to particular circumstances in each case, these countervailing institutions all lost their ability to contain market logic.

In serving as the *moral hardware* of our society, such institutions provided settings in which moral authority is publicly and credibly committed to the common good. In so doing, these institutions conveyed to people *moral software*, the values, sensibilities and support necessary for making wise, judicious decisions. As they deteriorated, little was left to inhibit the intrusion of market logic, the gist of which is that everything is for sale, that we must always strive to produce and consume more.

This transformation of our values has led to the crumbling of moral order. They are no longer American values, at least in the original sense, nor simply a matter of market logic, since they have not emerged in the same way in other market societies. We might think of these themes in terms of *American market culture* that is derived from American history, market logic, and refracted through the events of the last several decades.

The ambiguous character of this new culture reflects the complexity of social life in the modern world. Somehow nebulous and fluid but also potent and unrelenting, it seeps in to every space of our lives, contaminating all. Like water when it is contained and kept at the right level, market logic is extremely useful, even life-giving. As it leaks in to other places in sufficient amounts, though, market logic begins to corrode other aspects of society. The American Dream now strains under the weight of its own success as the market economy has become the market society. It is life in the market society with its hyper-individualism and obsession with money that is, in some ways, analogous to the Death Zone.

For some, entry into this Death Zone is intentional and active. The competition and potential returns hold great allure. For many others, life in the Death Zone is involuntary—either a matter of necessity or misunderstanding. That is, we work frantically because we feel that we must or we consume stupidly because we know no other way.

OVERVIEW

Firsthand observation, journalism, and especially social scientific research provide the main evidence for this argument.[9] I begin, in the next chapter, by reviewing key concepts in the debate about such matters, such as it is. There is a moral crisis embedded in our society, maintained through key social institutions and cultural values. While many on the Left and on the Right would agree with this statement, there is a striking lack of insight about this problem from either side. Although it is clear that there is much more that unites Americans than divides us, there do seem to be polarized ideological camps, each of which controls a swath of rhetorical ground and each of which is reluctant to seriously consider or borrow from the arguments of the other side. In chapter 2, I suggest that serious people from across the ideological spectrum can and should engage in productive discourse about how cultural values and social institutions both contribute to the moral crisis of our era.

The central values that have defined what it means to be American are as old as the country, or at least the terms have been with us that long. But their meaning has evolved in fundamental ways that are quite distinct from their original sense. In chapter 3, I trace the historical development of such values and the institutions that keep them alive. In particular, progress, freedom, prosperity, productivity, equality, and authority emerge as key concepts whose meanings have evolved in consequential ways that shape our current culture.

While this kind of incremental change has been significant, there were particular events and institutions that were especially important to the market culture that developed during the second half of the twentieth century. Drawing from the historical review of the previous chapter, I emphasize in chapter 4 the importance of these specific factors. How the expansion of market logic combined with the decline of civic life in general, and central countervailing institutions in particular, is the main story. Chapter 4 highlights how this shift began to unfold after World War II and came to fruition in the 1980s.

Since then, we have seen how market logic undermines morality in numerous institutions. Three particular areas of behavior in moral disarray bespeak a grave situation. While there are certainly some positive trends, each of these categories, what I respectively designate as economic life, civic life, and family life in chapters 5, 6, and 7, include a number of specific kinds of problematic behavior. And underneath the "moral malnutrition" in each case, we find seeping, unbounded market logic eroding the foundations of our society.[10] As Americans spend the bulk of their time and develop their most important relationships in these three kinds of settings, we can see how far-reaching this crisis is likely to be.

The growing pressures Americans feel to work, compete, and consume have become a kind of Death Zone, which is undermining our engagement in meaningful relationships. The only way this crisis can be resolved—and with it all the attendant problems of narcissism, corruption, greed, and waste—is to reconceive and rebuild the civil institutions that hold communities together. As grim as this picture is—and the reality is much more ominous than most people realize—there are hopeful signs. Even amid the power of expanding market logic, the human resources of anger and hope among ordinary people suggest such heartening possibilities are viable. Chapter 8 provides a brief summary of the argument and some preliminary thoughts about how such resources might be channeled into transformative ways to reorder our lives.

MISSING THE FOREST AND MOST OF THE TREES: WHAT'S USEFUL AND WHAT'S NOT IN CURRENT CONVERSATIONS

Crisis is a strong word. Or at least it used to be. Somewhere along the way, the breaking news of catastrophe, the e-mail warnings of imminent peril, the familiar mantra of emergency shouted by doomsayers, have all run together to form the background noise of our time. Disinterest, disbelief, or "tragedy fatigue" provoke many to cover their ears. With the way it smacks of arrogance and self-righteousness, invoking failed morality in particular is risky business. "Every generation," Alan Wolfe contends, "finds the morality of previous generations better than its own."[1] Robert Bork cautions, "one must not discount the great reservoir of self-interest that underlay much of the rhetoric of morality."[2] Obviously, great acts of idiocy and cruelty have been perpetrated throughout history in the name of morality.

Nevertheless, as flawed as many efforts to defend moral order are, there are real and powerful threats to our way of life that can rightly be thought of as moral. Our common life requires that individuals comply to a certain extent with standards of conduct not captured in law or utilitarian incentives. Society has needs.[3] We can neither surrender the notion that important ideals must be protected to serve the greater good nor ignore the fact that those principles are at times betrayed. And, of course, great acts of wisdom and compassion have also been carried out in the name of morality.

With these premises in mind, many of the conservative claims lamenting moral decline make perfect sense; Americans are behaving badly in ways that are destructive to themselves and others. It is quite possible, though, to view with compassion and empathy those persons suffering most from these problems, as some on the Left suggest, including those people making immoral choices themselves. Despite widespread commentary to the contrary, Americans of different political persuasions agree on the values of our society much more than they disagree.[4] Even around issues of serious dispute, such as abortion and gay rights, we have a great deal of (unpublicized) common ground. Most of us are very concerned about the same problems.

BRINGING MORALITY BACK IN

"Act only on that maxim whereby thou canst at the same time will that it should become a universal law."[5] Immanuel Kant's categorical imperative is a helpful starting point for understanding western morality. The notion that each of us should behave in a way that would not be harmful if everyone acted that way makes eminent sense and has proved an enduring principle. Thinking this rule a bit too rigid, though, John Stuart Mill proposed we should act in a way that produces the greatest happiness for all people.[6] The ideal moral order would be a setting where all are happy. Pursuing such a goal must necessarily involve a deep, abiding preoccupation with what is best for the common good, recognizing that the elusive ideal involves a delicate balance of collective and individual interests.[7]

In practice, of course, figuring out what is best for the greatest number of people is difficult. Any working definition of morality is functionally imperfect.[8] Émile Durkheim describes the moral framework of society as the "collective conscience."[9] It is comprised of shared cultural meanings and moral rules that most people accept as guideposts for ordering their behavior. The collective conscience is created by individuals, each of whom has a degree of influence over what is considered normal and right. By overtly affirming or simply living in accordance with the established moral rules, each individual contributes to the collective conscience. A person expresses, often implicitly, that, "this is the way things are done." Likewise, when enough individuals depart from such norms, even without much overt protest, they bring into question the legitimacy of the framework, which is one of the ways collective conscience changes.

On the other hand, the collective conscience also has profound influence on the individual. That is, individual conscience develops in the context of social groups. Our sense of what is right and wrong is shaped by what others communicate to us. As people around us declare, explicitly or implicitly, "this is the way things are," each individual comes to believe and ultimately internalize that understanding of the world.[10] This is true even in a culture like ours that celebrates "individuality" through specific gestures and symbols of independence. Thus we see everywhere huge cars, racy T-shirts, tattoos, trendy haircuts and other iconic expressions of rebelliousness even in the most milquetoast settings—that is, a patterned, predictable expression of "individuality."

In contrast to behavior driven by the threat of force or utilitarian gain, the moral sphere is based on normative, emotional, and symbolic incentives. It is comprised of the choices we make that are in some essential way voluntary. That is not to say that such incentives are trivial. Quite the contrary is true. Think of the power of guilt and humiliation or pride and respect. But it does mean that (unlike most of the behavior of, say, prisoners or slaves), our moral choices—whether they are sound or not—always implicate our own will.

In short, the "moral voice of the community" affects the "inner moral voice" of individuals, and vice versa.[11] Individuals are moral when their behavior reflects an expansive commitment to certain convictions they believe are valuable for their group, which they believe others should also follow. Society is moral when it protects the autonomy of individuals. Being moral thus means paying attention to those voices and encouraging others to do so as well. It involves grappling with the questions of what those voices are saying and who is in one's group. Interpreting moral principles, simply put, is an ongoing challenge and the boundaries of one's community or society are a moving target.

This sense of morality is neither universalistic nor absolute. But the wisest choices tend to consider the interests of the largest number of people possible over the long run. Needless to say, of course, some people do not share this understanding of morality. However, just because mainstream American values may be contradicted by those of the Taliban, to take one example, surely does not mean we should not try to articulate our defining morals. Furthermore, the same is true even, perhaps especially, when we are wrestling with moral shades of gray. While the practical challenge of such considerations is very difficult, the age of precarious environmental sustainability, global markets, and weapons of mass destruction offers no other choice. The stakes are simply too high for moral indifference to society's needs.

Our society has accomplished extraordinary feats in offering its members unprecedented wealth and freedom. Yet the collective conscience has deteriorated in its ability to shape the choices of individuals to the greater good.[12] The main result is consuming self-absorption and a related obsession with money. Contradicting Kant's and Mill's wisdom, many of our choices are completely unsustainable for the social collective. Under such favorable circumstances, that we are so far from realizing such ideals raises an obvious question: Why?

THE IRONIC NEGLECT OF MORALITY
IN SOCIAL SCIENCE

A wide range of social scientific studies critique various problems in contemporary society. In examining politics, education, family, religion, medicine, media, art, sports, popular culture, recreation, work, and consumption, such analyses have yielded numerous insights about how and why we live the way we do. They illuminate the strains and challenges in our lives and propose various solutions. All of this reflects great success in contemporary social analysis. We know a lot.

Despite the generally critical approach of most social research—the recognition that various arrangements in society are problematic and unnecessary—the issues are usually not couched in terms of morality.[13] Although most social scientists believe in personal responsibility and accountability—I have met very few who do not—they write little about it.[14]

The main emphases for progressives as well as sociologists—the latter being mostly a subset of the former—have been on material and structural arrangements in society.[15] There is scant indication in mainstream social research that we are facing a moral crisis that implicates not only institutions but also individuals, an unexpected trend in the discipline that historically has had the most to say about civic life.

In addition, the respect for how morality varies across cultures—which any thinking person has to grasp to some extent—sometimes leads to "moral colorblindness" in general.[16] Indeed, such complexity motivates many social scientists to never seriously think about the concept of morality. One problem here, as I have repeatedly argued with numerous colleagues reluctant to use the term at all, is that once we stop talking about morality, it is difficult to find a lexicon for describing what society needs from its members. That is, we stop speaking in ambitious ways about our common life.

A starting place for understanding our moral crisis is first establishing that there is one. And, as we will see, there is plenty of blame to go around. This situation is caused by numerous institutional failures, problematic cultural norms, as well as countless poor choices on the part of individuals. Moreover, one cannot really talk about patterns of individual choices and the operation of institutions in ways that are separate from one another. They are almost always necessarily entangled. Individuals make choices in the context of institutional pressures and incentives. History does not just happen; it is carried out by people.

THE PROBLEM OF VALUES

In the commentary that does recognize trouble, the explanations most prominent in public discourse today emphasize cultural values, clearly an important part of this story. Though preceded by a rich tradition of social criticism sometimes called "conservative," contemporary appraisals of cultural values suffer from several common shortcomings.[17]

The first is that the terms "values" and especially "culture" are used so indiscriminately as to provide little in the way of robust explanation. A good example of this problem can be found in the bestseller *Slouching*

Towards Gomorrah by Robert Bork. "'Culture,' as used here, refers to all human behavior and institutions, including popular entertainment, art, religion, education, scholarship, economic activity, science, technology, law, and morality."[18] The concept of culture is complex and has been defined in numerous ways by social scientists. But this all-inclusive sense of the term makes its use in *explaining* any particular thing difficult. In general, the many uses of the term *culture* necessitate clarifying its specific meaning in any particular application.

A related issue is the emphasis on "values" in accounting for the lousy choices people make. A deadbeat dad neglects his children because he lacks family values. A promiscuous young woman secretly sleeps around with countless partners because she never learned proper values. In one sense, the problem here is that these indictments sort of state the obvious. Of course someone who behaves badly is expressing some kind of poor judgment. More importantly, though, this kind of reasoning does not really account for where the values came from. The same is true with the cultural argument. The values, norms, beliefs, and symbols of a given social context, one of the common definitions of culture among social scientists, come from somewhere. That is, if we use cultural values to explain some kind of behavior, the question still remains, why? Why does this culture function this way? How did this culture develop this way?

Linking values to behavior is therefore the *first* step in a historical investigation. Inevitably, such inquiry leads to other kinds of factors, what social scientists call social structure, for example. In contrast to culture, this may include social organizations such as the family, schools, the legal system, or polity.[19] The strong links between culture and structure motivate many to treat them as one force.[20] Francis Fukuyama explains in his book, "I will not make use of this distinction between culture and social structure because it is often difficult to distinguish between the two; values and ideas shape concrete social relationships, and vice versa."[21] Fair enough. Despite this recognition of the linkages between culture and structure, though, the rhetorical emphasis often then shifts to just the component of values in culture, as in both Bork's and Fukuyama's work.[22]

I share the concern that many critics have regarding the importance of social virtue and its decline in our society. I also think cultural values are a useful starting place for understanding such matters. To fully explain this problem, though, we must necessarily grasp the historical development of particular social structures, including economic and political institutions, which have contributed to the rise and transformation of specific cultural values.

The other big problem with the dominant explanations that rely on cultural values is that they emphasize the wrong values. A common foil is the corrupt liberalism brought about by the 1960s, especially the sense of egalitarianism that developed at that time.[23] Certainly there were many important consequences of what transpired during that decade. But the protest movements and counterculture of the sixties did not emerge in a vacuum. And, contrary to various claims, they were the result of something more than a narcissistic generation spoiled by parents and agitated by rock and roll. The focus on radical egalitarianism is sometimes overstated. There are too many other societies with stronger traditions of social equality who have the same or less dramatic problems as the United States in terms of moral order.[24]

Moreover, despite the substantial rhetoric about equality and opportunity in this country, the bulk of resources are distributed in tremendously and increasingly unequal ways.[25] There is significantly more mobility in American society compared to many other industrialized societies, but there is also more extreme inequality, which partly motivates the ongoing advocacy of egalitarianism as an ideal. Identifying this ideology as the main cause of moral decline in this context, therefore, does not make much sense.

SHE STARTED IT! HOW FEMINISM WRECKED SOCIETY

Another element of modern liberalism fingered as a culprit behind moral decline is feminism.[26] The women's movement did facilitate broadening opportunities for women outside the home and engender more varied and ambitious sensibilities among women in terms of fulfillment and self-realization. Leaders like Betty Friedan, Gloria Steinem, and Hillary Clinton have at times belittled women who work (only) in the home. And just as there have been thoughtful, courageous activists seeking fairness and empowerment, there have surely also been narrow-minded, dogmatic ideologues willing to say and do anything. "Unspoken Traditional Family Values: Abuse, Alcoholism, Incest." "Don't Cook Dinner Tonight; Starve a Rat Today." Polemical messages found in slogans or bumper stickers, like these, reflect such extremism.[27] Partly as a result of such intemperance, two-thirds of women now refuse to identify themselves as feminists.[28]

Some may say feminists are simply narcissistic and unconcerned about the collective good of society; what we need is to restore the conventional nuclear family that thrived during the fifties.[29] Both these arguments ignore some basic facts. The idealized family of the 1950s never really existed. There was clear structure in the roles of bread-winning fathers and homemaking mothers, which three-fifths of all families had in 1950.[30] Children "knew their place." But underneath this visible facade was a more complex reality of intensely repressed individuality. The actual experience in many families of the fifties, especially among women, was painful and unjust.[31]

Zealots like Pat Robertson have used broad strokes redolent of Joseph McCarthy to attack any activity contrasting the idealized family of the fifties. "The feminist agenda is not about equal rights for women. It is a socialist, anti-family political movement that encourages women to leave their husbands, kill their children, practice witchcraft, destroy capitalism and become lesbians."[32]

Certainly some thoughtful feminists are socialistic, alienated by traditional family norms, critical of capitalism, and willing to abandon repressive relationships. As any serious historical account shows, however, there are good reasons why the women's liberation movement occurred in the first place, issues that implicated power relationships in advanced capitalism and the patriarchal family. It was and is at its core a fight for freedom and equality.

The change has been unsettling and not without costs, especially in the family, more so than many on the Left have been willing to acknowledge. Nevertheless, the conditions against which the women's movement fought were untenable. Violence against women, unequal economic opportunities and political representation, and repressive social norms were justly confronted.[33] And to the extent that such injustice persists, the battle rightly continues.

Despite the widespread aversion to feminist labels and rhetoric, a 1989 *New York Times* survey revealed that two-thirds of women and a majority of men agreed that "the United States continues to need a strong women's movement to push for changes that benefit women."[34] A recent CBS poll indicates that two-thirds of women believe the women's movement has made their lives better.[35]

Linking claims that are accurate (e.g., attributing critiques of family norms and of capitalism) to some that are outlandish but terrifying (e.g., accusations of intentions to murder children), as in the case of this denunciation of feminism, was exactly how McCarthy was able to do so much damage. However, the main problem with this kind of assault, which has somehow become a normal part of mainstream political discourse now, is that it neglects the underlying forces that gave rise to and persist in motivating the women's movement.

THE HOMOSEXUAL ASSAULT ON FAMILY

"Moms and dads, are you listening? This movement is THE greatest threat to your children," James Dobson warns.[36] Another moral scapegoat for society's problems revolves around gays and lesbians, and especially the goal of legalized same-sex marriage. Gays and lesbians are often lumped together with feminists as the offenders responsible for everything from moral decay to God's wrath. Two days after September 11, Jerry Falwell exclaimed, "God continues to lift the curtain and allow the enemies of America to give us probably what we deserve." Why? "I really believe that the pagans, and the abortionists, and the feminists, and the gays and the lesbians who are actively trying to make that an alternative lifestyle, the A.C.L.U., People for the American Way—all of them who have tried to secularize America—I point the finger in their face and say, 'You helped this happen.'"[37]

More recently, John Hagee declared that, "All hurricanes are acts of God, because God controls the heavens. I believe that New Orleans had a level of sin that was offensive to God, and they were recipients of the judgment of God for that . . . there was to be a homosexual parade there on the Monday that the Katrina came. And the promise of that parade was that it would was going to reach a level of sexuality never demon-strated before in any of the other gay pride parades."[38]

Such preposterous claims could be dismissed if they were not spoken by influential people who command the attention of tens of millions of conservative Christians as well as important and mainstream conserva-tive leaders like George Bush, Mitt Romney, Rick Santorum, and John McCain. In April of 2008, the Religion News Service released a list of the ten most influential GOP "King Makers" who had influence on the Republican campaign. It included Dobson, Tony Perkins, Rod Parsley, and others who proclaim militant antihomosexual stances.

By 1980, one estimate suggests, some 61 million people were tun-ing in to evangelical television and radio programs.[39] While the likes of Falwell and Robertson speak for many fundamentalist Christians, they are some of the most reviled figures in public life and do not speak for more sophisticated conservatives. However, there are other more nu-anced but nevertheless problematic assertions about the role of gays and lesbians in the decline of moral order in America. "Gay marriage is not some sideline issue," the columnist Maggie Gallagher recently declared, "it *is* the marriage debate."[40] Once the third-ranking Republican leader of the Senate, Rick Santorum wrote that advocacy for gay marriage represents just "the latest liberal assault" on the "natural family."[41] The result of this "dangerous social experiment," Zell Miller suggested of "same sex marriage," will be disastrous. "Over time, if not stopped, this practice will destroy the traditional family. It will affect our children in a terrible, harmful, and lasting way for generations to come."[42] America will lose a common set of values if same-sex marriage is legalized.[43] In that event, "Losing this battle means losing the idea that children need mothers and fathers. It means losing the marriage debate. It means los-ing limited government. It means losing American civilization. It means losing, period."[44] Expanding the rights and amplifying voices of gays and lesbians in our society would no doubt be enormously significant. But civilization does not rest on this single issue. Regardless, this kind of hyperbole detracts from the most serious threats to the family, and it is strident enough to make some wonder whether there is at least some truth in it.

The assault on gay and lesbian rights neglects several important issues. First, other factors are much more important in determining the vitality and moral order of the American family. This small minority—gays and lesbians comprise perhaps 3 percent of the population—hardly has the power to determine family norms across the land in a way that can account for the transformation of the last fifty years.

Insofar as the gestures directed against gays and lesbians are really just about bigotry—which certainly appears to be the case for some but not all adversaries—its expression will have little impact on the well-being of the family. The real forces behind changes in the family involve external pressures and internal choices of family members that have almost nothing to do with sexuality (as outlined in chapter 7).

Second, from a practical point of view, homosexual Americans are simply here to stay. Whether they are comfortably situated in the context of legal marriage or formal definitions of family, or openly embraced in our communities, they are in fact part of who we are. Recent research suggests that most Americans are increasingly tolerant of gay and lesbian lifestyles but still resistant to legalized marriage and adoption rights.[45] Even that opposition is shrinking. One poll reports a decline in the number of Americans who "strongly oppose gay marriage"—down from 42 percent in 2004 to 28 in 2006. The proportion that supports same sex marriage has grown to more than 42 percent.[46]

Third, gay and lesbian parents are as effective as straight parents.[47] As Bill O'Reilly has rightly acknowledged in his book, *Culture Warrior*, "A variety of scientific studies have shown that kids raised by gay parents usually turn out the same way children in traditional homes do."[48] Despite a huge body of research confirming this finding, we continue to hear the warnings of alarmist propaganda charging gays and lesbians as morally unfit caregivers.

What seems puzzling about the outrage expressed over homosexual rights is that the issue has so little to do with the most extreme problems of moral decline. That is, deteriorating community life, increased violence and incivility, unhealthy lifestyles, substance abuse, greed, and consumerism have no connection. The real problems in the family, certainly the increasing rates of divorce, have nothing to do with gay and lesbian rights or lifestyles.

Even the vast bulk of cruddy entertainment is unrelated to either same-sex relations or the subcultural norms among gays and lesbians. If anything, most of what we see and hear in popular culture—raunchy

MTV videos, nudity on programs like *NYPD Blue* and vulgar shows like *The Bachelor* and *Temptation Island*—all affirm a kind of heterosexual degradation.

Overall, despite all the attention that the issue of gay and lesbian rights generates—including in almost every major religious denomination—it is not a significant force in causing the moral failures of our time. If the issue of gay marriage somehow disappeared along with all its advocates and exemplars (were such an imagined purge possible), virtually all the strains that other families face today would still be in place.

It appears that the fuss about homosexuality is the *result* of moral disorder rather than the *cause* of it. For some, this particular encounter with the "other" has provided a convenient peg to mistakenly hang fears associated with the transformation of the family. More broadly, the complexity and uncertainty of modern life, which is genuinely overwhelming for many of us, motivates a profound sense of protectiveness regarding what order we are able to discern. Certainly that includes the natural order or God's plan.

Setting aside biological and theological questions about sexuality, which are in fact quite substantial and unsettled, the main problem with this defensive crouch is that it will not provide any shield from the real issues. As with the taboos of intimate relationships that cross class, religion, and race, we will in time recognize that stability, respect, community, and love are the bases of a viable family, not the particular characteristics of the individuals involved.

MARKET MORALITY

Another argument about modern liberalism's contribution to society's ills pertains to disruption of the market. Echoing Adam Smith, champions of free-market fundamentalism maintain that the market has the capacity to harness individual incentives in the service of the collective good. The premise is that rational self-interest guides all behavior.[49] The core principles of supply and demand enable the production of what is desired while facilitating the eradication of that which is not.

According to this perspective, this organizational logic can help institutions meet the collective needs of society. In a vastly complex modern

world, the market's ability to arbitrate among the many different interests
of people—some 300 million of them in the United States alone—is critically important. Businesses, banks, schools, hospitals, government, and
most other large organizations can all benefit from rational market logic.

One version of market morality links "economic and spiritual freedoms." "God is in favor of freedom, property, ownership, competition,
diligence, work and acquisition. All of this is taught in the Word of God,
in both the Old and New Testaments," Jerry Falwell once declared,
"people should have the right to own property, to work hard, to achieve,
to earn, and to win."[50] The "prosperity gospel" preached by new generations of Christian leaders argues the same thing.

The purely free-market-oriented understanding of this connection
goes further in attributing capitalists with special intrinsic virtue. Dinesh
D'Souza argues in *The Virtue of Prosperity* that to participate in the
market, especially as an owner of a business, is to contribute to the well-
being of society.

> The moral argument for capitalism is that it makes us better people be-
> cause it puts our imagination and our efforts at the behest of the people.
> Success is defined as the ability to serve the needs and desires of others.
> There is no reason whatsoever for businessmen and businesswomen to
> feel guilty about being successful, because their success is the proof that
> they have effectively met the wants of their fellow human beings and
> thus earned a just reward. More than any social type, except perhaps the
> clergy, the capitalist is, in his everyday conduct, oriented to the task of
> helping and serving others.[51]

Conversely, according to this perspective, anything that inhibits successful business is viewed as a moral problem. The most consequential
interference with the moral order enabled through market processes,
therefore, is government intervention.[52] It exacerbates bureaucratic in-
efficiency, causes dysfunctional social dependence, undermines creativity and ambition, serves narrow interest group priorities, and politicizes
otherwise rational economic processes.

For these reasons, Milton Friedman argued that government should
not control minimum wage rates, economic output, rent parameters, or
tariffs. It should not maintain social security, public housing, municipal
or national parks, or toll roads. There is no need for it to draft people

into the military or restrict private mail systems. And of course government ought not to regulate industries.[53]

This yarn is not without merit, not entirely. Rationally organized economic firms can be very effective. Historically, they were critically important in establishing the rule of law and the possibilities for democracy.[54] In countless cases, well-run corporations have proven to be extremely efficient, creative, and valuable in the advance of human civilization. Think of the wonders produced by General Electric, McDonnell Douglas, and Microsoft.

And it is no chore to recognize the enormous failures of government. The lumbering bureaucracy and corrupt interests embedded in Washington make front-page news every day. The main problem with the connection drawn between market logic and moral order, however, is that it only holds for some of the people some of the time.

In particular, it holds for the "haves" on a good day. That is, those who enjoy profits in a competitive system by definition receive the greatest returns. They benefit from the industriousness of capitalist firms, the richness of civic life, and the security of prosperity. The others, the "have-nots," do not have the same access to such gains. For a host of reasons, restricted competition and incomplete information, which are regularly part of market transactions, guarantee that markets will not function in the same beneficial way for everyone involved.[55] Whether a small number of firms dominates an industry, as so often happens (e.g., computers, mass media, soda), or consumers lack basic knowledge about how to shop (e.g., medical expertise, banking), some people are systematically disadvantaged.

In any case, the ethos of competitiveness itself is not really the best basis for moral order.[56] But even when it fosters imagination and ambition, since markets are not always competitive or profitable, there are inevitably some on the short end. Moreover, there is now a common practice of socializing costs and privatizing benefits of certain enterprises.[57] Whether it is public financing of stadiums, the overuse of natural resources in business, government bailouts of failed corporations, or the taxpayer-funded U.S. Air Force training of pilots who end up with jobs for commercial airlines, there are plenty of examples. There has never been a market system that did not encompass significant poverty. Sometimes the poor are out of sight, perhaps in a foreign country, as in the case for much of America's producing class today, but that does not mean they are not a part of the system.

Another problem here is that not every day is a good day. Market logic can only serve moral order when the system is profitable.[58] When desirable goods and services cannot be bought, for whatever reason, they are not offered. The needs they would serve go unmet. Unpurchased food or unrented apartments help no one. A depression therefore creates problems for everyone, especially those without any reserves.

More importantly, goods and services that are intrinsically difficult to sell, such as sound inexpensive housing or drugs for rare diseases, are less likely to be produced in the first place. The system does not reliably produce that which is not profitable. Since there are so many worthy aspects of meaningful life that are not in any way lucrative or cannot be easily shown to be profitable, this creates serious problems. Think of safe public parks, engaging art, attractive architecture, long-term environmental viability, preventative medical care, public television, enlightened education, active religious life, amateur sports, or just plain old free time.

Even on a good day, most beneficiaries of a competitive market system are not likely to dwell on these matters since they are not the forces that created their success. And if they do invest in the public good (beyond the goal of exchange D'Souza celebrates), their focus is likely to be quite local. That is why we see such lovely parks, buildings and streets in affluent neighborhoods, but not run-down schools or sprawling retail stores.[59]

None of this is to suggest that government has all the answers or that another kind of economic system has demonstrated itself to be superior to capitalism. Rather, I simply want to clarify here that the link between market logic and moral order is very limited. "Distrustful of compartmentalization, inclined toward expansion, resentful of the limits imposed by time, space, and culture," Alan Wolfe observes, "the market is a poor instrument for sensitizing individuals to the complexities and paradoxes of moral obligations under modern conditions."[60] Such concerns would distract from what Milton Friedman holds to be the "one and only social responsibility of business," to increase profits.[61]

As a CBS vice president for television explained to the sociologist Todd Gitlin, "I'm not interested in culture. I'm not interested in pro-social values. I have only one interest. That's whether people watch the program. That's my definition of good, that's my definition of bad."[62]

Rational economic behavior certainly contributes mightily to the well-being of society. But to really understand what makes for sane and healthy moral order, most of our attention should be directed elsewhere.[63] Moral authority is not championed by capitalists. As they themselves know, that is not their job. Nor is it, necessarily, undermined by those who critique the operation and practices of our economy.

For those urgently concerned about moral decay, the unquestioning defense of the free market is a strange commitment indeed.[64] The confusion is derived from two misguided rationales. The first is treating socioeconomic status and merit as the same qualities.[65] In this vision, society is already appropriately ordered because the most moral and deserving people receive the greatest returns. The most worthy are the most wealthy.

The conflation of these correlated but discrete forces thereby enables the neglect of other factors that contribute to achievement (e.g., family, neighborhood, education, employment, discrimination). Even on its own terms, this argument confuses competitiveness and performance for moral worth. People are not paid a lot because they are generous and compassionate.

The other rationale attaches inordinate value to rules and laws, which many capitalists are quite diligent in following. But such a view strips people of moral agency.[66] By this logic, it is the law that is moral, not the individual. Shifting focus away from personal responsibility or values diminishes the possibilities for moral order in the face of new challenges unaddressed in law. Plus, as noted above, the market serves the collective good only in limited ways.

There will always be vitally important aspects of social life not subject to market logic and not attended to by agents of the market, no matter how conscientious they are in following the rules[67]—just like the bonuses AIG executives recently paid to themselves out of government monies offered to bail out the investment firm.[68] Some commentators recognized the actions as legal, but most observers found them to be morally dubious.

One of the problems with the contention that capitalism is the main basis for moral order is the conceptualization of capitalism itself. Most discussion of the matter, whether from critics or advocates, suggests that capitalism represents a single condition that is present or absent. A society is capitalistic or not. We are the United States or the Soviet Union. And within the scholarship that studies the variation among capitalist countries, there is often little more than lip service paid to the importance of culture and history.[69]

However, as Robert Kuttner contends, "Contrary to both Marx and to Chicago economists, there are huge aspects of socioeconomic life that are culturally conditioned, and cannot be usefully comprehended as merely material calculations at one remove."[70] It makes more sense to recognize that the dynamics of culture and other institutions affect the character and consequences of capitalist economies in meaningful ways. Blind commitment to market logic and its expansion, without any concern for other factors, is economically short-sighted and morally disastrous.[71]

There is great risk (and opportunity) as the country comes to terms with the recent economic crisis. The attempt to repair the damage to our economy, to restore business confidence, and reestablish growth is an understandable focus. Certainly, those are important objectives. But the risk is in believing that our problems fundamentally revolve around market value. Thinking about how to fix our economic system without any attention to the ethics and values people in the system hold will not address the underlying fault lines that led to this upheaval in the first place.

CONSIDERING THE EFFECTS AND CAUSES OF CULTURE

Despite these problems with its common uses, the notion of culture is a promising concept for explaining some of our choices. Fukuyama's initial definition, "inherited ethical habit," is a credible one.[72] Contrary to some misuses of the term, when applied appropriately to the behavioral norms of a given social setting, the concept is very useful. It allows for sympathetic critique of certain people without demonizing them. It empowers individuals and groups with agency. They act in history;

they make history. And culture, properly understood, allows for change. It involves contingent actions that shape the historical trajectories of a people.

Focusing on culture allows us to recognize that if "we" were exposed to the same lessons and material conditions as "they," we would likely develop similar ethical habits. Such an empathetic perspective allows us to evaluate the collective sanity or character of an unfamiliar people without reifying their differences, demonizing them, or reducing them to a caricature. But studying history with an emphasis on culture also enables us to recognize the importance of agency or free will. That is, individuals and groups have the capacity to make choices in any given moment that may shape their future.

A cultural approach is more likely to avoid one of the main pitfalls of strictly "structural" approaches in social science, which emphasize the durability and power of large institutions and neglect the importance of human agency. The actions of people do matter. Most significant turns in history were the result of such action. Respecting the freedom of all individuals to make that kind of choice, to recognize each person as a potential player in history, is another strength of cultural analysis.

By definition, culture is subject to change but not easily given to it. The symbols and stories developed in a certain culture are typically robust and well defended enough not to melt under the first offensive assault. Over time, though, the choices people make in serving particular priorities can shift.

What is constructed can be deconstructed. Studying the continuities in culture facilitates insights into this kind of ambiguous development in which things change but stay the same. To understand culture, though, we necessarily must also pay attention to the important institutions in a given context. This allows us to explain the development of specific values and the actions derived from them.

Only by examining these different pieces of the puzzle over time—that is the landscape of a society's way of life—can we have any confidence that we have identified the causes of the current problems in question. These are critical elements in grasping the historical processes which have led to the habits we have now inherited, the topic of the next chapter.

CONCLUSION

A lot of conversations about morality lead nowhere. The Left avoids using the vocabulary of morality for the most part (except in reference to
those who wield power). There is little discussion of bad choices or good
choices, of character. The problem here is in neglecting the power and
autonomy of individuals. We almost always have choices. Consciousness
guarantees that. Some choices are terribly costly and some are like falling off a log. Understanding probabilities, though, does not exclude the
possibility that extraordinary choices could be made. At any given moment, you could drive your car off the road, or not; you could just stay
on the conveyor belt, or not. The choice is yours, always.

On the Right, the problem is more about the underlying explanations.
Comfortable, even exuberant, in the use of moralistic rhetoric, the Right
often ignores the basis of morality. In this approach, individuals seem to
make choices in a vacuum, either because they are inherently noble or
inherently base. That is, individuality is essentialized. The problem here
is neglecting the ways different choices become available and understood. This error is most commonly made among proponents of market
fundamentalism who reduce success, ability, merit, and morality to the
same element of individuality.[73]

Despite the problems with these various arguments that currently domi-
nate public discourse, the basic point that a crisis of cultural values un-
derlies our moral disorder is dead on. The key to understanding how this
situation came about, however, requires a bit of investigation. It cannot be
casually explained by the specific flaws of those acting most immorally.

On the other hand, we do not have to identify the sweeping arc of history, acknowledge the death of God, or seek the Second Coming for any
hopes of moral order. Rather, my modest argument is that particular
choices can be made that will foster morality. Specific institutions can
play a large or small role in shaping our ethical habits that will enable
different kinds of choices.[74]

History is composed of both powerful, long-term forces that are difficult to derail as well as meaningful choices that are highly contingent
and consequential.[75] The incredible, abrupt shifts in the currents of history resulting from specific decisions illustrate this point. Think of the

American Revolution, the assassination of Lincoln, or the development of nuclear power, for instance, or all the other decisive events that were neither inevitable nor predicted.

That we should arrive here, at this moment, certainly does not represent any kind of inevitable course of history. There is hope in the elusive, conditional logic of history because it means that whatever current trajectory we discern is likely not an accurate projection of the possibilities. Such potentialities surely encompass grim scenarios but also some heretofore unimagined future of promise and opportunity.

With this premise in mind, we can recognize that there was once a balance of institutional influences in American life that facilitated greater concern for relationships and the common good. I do not suggest that we should—or could—return to a previous era. But we can learn from such success, as well as the failures, in seeking better balance in the future. First, though, how we lost that balance is the topic of the next chapter.

3

SOCIAL CHANGE AND
CONTINUITY IN U.S. HISTORY

There is little in the dominant belief systems of our society that is inevitable, universal, or fixed. Each of us is socialized to accept certain values developed by previous generations. They did not create cultural beliefs in a vacuum, but like generations before and after them, put their own imprint on the values and symbols of the day. Each generation brings to the traditions handed to them particular experiences shaped by trends and events of their era, which then affects the contributions they make to the legacy handed off to subsequent generations.

Such traditions are necessarily layered and multifaceted, but there are core symbols, which contain the most important values, around which the culture orbits. To understand the dominant values of our day, including those underpinning family, civic, and economic life, why they compel us and why they endure, we must trace their development back through generations that imbued them with the status they now have. In this investigation, six central themes emerge: progress, freedom, prosperity, productivity, equality, and authority.

UNUSUAL TALENTS, SPECIAL INSTITUTIONS, AND RUTHLESS CONQUEST AT THE FOUNDING

An appropriate starting point is the founding of the nation. A number of complex factors led to Europe's dominant position in the eighteenth century, especially that of England.[1] The main causes of the American Revolution encompassed questions of governance, and specifically the colonists' grievance against being taxed without political representation. The ground for this protest was made fertile by the motivations for more freedom that brought colonists to the new world in the first place. In the decades preceding the rebellion, Enlightenment sensibilities of progress and liberty permeated the colonists' political culture. In addition to the circumstances that sparked the uprising and the dynamics of the revolution itself, several other distinctive factors contributed to the particular character of the new nation.

First, that generation of colonists was unusually industrious, practical, and ambitious. The Founders themselves were a remarkable group of talented and able men. Gifted farmers, professionals, soldiers, and statesmen brought significant resources to the challenges of the day. Their motives to do so were partly derived from a deep commitment to the public good. In addition to varied priorities, the Founders had a common goal that transcended their differences, drew them into compromise, and became part of an enduring communitarian sensibility.[2] In effect, the United States was from the beginning comprised of a self-selected group of immigrants who were highly motivated, industrious, and civic-minded.[3]

Second, the colonists imported three very important kinds of institutions to the new land. They drew from the economic lessons of Europe, establishing a market economy from the outset. This entailed a strong commitment to productivity, that is, the spirit of capitalism, but also avid consumerism. They also borrowed heavily from the relatively new conventions of parliamentary government. Over time, the centralized state provided key legal and regulatory systems that supported the market. In so doing, they brought to bear two of the guiding principles of liberalism—the primacy of individual freedom and representative government—in service of modern capitalism.[4]

From the beginning, the operations of the market and state were mediated through the institutions of vibrant civil society. Religious organizations, fraternal brotherhoods, women's associations, veterans' associations, and social movements nurtured the noncapitalist moral values so critical to balancing the "rationality" of the market and the authority of the state.[5] Inspired by their contemporary, Adam Smith—author of not just *The Wealth of Nations*, but also *The Theory of Moral Sentiments*— the Founders recognized the importance of moral principles established by the people themselves and protected in other institutions. Generally large, "translocal," and driven by citizen-organizers, such organizations were explicitly oriented toward national issues facing the country.[6]

As critical as these institutions were to the moral character of the nation, each was established in ways that advanced the interests of the dominant classes. Both the sense of community and individuality embedded in the country's origins were entangled with the highly stratified class system.[7] At the center of this arrangement was a legal and moral tension between the economic rights associated with capitalism and the political rights associated with democracy.[8]

A third circumstance was the effectively unlimited natural resources appropriated in the new land. The conquest of the native tribes of North America reflected a complex understanding of freedom delimited to certain people, a problem that would persist and escalate over time. In the beginning, though, it allowed for the co-optation of huge natural resources stretching west.[9] The agrarian context of the colonists also contributed to a self-reliant, hardy sensibility that endured as an American ideal. It was the basis for family-centered life as well, which had rippling implications for socialization into the assiduous, ambitious national ethos.

While the American experiment represented a unique attempt to build a just and prosperous society, it contradicted its own ideals from the very beginning. The arrangements of the new society would not have been possible without the assault on native peoples—which enabled the appropriation of natural resources—and the institution of slavery—which provided cheap labor.[10] The class structure preceding and advanced by the revolution involved systematic inequality that would persist for generations.

The paradoxes built into the Constitution and manifest in the lived experience of Americans in the late eighteenth and early nineteenth centuries represented complex values inherently in tension with one another. Inalienable rights did not extend to all. Political equality was limited, which sometimes undermined the competitiveness of markets. Noble ideals of liberty, equality, and progress shaped the young nation's character in profound, enduring ways. The contrasting goals and institutions of unequal power were also from the beginning important and lasting.[11]

Despite these contradicting forces, victory in the revolution provided a sense of resolution and possibility for many. For most American citizens, the early decades of the new country were promising indeed. A youthful population of industrious immigrants set up a competitive market economy and a representative government, at least ostensibly intended to oversee the economy with a light touch, drew from seemingly endless resources, and began utilizing rapidly developing new technology.

It was the special combination of ideals (freedom and progress), the establishment of key institutions (the market economy, democratic government, and civic organizations), the abundance of resources, and the particular sensibilities of the dominant classes that made the promise good. That generation was keenly aware of the need for individual rights protected from arbitrary authority, at least for citizens, as well as the importance of civil society, volunteering personal contributions, and sacrifices in service of the young nation's security and prosperity.[12] The compromise of sectional and individual interests enabled the rise of the new nation. The formation of the nation-state then allowed the colonists to stand against the forces of the Crown and other foreign interests. Only with such commitment to collective well-being could the project have endured.

INDUSTRIALIZATION, CIVIL WAR, AND THE FORMATION OF NATIONAL IDENTITY

The most important development for the United States during the nineteenth century was the dramatic, relentless growth of industrialization. At the beginning of the century, agrarian interests were supreme. Some 90 percent of the population still worked on small self-sufficient farms in 1790.[13] Within a hundred years, industry's new domination would be secure. The modern pricing system was also established during the first half of that century, setting in motion the forces of supply and demand on a broad scale.[14] Increasingly, everything had a price; everything could be bought and owned. This rapid economic shift from agriculture to industry also sparked a complex dispute over the meaning of freedom.

This struggle came to a head in the Civil War. The central clash over slavery encompassed several other disagreements. A sensitive issue since the founding of the nation, states' rights was a continual quandary of governance. Related to that dilemma, the moral question of the status of people of African descent, which had been purposely left ambiguous in the Constitution, proved enduring and volatile. The impasse also reflected disputed claims on how to expand the economy for a rapidly growing population.

Southern planters were then economically dominant. But aspirations for more homestead farms spreading to the west became widespread and industry grew quickly. As all of these issues were intertwined, many people attached differing levels of significance to each aspect of the conflict. Given the ambiguity of the Constitution in relation to these questions, there was a great deal of tension throughout the first half of the nineteenth century. As the Union added more states, the disagreements intensified, always orbiting around the question of slavery.[15]

Among the many consequences of the most deadly conflict in U.S. history, the Civil War settled a number of unresolved questions. The federal government emerged stronger as states' rights receded. Legal slavery was abolished. And the planter economy was greatly curtailed. Local communities still thrived, but the basis for identity began to shift from states and regions to nation.[16] In that way, the Civil War represented a convergence of long-term historical processes. The relentless march of industrialization gained great momentum after that defining event.[17] Gemeinschaft persisted, but Gesellschaft emerged forcefully during this time. Simultaneously, the distinction between private and public life became more pronounced.[18] Increasingly, work was public and family was private.

The expansion of market logic attached a monetary value to every-thing, straining the historically complementary connection between the economy and civil society.[19] The new technology and new means of exchange helped bring about the Gilded Age, which produced the first billion-dollar corporation, United States Steel, and the first billionaire, John D. Rockefeller Sr. Other large, modern, industrial firms formed within a few short years and a number of men got very rich.[20]

Like the Revolutionary War, though, the Civil War also reaffirmed the collective nature of Americans' ambitions. The half-century follow-ing the war brought the greatest expansion of voluntary associations in American history.[21] The war reminded Americans in the North and South, as well as the West, of their shared destiny. As public conscious-ness was nationalized, the United States were transformed into a sin-gular noun. Having been keenly aware of attachments to something important, something worth fighting and dying for, the outcome of the war motivated organization of and advocacy for broad agendas.

Industrialization spread rapidly over the next fifty years.[22] Cotton declined, undermining the planter culture, while iron, steel, petroleum, electrical products, rubber, automobiles, railroads, and numerous other industries proliferated. Cities shot out of the ground as populations grew around production centers. The new capitalized industry and the mechanization of farming and of well established crafts transformed the labor force into proletarian workers.

IMMIGRATION, INTERNATIONAL WAR, AND THE ADVENT OF THE AMERICAN CENTURY

The demand for less-skilled labor created enormous opportunities that lured scores of immigrants. During the second half of the nineteenth century and especially the first half of the twentieth, they poured in to the United States.[23] The surge also included large numbers of people, especially African Americans, relocating from the rural South to urban areas, both in the South and North.[24] The opportunities for industrial work and then the curtailing of foreign immigration during World War I also facilitated this large movement.

Just as the first generations of colonists, these migrants arriving from other countries and regions self-selected in important ways.

"The typical behavioral profile of the successful migrant that emerges from international research," observes the psychologist Peter C. Whybrow, "is that of an independent-minded and socially competitive individual who is restless (and often impulsive in decision making) and driven to succeed."[25] As risky as relocation was, burgeoning demand for labor provided substantive opportunities for most groups willing to try it.

For the first three decades of the new century, the percentage of the population that was foreign-born remained in double digits, peaking just before World War I around 15 percent.[26] The most economically successful immigrant groups also formed enclaves with others from their countries of origin. For instance, a small business owner might hire a young man from his country of origin, pay him less than the going rate, thereby gaining a competitive advantage in exchange for guidance, training, and future opportunities. The employee's family might then offer other in-kind goods or services to the business owner's family, and so on.[27] Just as ethnic enclaves were producing coherent, upwardly mobile communities, the newcomers were also assimilating into American life in measured steps.

The early decades of the twentieth century thus produced vibrant urban settings. The home became an increasingly private setting where the nuclear family lived, but it remained situated in concentric circles of civic life.[28] While straddling the familiar traditions of home and enculturation in a new world, and balancing individual aspirations with communal obligations, many new Americans "made it."

Again, some were left out in ways that created long-lasting problems. Urban crime and poverty were more difficult than that experienced in rural settings. The ideals of American democracy coupled with the reality of inequality proved an unrelenting dilemma.[29] For many Americans, though, the promise of freedom was real. Civic life flourished during this period.

Industrialization motivated the formation of workers' associations. Immigration facilitated the burgeoning of ethnically based groups. And expanding cities generated various social problems that then spawned a host of organizations oriented toward reform and charity.[30] Partly in response to the needs of such newcomers as well as the greed and urban squalor that had gotten out of control in the previous age, the Progressive Era, as this period came to be known, entailed a series of consequential reforms that improved the working conditions of laborers and inhibited the formation of monopolies.

As international war ripped through Europe during the First World War, Americans were reminded of the significance of national boundaries and identity. Again, voluntary associations proliferated during the years following the war.[31] Despite the unifying impact in the United States of that international conflict, though, the following years also evinced a heightened degree of individualism.

Many of the trends of previous decades converged to produce a marked departure from the country's agrarian past. Mechanization of industry contributed to immense productivity. Frederick Taylor, who published *The Principles of Scientific Management* in 1911, was instrumental in bringing about a new, modern sense of efficiency, hierarchy, and organization in industry. Large corporations with increasingly massive holdings developed innovative forms of rational management based on "Taylorism."[32]

New products and new prosperity gave rise to a consumer class. Anxieties about the perceived loss of morality from a previous age, the promise of opportunity in the new age, and the influx of large numbers of immigrants of differing cultural and ethnic backgrounds made for significant tension. The widespread opportunities available to many contrasted with the reality of intensely concentrated wealth under the control of a small number of corporations and families. This growing polarization, however, was disrupted by a national crisis, the Great Depression. The resentment among laboring classes that had developed in the twenties gave way to an urgent struggle for survival and the indulgence of the affluent quickly subsided in recognition of a broad economic catastrophe.[33]

CONFIDENCE IN CRISIS, AND THE NEW DEAL REALIGNMENT

It was in this context that capitalists were deemed culpable for the excesses of the era as well as the crisis of the day. Herbert Hoover's administration, closely identified with business interests, was held responsible, leading to the landslide victory for Franklin Roosevelt in 1932.

In an effort to stem the crisis, Roosevelt led the federal government in enacting a stunning range of legislation.

Cobbling together a broad combination of interests, the New Deal fundamentally altered the role of government.[34] Social reformers, urban planners, southern planters, racial progressives, labor unions, certain industrial capitalists, and others all joined the miraculously balanced New Deal coalition. Provisions for regulation of industry, social welfare, and collective bargaining were all central to this transformation in government. In 1945 the top marginal income rate rose to 94 percent.[35]

Just as the country came to accept the need for an expansive, active federal government, that generation also embraced a broad sense of civic life and personal responsibility. The economic crisis taught painful lessons of discipline, thrift, *and* interdependence. While the Roosevelt administration accomplished great feats in alleviating its effects, the most significant factor rejuvenating the country's economy was World War II.[36] Few events in history were more consequential than this unprecedented global conflagration that killed 60 million people.

The ultimate success of Roosevelt and his counterparts in the Allied powers further enhanced the position of government at home. If the Depression engendered a complex sense of responsibility for one's self and neighbor, the war facilitated a complex sense of patriotism and internationalism. Americans, many of whom had been immigrants, considered their involvement in the war heroic, both in terms of U.S. interests and that of other free peoples. This was again perceived as an important lesson on the costs and rewards of freedom.

On the heels of enduring the Depression and winning the war, confidence in government and other institutions deepened.[37] The immediate aftermath of the war, however, entailed a political backlash against government's expanded role during the previous decade. The massive strike wave of 1946 and the antilabor Taft-Hartley Act of 1947 reflected unresolved tensions between labor and management in the industrial era.[38]

The upshot was a degree of leverage restored to employers relative to the gains organized labor had attained during the Roosevelt years. After victory in the war, U.S. international policy helped open vast new markets for American products, which contributed to prosperity at home. Corporations in a wide range of industries grew at staggering rates. Their giant enterprises necessitated much larger, more complex bureaucratic organization. The trend of increasingly concentrated corporate power begun in the Gilded Age picked up pace rapidly.[39]

By the end of the forties, however, the country's growing affluence took the sting out of the labor movement's declining leverage and brought even more Americans into the growing middle classes.[40] For many, the notion of "progress" rooted in the nation's origins took a new form in this era: new opportunities, new products, new promise. Being a good citizen started to mean being a good consumer.[41]

Within five years of the war's end, household spending for food rose 33 percent and for clothing 20 percent, and spending for home furnishings and appliances grew 240 percent. In the fifties, real wages increased more than they had in fifty years.[42] Reversing a hundred-year-old pattern of declining hours of work, Americans also began working harder during this time, a pattern that would gain momentum in the coming decades. The growing prosperity and security only served to affirm and motivate rigorous working patterns among professionals throughout the workforce.[43]

The logic of Henry Ford's assembly line was applied to food, hotels, homes, stores, and many other kinds of goods. Mass produced, standardized, affordable goods thus became available to huge portions of the population. McDonald's set a compelling example of rationalized, efficient, available products. Similar organizing principles were used by Holiday Inn, E. J. Korvette, Levittown, and many other companies and industries. What had previously been special conveniences and comforts became normal for a majority of Americans. Propped up as the most fundamental or even sacred institution, family was the main setting for socialization, fun, and recreation, as well as a crucial symbol in the fight against Communism.[44]

PROSPERITY, INDIVIDUALISM, AND FEAR IN THE FIFTIES

As an expression of patriotism, buying a home and filling it with more things was central to the new suburban, middle-class lifestyle. Twenty-three percent of Americans lived in the suburbs in 1950. By 1980, that proportion would be 45 percent. The farm population would shrink from 23 percent in 1940 to 2 percent in 1987.[45]

Americans grew accustomed to shopping as the postwar economy hummed. The number of "shopping centers" in 1957, 940, doubled by 1960 and then doubled again by 1963.[46] "Planned obsolescence" became a working principle first in the garment industry, then in automobiles.[47] By the end of the fifties, consumer goods across industries were repeatedly restyled from year to year.

Suburban households of the fifties could live with a level of affluence and independence rarely known among other generations. Gross national product (GNP) rose some 37 percent in ten years.[48] A cultural shift occurred as a "middle class" identity replaced the "working class" ethos. As the American Dream became more real to more people, including ethnic and racial minorities, a strong sense of individualism became more expansive.[49]

Less dependent on the resources of the immigrant community and less vulnerable to the vicissitudes of the economy, many Americans eagerly embraced the comforts of suburban life. In time, the appeal of the cultural lifestyle overshadowed the actual income available in the burgeoning economy. Between 1945 and 1960 consumer credit increased elevenfold; installment credit in particular jumped by a factor of nineteen.[50]

Another related change occurred as cultural icons shifted from being heroes of production, such as the leaders of industry and finance, to heroes of consumption, that is, Hollywood stars and other celebrities.[51] The logic of consumption spread beyond goods to people. Their lives were commodified in the form of print media, radio, and TV exposés. *People*, *The Johnny Carson Show*, and other precursors to the *National Enquirer*, *The Late Show with David Letterman*, and *Entertainment Tonight* became hugely popular.

Replacing public spaces for entertainment such as theaters, television emerged as the main medium for this shift. Between 1948 and 1955, two-thirds of American households acquired TVs; almost 90 percent of them would have a television by 1960, usually in the "family room."[52]

The combination of several factors, however, distinguished these indulgent impulses of the fifties. Few survivors had forgotten the experiences and lessons of recent years. Though many who had weathered the Great Depression sought to provide their children with a comfortable lifestyle, economic security was not taken for granted. Government and other institutions had a central role to play in holding the country together, in protecting the American way of life.[53] This included advancing prosperity, promoting family, and defending against the real dangers loose in the world.[54]

The apparent calm and consensus of the era, however, obscured underlying complexities. Even in this time of peace and prosperity, many were left out. Women and minorities remained legally excluded from various rights and opportunities white men enjoyed. The new culture exerted inordinate pressures on women to invest fully in a particular image of feminine domesticity, and severely ostracized those who did not comply. Despite new labor-saving devices, women spent more time on housework.[55]

Persecution of blacks, through both illegal and legal means, in the South and elsewhere, remained common. Neither the unprecedented prosperity nor the patriotic rhetoric of American unity erased intense material inequality. Twenty-five percent of the nation's population was poor in 1955.[56]

The Depression and especially World War II had made such inequality more conspicuous. Americans had suffered and died together. The national crises and the hopes and expectations for affluence, freedom, and modernization that followed stood in increasingly stark contrast to the reality of life among subordinated groups.[57]

And other circumstances troubled Americans. The grim threat of Stalin represented evil that was real and immediate. Such genuine malevolence had been encountered in the form of Hitler, and the horrendous stakes had been witnessed in London, Dresden, and many other places in Europe, and especially in Hiroshima and Nagasaki.

The resulting fear magnified differences among those protective of conventional American institutions versus critics, radicals, and idealists skeptical of the establishment.[58] Throughout the fifties, however, such dissent was largely squelched in most mainstream institutions by anti-Communist centrists. This included various organizations associated with the private sector, religion, organized labor, the media, and of course, government.[59]

Under the weight of burdensome memories of the Depression and the war, and fed by the ongoing threats associated with the Cold War, these institutions contributed to a kind of American orthodoxy. There was, according to this sensibility, a right way to do things, a proper way to live and think.

This was the era in which the voice of Senator Joseph McCarthy found an eager audience. The consuming fear of Communism translated easily into apprehension about anyone who was defiant, deviant, or just different. More than any other decade of the century, the fifties fostered rigid obedience to authority. Some Americans found a degree of security in such clarity. For many others, though, the sanctions against dissenters were repressive. The acquiescence to the outlandish claims of McCarthy and his ilk was just the most extreme manifestation of such conformity.[60]

Institutional officials wielded unusual influence, for instance, in government, corporations, religion, and schools.[61] Established norms in the family, workplace, and civic life in general were carefully adhered to, at least in public settings. By the end of the fifties, American life was much more privatized. The expression of views or opinions consistent with dominant ideology could be shared publicly. Those that differed were swept under the newly purchased rug at home.

Thus, the individualism associated with economic opportunities and prosperity was tempered by a type of conformity with established institutional authority.[62] In 1964, some 62 percent of Americans trusted the federal government "to do the right thing most of the time."[63] These forces—individualism and institutional compliance—countervailing in that moment, would prove very consequential in the decades to come as the balance shifted.

DISOBEDIENCE TO AUTHORITY

The women's and civil rights movements had deep roots, but the modern versions began in earnest after World War II.[64] Women and minorities played important roles in the national effort during the war years. Some women who had taken on "men's work" during the war found the return to narrowly defined domestic roles constraining.[65] For blacks who had served in combat and were greeted with a hero's welcome in Europe, to arrive home to segregation and subordination was a bitter awakening.[66]

These feelings matured some in the fifties but were constrained by the conservative pressures of dominant institutions. They cohered further and found powerful expression in broad social movements that fomented during the 1960s. Many observers identify the Port Huron Statement adopted in 1962 by the Students for a Democratic Society as a crucial document that reflected and spurred key sentiments of that era, especially among young people.[67]

It advocated "the establishment of a democracy of individual partici-pation governed by two central aims: that the individual share in those social decisions determining the quality and direction of his life; that so-ciety be organized to encourage independence in men and provide the media for their common participation."[68] The patterns of "privatization and conformity" so prevalent during the previous decade were replaced by values of "the politicization of society, individual fulfillment, and the legitimation of dissent."[69] As the personal became political and vice versa, the relationship between individual Americans and institutional authorities changed.

The recorded history of the Great Depression and World War II was less powerful in the consciousness of younger generations than the actual memories were to that of older ones. While fears associated with the Cold War persisted, many young people found immediate problems at home more troubling. Stifling social norms of mainstream suburban life were not just restrictive. Considered by many to be op-pressive and corrupting, they contributed to the development of youth counterculture.[70]

Rather than looking to government and other institutions for guid-ance and solutions to problems, many Americans—including young people and those with more left-leaning views whose agendas had been marginalized during the previous decade—increasingly saw such authority as the source of trouble.[71] This environment proved fertile ground for social movements that had been alive but largely dormant for some time.

The epic struggle of World War II reflected an ordered world for Americans. The enemy was evil. The ambivalence of the sixties, in contrast, reflected growing skepticism and a loss of innocence. The shock of Kennedy's assassination in 1963 produced a coherent sense of this new reality. American life was vulnerable. The spreading disquiet was greatly energized by doubts about the Vietnam War, which the United States entered in 1964. Warned of the dangers of the "military industrial complex" by President Eisenhower, uncertain of the particular role of Vietnam in global politics and its connection to American interests, U.S. citizens of this generation never felt the kind of support or patriotism that World War II had engendered.[72]

For young people, the perception of a misguided, corrupt government and the fear of death among those who might be called to arms made the Asian conflict a true nightmare. After some 2.5 million American men served in Vietnam, with 300,000 injured and 58,000 killed, and after the outcome proved unsuccessful and the returning veterans were greeted with hostility and pity, the nation never came to terms with the ambivalence of the conflict.[73] The painful, unsettled history of this event parallels the strong, contradicting, and ambivalent feelings many Americans still have about the entire decade.[74]

In overlapping efforts, activists organized around the rights of Native Americans, prisoners, and workers, opposition to the war, as well as the civil rights, gay rights, and women's liberation movements. Those circumstances also gave rise to forces broader and perhaps more consequential than the many specific social movements of the era. Counterculture found various expressions, none more pervasive than popular music. In 1969, 400,000 young people gathered in Woodstock, New York, to listen to music, protest, and have fun. The oppositional culture of young people denounced the customs and norms of society in general, the goals of "success" and even the notion of institutional authority itself.[75]

Young people born in the fifties, the period now idealized in some circles as the heyday of the nuclear family, lashed out in numerous ways in the years that followed, contributing to sharp increases in drug use, sexual activity, delinquency, out-of-wedlock births, and other aberrant behaviors.[76] New notions of femininity and masculinity emerged, which emphasized greater independence and self-realization, and stirred up centrifugal pressures in the family.[77]

Various other factors helped strain the standing of institutional authority as well. McCarthyism had damaged the credibility of government in the fifties. Americans increasingly questioned a broad range of U.S. practices and policies in international relations. The Bay of Pigs fiasco exemplified the perceived problems of hypocrisy and incompetence. Americans, young as well as old, were further alienated by the debacle in Vietnam. And the Watergate scandal permanently altered American political culture.[78] All of these institutional failures valorized the politics of dissent.

Certainly long-term pressures had been building against the institutional establishment in general. Despite the truncating view of hindsight that tempts us to lump them all together, though, the protest movements were diverse and complex. The modernizing society had promised much to its citizens that it withheld from some groups, such as African Americans and Native Americans. It promoted its defining value of individualism while also dictating to women that they had limited individuality. It celebrated inclusive government in contrast to totalitarian regimes abroad while marginalizing those outside the political center at home.[79]

There was also an element of naive, self-absorbed, insolent youthfulness, enabled through affluence and unburdened by harsh memories of depression and war. These qualities complemented the impulse to stand against the rigid and repressive establishment that had been so intrusive and overbearing the previous decade.[80] But any dismissive indictment of that generation ignores the glaring paradox of celebrated values integral to our cultural legacy—freedom and equality—in the context of institutional authoritarianism and social injustice. They did not have all the answers and did not grasp the implications of all their actions but they fought deeply American causes related to individual rights and governmental accountability.

The credibility of the establishment, Samuel Huntington suggests, was greatly weakened.

The essence of the democratic surge of the 1960s was a general challenge to existing systems of authority, public and private. In one form or another, this challenge manifested itself in the family, the university, business, public and private associations, politics, the governmental bureaucracy, and the military services. People no longer felt the same obligation to obey those whom they had previously considered superior to themselves in age, rank, status, expertise, character, or talent.[81]

This was a decisive development. Moral authority was never restored to the core institutions confronted by the protest movements of that decade.[82] Indeed, the notion of institutional moral authority itself would thereafter remain a problematic, precarious ideal, more often interrogated than not, and never taken for granted again.[83] We have become much more comfortable "booing the judges," muses Lynne Truss. "Authority is largely perceived as a kind of personal insult which must be challenged."[84]

The skepticism about authority in conventional institutions encompassed both large-scale organizations such as government and the social norms of more intimate settings like family. "How much of the time do you think you can trust the government in Washington to do what is right?" In the sixties, some three-fourths said "always" or "most of the time," compared to one-fifth to one-third by the nineties.[85] Traditional family and sexual norms were much in question.[86] What was celebrated or tolerated in the previous era—including highly prescribed roles—became dubious. As Ruth Rosen notes, "Marriage—already battered by growing divorce rates, the values of the counterculture, and new ideas about sexual freedom—began to seem like just one of the many lifestyles that men and women might choose."[87]

One part of the establishment that was not unhinged in the same way as most other institutions, however, was the market. In *The Conquest of Cool*, Thomas Frank details how the countercultural agenda young people pursued ended up being immensely liberating for various industries, most importantly advertising. Kids who acted up in protest of injustice, in response to overbearing grown-ups, or just for fun, helped loosen the creative imagination of advertisers and consumers alike. Not only were marketers able to get in touch with what it meant to be "hip," but their greatest triumph from the perspective of the industries in which they worked was making indulgent consumption "cool."[88]

Between 1955 and 1959, advertising expenditures jumped from $3 billion to $11 billion.[89] In 1965 the chair of the board at Macy's presciently declared, "Our economy keeps growing because our ability to consume is endless. The consumer goes on spending regardless of how many possessions he has. The luxuries of today are the necessities of tomorrow."[90] By that same year, the top marginal tax rate had slipped down to 70 percent.[91]

"Men of the world, arise! The revolution has begun and fashion is at the barricades. Charge into Chapman's shops for men and lead the way to this new found freedom in men's clothes."[92] This 1968 retail advertisement was part of a vast shift toward embracing, absorbing, and exploiting dissent. Who's cooler than a rebel? So you better buy this. This change in how industry leaders thought about communicating with consumers constitutes a sharp turning point that is generally obscured by all the other turmoil of the era.

But the effects of this conflation of commerce and counterculture continue to shape our society, as the sale of torn jeans in Macy's and the appearance of virtually naked, "rebellious" teenagers on MTV illustrate.[93] We look to the margins for style and recognize subversion in fashion. Those critics who lambaste young people of the sixties for their pleasure-seeking rightly identify this kind of hip consumerism. What was portrayed as principled dissent sometimes morphed into selfish materialism. But a crucial and neglected part of this story involves the encouragement and opportunity the market afforded them.

CENTRIFUGAL SEVENTIES

On the heels of all these developments, it is not surprising that this period also marked a transition in civic life, as social capital throughout various contexts began to decline precipitously in the early 1970s.[94] Public spaces were increasingly privatized and commercialized in shopping centers, 17,520 of them by 1976, with a whole range of shops and services, where the central activity was consumption.[95]

The idealism of the sixties mostly lived on in specific social movements in the following decade. Some won decisively, some were suppressed, and some just fizzled. Many of the successful movements continued to evolve and actually gained more members and more influence in the seventies.[96] But a lot of them became specialized and isolated. In the broader society, a more cynical sense of politics and social life prevailed.[97]

This growing malaise was compounded by economic stagnation, declining wages, fuel shortages, and humiliation in global politics, nothing so dramatic as the Great Depression but a perceptible decline nonetheless.[98] Annual expenditures on advertising were up to $50 billion in 1979.[99] And it paid off. Americans were spending money they did not have, both individually and collectively. Prior to this decade, the country had enjoyed a foreign trade surplus. By 1980, the trade deficit was $25,480,000,000 and by 1988 that figure would be $127,215,000,000.[100]

Real income of the bottom 40 percent of the population fell by about 11 percent between 1979 and 1986, while the top 1 percent gained 20 percent.[101] In addition to complex economic factors, government policies in the Nixon and Carter administrations enabled this increasing inequality. Both administrations took major steps to deregulate large swaths of industry.[102]

With all these problems, the mess appeared to many Americans too complex for real solutions. As the two great institutions of the economy and government were floundering, other indications of trouble were evident throughout everyday life. Violent crime, substance abuse, urban decay, family breakup, and child abuse were all getting worse.[103] The debate about gender roles intensified during the seventies as more extreme views calcified on different sides. "A 1980 Gallup poll reported that 45 percent of Americans felt family life had gotten worse over the past decade; only 37 percent thought it had improved."[104]

The expression of dissent and questioning of authority became more normative but less purposeful and coherent. This shift encouraged a kind of self-absorption, which was not altogether new but was manifest in powerful ways during this time.[105] Unconstrained by institutional authority (á la the fifties) and untethered by political ideals (expressed in the sixties), individualism yielded to narcissism.

Though various forces over the course of the twentieth century mediated the momentum of this shift, the seventies offered some of the most vivid images. The same decade gave rise to punk rock, *M.A.S.H.*, and *Taxi Driver*, but *Saturday Night Fever*, *Charlie's Angels*, and *The Brady*

Bunch are more widely associated with the zeitgeist of that time. The unresolved resentments of the previous era were put on the back burner obscured by freshly forward-looking and cheerful pop culture.

LEADERSHIP WITHOUT AUTHORITY

Shifting political terrain having weakened it for years, the old New Deal order finally crumpled conclusively upon the election of Ronald Reagan in 1980.[106] As real wages continued to decline throughout the seventies and eighties, the salaries of top executives climbed rapidly. This period of intensifying stratification further validated the deepening sense of individualism, which complemented a particular notion of national pride that Reagan helped foster.[107] The pursuit of individual happiness, available in the United States, stood in stark contrast to the corrupt empire of the Soviet Union. Reagan helped Americans recall the special value of our national heritage.

But the question of how we use that freedom had begun to simmer as unease about the loss of community spread. "There is no such thing as Society. There are individual men and women, and there are families," Margaret Thatcher famously declared in 1985. Unsurprisingly, apathy toward society's interests, if there really was such a thing, was expressed in numerous ways.

One manifestation was a wave of outrageous white collar crimes and other corporate excesses, or what Charles Derber describes as the "economic wilding of America."[108] Michael Milkin, Ivan Boesky, Charlie Atkins, and other criminals of their ilk typified the costs of deregulation and coddling of business interests. The savings and loan scandal of the late eighties, which cost the taxpayers some $500,000,000, further implicated national economic policy. Remaining political efforts to advocate for progress and reform were increasingly carried out by paid staff as opposed to grassroots organizers.[109]

More broadly, this environment cheapened the American heritage of individualism further, spawning the self-absorbed pursuit of a quick buck.[110] The collectivism served by unions, which had been in decline for some time, was only further weakened by this broad cultural sensibility and coordinated efforts on the part of government and corporations to shift the balance of power in favor of management. A broad pattern of deindustrialization brought about by technological innovation and relocation of manufacturing industries also undermined the economic and political leverage of organized labor.[111] By the end of the eighties, the American Federation of Labor–Congress of Industrial Organizations (AFL–CIO) was an inert, frail shell of its former self.[112]

Institutions as varied as government and the family deteriorated in other ways in this context. The suspicion directed toward government, the view that it was manipulated by "big interests," grew throughout this period.[113] The years between 1980 and 1985 entailed the highest rates of divorce in the country's history.[114] Even as President Reagan was renewing claims of American preeminence, Americans were confronted by familiar problems of poverty and child abuse as well as new epidemics, including crack and AIDS, all of which served to further divide the nation.[115]

The explosion of the space shuttle *Challenger* in January of 1986 made visible to all the deadly thin line between national pride and anguish. The Chernobyl disaster a few months later reminded us of the the stakes everyone was facing. Such concerns tempered the elation of victory when the Berlin wall finally fell in 1989, the Cold War won.

The combative Republican political strategist Lee Atwater, who helped effect the Reagan revolution, reflected on that era as he was dying of a brain tumor in 1991.

> My illness helped me see that what was missing in society is what was missing in me: a little heart, a little brotherhood. . . . The 80s were about acquiring—acquiring wealth, power, prestige. I know. I acquired more wealth, power and prestige than most. But you can acquire all you want and still feel empty. . . . It took a deadly illness to put me eye to eye with that truth, but it is a truth that the country, caught up in its ruthless ambitions and moral decay, can learn on my dime.[116]

While heartening to many liberals, the election of Bill Clinton in 1992 did little to curtail a number of these trends and intensified growing tensions among Americans on different sides of the political spectrum. Whether equivocating about what it means to smoke marijuana, have sex, or tell the truth, Clinton evinced a tricky ability to avoid clear judgments of dominant moral categories of right and wrong.

This ambiguity and Clinton's liberal agenda further exacerbated the ambivalence with which Americans recalled the turmoil of the sixties. His leadership affirmed the spreading sense of cultural relativism through which experience and subjective perspectives provide the basis for moral categories.[117] At the same time, though, a backlash was well under way as the champions of a more orthodox moral order resisted this shift.

The nineties became a time of moralism without moral order. The concern for morality did not translate into the kind of widespread respect and deference for institutional authorities that had characterized previous decades. By 1994 only 19 percent of Americans trusted the federal government to do the right thing.[118] And what authority was preserved by government and other institutions could not ameliorate the increasingly pervasive anxiety and tension felt by Americans.[119]

Alongside all the apprehensions described above, many Americans experienced the final years of the twentieth century as a period of prosperity. Budget surpluses and continuing productivity reflected healthy economic growth.[120] Confidence in free-market logic motivated repeal of the Glass-Steagall Act in 1999, which had been one of the main laws regulating the banking industry for over sixty-five years.[121]

CROSSING BOUNDARIES

The approach of the new millennium brought to mind a sense of history, an awareness of struggles of the past and the possibilities of the future. One important trend in particular was recognized by many as a source of profound social change. Echoing the dramatic transformation of the Industrial Revolution, the rapid development of computer technology contributed to an information revolution. The speed and volume of information that spread through the use of computers altered fundamental perceptions of time and space.

While we begin trying to make sense of the consequences of this radical transformation in how we communicate, two patterns are clear. Americans are interacting with a larger number of people via digital technology. And the character of those interactions is different than social ties of previous eras. The media allow for more efficient, frank, and egalitarian interaction than face-to-face talk, which is partly why we are so inclined to join in.

But the new technological communication also enables more staged, manipulated "presentation of self" or personal branding because it lacks the physical, perceptible aspect of personal contact and, often, the accountability of more than two persons.[122] If the candor is volatile or the cultivated impressions not credible, that's okay because the interactions are more intermittent, short-lived, and superficial.

Again, we see a twist on old themes. The sense of productivity and progress—doing something faster in new ways with the hope of better outcomes—has compelled the rapid spread of wireless phones, Blackberries, desktop computers, iPods, and the like. Fewer than a quarter of American adults owned mobile phones in 1995, compared to 53 percent in 2000, and two-thirds in 2004.[123] Likewise, just 11 percent of U.S. households had online access in 1994, but by 1998 the proportion was 26.2, and in 2000 it was 41.5.[124] In 2006, 73 percent of adults went online each day.[125]

This phenomenal cultural diffusion represents a broad shift we cannot yet fully comprehend. The new technologies have blurred boundaries, allowing the rapid movement of people, capital, and especially information.[126] The technology itself is dynamic, much of it turning over to new versions faster than a lot of individuals and organizations can keep up with. The very real and remarkable benefits are grasped by many, as the rapid growth in use demonstrates.[127] However, the drawbacks are not as clearly understood.[128] For example, a new "digital divide" has developed, which reflects tremendously divergent trajectories in life for those with or without access to innovative computer technology, further exacerbating the increasing social inequality of American society.[129]

Despite the meaningful possibilities of computer technology, however, those with access give inordinate attention to trivial information and juvenile games. The Internet can be used for a lot of things, but our current patterns largely revolve around commerce, sex, and celebrity.[130] Virtually all of the most frequently researched subjects on Google in the new millennium are highly marketed popular culture icons like Britney Spears, Harry Potter, and Brad Pitt.[131] Such diversions cannot be blamed on the technology per se. Rather, the expansive market culture has accustomed us to such escapism. During 2001, $230 billion was spent on advertising in the United States, a nearly 750 percent increase in four decades.[132] Whether or not we blame it on advertising, the way the new technology is used reminds us that information and wisdom are not the same thing.[133]

Indeed, there is much about digital communication that is in no way durable. Relationships and identity are increasingly considered provisional. As "planned obsolescence" shapes cycles of production and consumption of material goods, a new kind of intended disposability coincides with the digital age. Beyond clothes, cars, and houses, we are becoming accustomed to trading in emotions, convictions, "friends," and confidants.[134] Given recent patterns in other media, it will be interesting to see whether the power of the Internet with all its diffuse, free, creative possibilities can be harnessed, managed, or regulated.[135]

FROM BAD TO WORSE

In general, the privatization of public goods has been spreading.[136] Starbucks operates in public libraries and on state university campuses. Cell phones replace public telephones. Political campaigns are funded through private donations (sometimes by the candidates themselves) on a scale never seen before. An estimated one in six Americans lives under the protection of privately hired police in some kind of self-contained community.[137] Lizabeth Cohen describes in *A Consumers' Republic* a trend that began after World War II and has gained ever-greater momentum: Americans define themselves as citizens and consumers. Citizenship and consumerism are now inextricably enmeshed—a kind of synergy that will likely play out on the Internet in interesting, consequential ways.

This awkward coupling notwithstanding, patriotism surged in recent years. If the defining trend of the era—technological innovation—blurred boundaries, the single most important event of the new millennium undermined the notion of coherent boundaries further on September 11, 2001. The assault on the United States of America by a shadowy enemy shocked us into recognition that our national borders are porous. Not a nation, a people, a religion, or a conventional social movement, the fundamentalist Islamic terrorists themselves resisted familiar categories and did not fit with previous understandings of global politics dominant in American society.

As this new threat and new sense of vulnerability startled Americans, we were reminded of our rich history of struggles for freedom. Though our borders were not as secure as we had imagined, this attack fostered a sense of pride and coherence in the American identity not felt in some time. But soon after this event brought us together, new centrifugal pressures began pulling us apart. The usual rejuvenation of civic life on the heels of warfare did not take place.[138]

The troubled presidency of George W. Bush further aggravated a strongly polarized political culture. Though his leadership during the early weeks after 9/11 was widely praised, the country soon became intensely divided about the war in Iraq. By the end of his second term, public confidence in the president, and more generally in the direction of the country, reached the lowest point in decades.

"Mission Accomplished," Abu Ghraib, Valerie Plame, Guantanamo, Pat Tillman, Katrina, phone tapping, waterboarding, Walter Reed Hospital, and all the other dreadful headlines seemed endless. Large tax cuts benefited few but the most wealthy.[139] Unresolved conflicts in Afghanistan and Iraq, growing instability throughout the region, including in Israel, diminished American credibility around the world, scores of domestic problems, including deteriorating infrastructure, and most importantly, a projected $1.2 trillion deficit for the final year of his term, motivated many commentators to suggest that Bush had been the worst president in American history.[140]

A NEW DIRECTION?

Strange things happened in 2008. As one scandal after another tumbled through Wall Street, the biggest fraud in history, the theft of more than $60 billion by Bernie Madoff, was just another news story. While the scale of such corruption was difficult for most Americans to conceive, the reality of a deepening recession was familiar and immediate.

A sharp drop in American housing prices during the summer of 2007 and then the crash of the "subprime" mortgage loan market led to a glut of unsold houses. A related crisis in the financial industry in the spring of 2008 occurred at the same time as a decline in the consumer price index (CPI), the first since 1955. As the global banking industry collapsed the following fall, the Federal Reserve, the Treasury Department, and Congress all made frantic efforts to avoid a genuine economic disaster.[141]

By December, falling housing prices had contributed to $50 thousand lost per household. When venerable firms such as American International Group, Lehman Brothers, Bear Stearns, Merrill Lynch, Ford, Chrysler, and General Motors faced the very real prospect of bankruptcy, the federal government spent trillions of dollars on no fewer than six bailouts.[142]

In one of the first ambitious attempts to make sense of the economy during this time, Richard A. Posner characterized this "depression" as "par for the course."

> As far as one can judge on the basis of what is known today (obviously an important qualification), the depression is the result of normal business activity in a laissez-faire economic regime—more precisely, it is an event consistent with the normal operations of economic markets. Bankers and consumers alike seem on the whole to have been acting in conformity with their rational self-interest throughout the period that saw the increase in risky banking practices, the swelling and bursting of the housing bubble, and a reduction in the rate of personal savings combined with an increase in the riskiness of those savings.[143]

This was not a problem fundamentally resulting from government policy, except insofar as the long-term deregulation movement (which began in the 1970s and culminated in the repeal of the Glass-Steagall Act in 1999, and the tolerance of new unregulated financial institutions) left the way open for the kinds of risks bankers and consumers alike were tempted to take.[144]

Undaunted, committed defenders of the market, such as syndicated columnist Cal Thomas, resist the possibility that government can help or that the market can hurt our common life.

> As government acquires the auto industry and seeks to own health care; as it plans to take more money from the productive in order to subsidize the unproductive or less productive; as government evolves

from nanny to a cruel and abusive guardian that will rob the individual of incentive and punish those who manage to succeed with crippling regulations and higher taxes, where are the champions of liberty and personal responsibility?[145]

During this period, nevertheless, it became very clear that the majority of Americans were eager for a different direction.[146] Fifty-three percent of the electorate voted for an African American, who ran his presidential campaign on the promise of change, electrifying the world and surprising even themselves. Still more people expressed confidence in Barack Obama's leadership after his inauguration. A 69 percent approval rating at that time, one of the highest in the history of presidential polling, seemed to reflect more than a partisan victory.[147] Where this combination of widespread frustration and intense desire for a fresh start will lead is very much an open question.

CONCLUSION

This review reveals the evolution of key values most relevant to our current situation. To conclude this chapter, I will briefly comment on these defining ideals that were important from the founding but have changed in significant ways. With an ocean and a revolution to separate it from its European roots, the United States was in a special position to embrace the Enlightenment principle of *progress*. Looking forward, Americans eagerly sought out the new and faced the unfamiliar. Even in the context of radical social change during the nation's first century, though, enough people still knew, or were themselves, immigrant Americans so as to retain some real sense of a past set elsewhere. After immigration was curtailed in the early decades of the twentieth century, the break became more complete and an expanded sense of progress surged. As the melting pot expected and rewarded assimilation, Americans embraced what was "new and improved."

This change gained momentum throughout the middle and second half of the twentieth century. From a fascination with novel ideas, products, and experiences and a complementary aversion to the old and traditional, the result has become scarce memory for situating and interpreting the way we live.[148] We seek out the newest version of products we already have so impatiently that we will accept the sprawl of additional shopping centers that make them available.[149] The current notion of "progress," though clearly rooted in the old, is in some sense quite new but not improved.

This sense of progress at the founding encompassed the goal of expanding *liberty*. The most important and historically contested ideal in the American experience is freedom. Despite some fairly unqualified language about "inalienable rights" and the like, the Founders recognized the complexity of this ideal, its varied meanings, and the ongoing need for its negotiation. The narrative presented in this chapter reveals how this burdened ideal has been strained by discrimination, yearning for prosperity, the desire for order and security, skepticism of institutional authority, and the related impulse to privatize large portions of our life. A widespread appreciation of the complexity inherent in this sacred American principle endures in spite of such pressures.

The most prominent element of freedom in public memory and contemporary discourse, though, has become protecting the pursuit of property. The main impediment to this kind of freedom is the state. Since the end of the New Deal order in the early 1980s, there has been a growing sense that government must be vigilantly restrained and kept out of our lives. Certainly there is talk of freedom from government surveillance and similar encroachments, freedom to drive fast or watch profanity on TV. But what has dominated public discourse in this regard seems to be the individual ability to make money, including specifically minimal taxation and regulation, the most common impositions of government.

This preoccupation contributes to acceptance of incessant marketing and insatiable consumption. Whatever the laws are, we have become accustomed to advertisements in virtually every space of our lives, not just hanging on the signs along the road or popping up on our screen, but blaring into our living room and amplified over the airwaves. And the main expression of "individuality" is to consume voluminously in distinctive, exhibitionist ways.

Another related aspiration built in to the American Dream is *prosperity*. The triumph of the Pilgrims' survival in 1621 celebrated at the original Thanksgiving signified humble recognition of their vulnerability and the hopes for ongoing welfare. Jefferson's defining phrase, "pursuit of happiness," was derived in part from Adam Smith's pursuit of "property" and John Locke's pursuit of "estate." Public memory retained an important blend of humility and ambition in these linked quests up through the middle of the twentieth century. Those who encountered the changes triggered by industrialization, immigration, war, and depression nurtured dreams of security for their children against the genuine threats they had endured.

After World War II, though, such goals broadened. As the economy and consumer classes grew, such ambitions did too. And they were largely fulfilled as the output and affluence of the society improved dramatically for more than three decades. Early on, the urgent hope of survival had become the rational fulfillment of authentic needs. After consumerism spread and became more privatized, by the 1980s, hungry desires were transformed into insatiable wishes. The humble pursuit of happiness is now the harried hunt for more.

The explicit goal of prosperity was from the beginning served through another implicitly prized value, *productivity*. The early colonists and all the immigrants that followed included a disproportionate number of industrious, motivated people. For some, this quality was the result of the Protestant ethic, for others the special self-selecting combination of risks and opportunities inherent in the immigrant experience. For whatever reason, Americans have always worked hard. It is ironic, though, that as the wealth and labor-saving technology of our society have dramatically accumulated over the decades, this urgent sense of productivity has, if anything, gained momentum.

The more important development is that this sensibility has swept into other parts of our lives beyond work, in the home, in school, even in recreation. We do not only wish to have more, we wish to do more. Competition has been woven into the fabric of our lives, for the top job, the nicest house, the most successful child, the best parking spot, and so on.

The goal of having and doing more makes problematic the next theme, *equality*. Our economic system has always yielded uncommon opportunity to realize unusual prosperity. That is, compared to other industrialized societies, there have been greater possibilities for turning a little into a lot. While the ongoing development of technological innovations, the persistent competitive advantage in global exchange, and the ever-growing affluence keep it from being a zero-sum game, however, the game is nevertheless rigged. The American Dream is predicated on an uneven distribution of resources.

This was true at the beginning with Native Americans, Africans, as well as Europeans and others in the laboring classes on the short end of things. And the stratification system has continued to facilitate hugely concentrated wealth. While there is less absolute poverty and less injustice based on ascribed status such as race and gender, there is now more unnecessary poverty than ever before. That is, we have the aggregate wealth to essentially eliminate poverty, but do not. There is simply no material basis for people in our society not having first-rate medicine, education, or housing, for example.[150] The poor and working classes contain disproportionate numbers of children, women, and people of color, many of whom work for the security that eludes them.

Given the pervasive rhetoric of the American Dream and the exorbitant expectations for comfort and leisure, it is easy to see why so many people become frustrated and angry. And it is also not difficult to grasp how their piercing complaints then alienate many affluent Americans who feel they have earned their way. While not as hideous as genocide or slavery, this gap between the talk and experience of what is possible nevertheless reflects a significant moral failure of our time and contributes mightily to ongoing strife.

The final issue worth emphasizing is *authority*. Though less iconic as an American ideal than the other themes mentioned here, it has been central to our ethos since the break with King George III. The transfer of power from a monarchy to a republic, the shift from traditional authority to legal rational authority, to use Max Weber's terms, represented a defining and decisively American moment of modernity. Who you are now matters less than what you do, especially in relation to the laws of modern government. Beyond that, though, the entire notion of authority is in question.[151]

The Founders are regarded in our public memory as people of uncommon talent who explicitly recognized the threat of authority. Conversely, our leaders today are often considered individuals of modest ability unwilling to acknowledge the risks of power. Whether or not this dichotomy is fair, it reflects an important transformation in how Americans think about leadership, and more broadly, the authority of institutions in general. Various forces converged in the 1960s to pull back the curtain. Reacting to specific failures of institutional leaders and to old, unresolved problems, such as those related to inequality described in the last paragraph, that generation of protesters assaulted the notion of anyone being in charge.

This saga, combined with the staggeringly complex problems of modern society, and new institutional failures, seems to have permanently complicated the idea of moral authority. Even those who champion the cause of this candidate or that chief do so with knowing cynicism about the necessary evils of leadership. And many more take comfort in ignoring the fray. In this way the burdens and skepticism of public leadership have led us to cede power to people willing and able to work in more concealed settings. This includes those maneuvering among market forces. The upshot is a great lack of credible, public, moral leaders.

4

TRIUMPH OF THE MARKET

A common complaint of conservatives is that government has exceeded its appropriate boundaries by way of regulation, surveillance, and especially taxation. On the other hand, we also hear criticism from liberals decrying the influence of religion in public life, particularly in terms of moralistic judgment. Both sides make credible arguments but ignore the big elephant in the room. The influence of the market is substantially more authoritative than the most powerful elements of either the polity or civil society.

In addition to the colossal leverage of multinational firms "too big to fail," think of how frequently advertisements, job opportunities, work pressures, or consumption habits shape our choices. Or ask the inverse question. What choices are not affected by such forces? Then we can perhaps think more clearly about which institutional sphere has become too intrusive.

There is no society without an economy. Of all the different kinds of economic systems different societies have created, free market capitalism has proven itself to be the most productive. It generates sophisticated institutions that serve education, innovation, and creativity. In encouraging the development of rational law and various forms of individual freedom associated with it over time, capitalism also undermines traditional sources of domination associated with racial, ethnic, gender, and religious discrimination.

In the history of the world, these are neither incidental nor inevitable patterns; they reflect immense accomplishments in the advancement of human society. As with the history of our own young nation, the development of capitalism was determined by broad institutional forces as well as particular consequential choices people made at momentous turning points. Both the institutions and actions were shaped by important ideas and values.

Given all of these appealing aspects of our economic system, wouldn't it make sense to want the influence of the market to grow? Don't we want to promote the relevant ideas and values? The obvious answer is, yes, to a certain point. But too much of anything is bad. When the logic and force of any given institution expands past a certain threshold, history shows that serious problems inevitably unfold. Whether it is government, religion, the military, or the family, for instance, we do not have to look far to find troubling examples across the world. Think of state socialism, fundamentalist theocracy, military juntas, or rigidly divided ethnic clans.

In our society, the logic and force of the economic system has crossed that threshold. Forget about Max Weber's "Protestant ethic," even the original "spirit of capitalism" is itself now antiquated. The notion of judiciously borrowing money, perhaps to invest in a business or make a down payment on a home, has ballooned to the point of stretching as far as possible in order to get more and bigger stuff. This growing tolerance for debt is accompanied by a frantic need to be productive, one enduring element of the old work ethic, but now in all aspects of life.

The venerated ideals of freedom, equality, and progress, as well as related but less explicitly celebrated notions of prosperity, productivity, and authority reflect defining elements of the American ethos. Another set of overlapping goals has been integral to this story as well. These more generically capitalistic themes include efficiency, technological innovation, and profit (which are discussed in the next three chapters). That is, each of these ideas has been very important in American history but has been less explicitly extolled as American.

The fact that I am describing two sets of ideas, one identified as American and the other capitalistic, reflects an important distinction.

The United States of America and capitalism are not the same thing. The first contains the best example of the latter, but an economic system is only one type of institution among others that shape a large, complex society like contemporary America.

THE AMERICAN ETHIC AND THE SPIRIT OF CAPITALISM

There are in fact many different capitalistic nations, quite varied in terms of language, religion, government, and, ultimately, the way people live. Despite the intrinsically expansive logic of the market system, capitalism has not been able to reduce all of these different societies to indistinguishable copies precisely because of the importance of other institutional forces.[1] For example, we see tremendous cultural variation between capitalistic countries like Brazil, Germany, Israel, and Japan.

Contrary to claims about the final triumph of liberal democracy or the end of history, the differences among various industrialized societies will surely continue to be significant. As important as the political economy of a society is, there are other powerful forces in history, not to mention lots of real variation within the category of liberal democracy. If that is correct, then the main question about our own society is, how did the values of the market so thoroughly penetrate the values of the United States? What happened to the noble ideals that defined who we Americans are to one another and to the world?

The answer involves the relative weakening of noneconomic social institutions, which accelerated decisively in the second half of the twentieth century. There once was in our republic a balance of institutional forces composed of the state, the market, and civil society. At first, the market and civil society acted in concert to contain the exertion of government authority.[2] Over time, the market's influence grew, shaping government to serve its interests and nudging civil society to the side. Along the way, the market economy became the market society.[3] The logic of commodification in the economic sphere spread to other parts of society. There were no longer any limits to the value that could be placed on nature or humanity.

Everything now has a price, including experiences, personalities, and public goods, including, at times, government itself. We now know that whether it is climbing Mount Everest, traveling in space, spending the night in the Lincoln bedroom, adopting a child, having someone else raise your children, or acquiring a new body part, anything can be bought. That means anything can be sold.[4] At the very least, that is a powerfully magnetic idea in our culture.

It is impossible to identify one turning point in this narrative. But among the essential defining moments, one was clearly the conflagration of World War II, which drew the world's attention to this vibrant, young nation as we participated in international politics and deepened Americans' own sense of *national* destiny (relative to region, state, ethnicity, religion, and other sources of identity). As a transformative event, the war set the stage for the cultural shift that followed in the middle of the twentieth century.

In that context, the rigid assertion of institutional authority in 1950s America, combined with deep-seated resentments about unequal access to power, gave rise to the protests and antiestablishment social movements of the 1960s. Civil society has been weakened ever since, throwing the previous institutional balance further out of whack. The result is that civil institutions no longer have the strength to contain market forces, and individuals no longer have the moral framework provided by such institutions to screen the influence of market logic in their lives. Unfit for this latter task in any case, the state has its hands full in governing a society that has rapidly grown larger and more complex.

That is, in terms of the resources, energy, and attention that society collectively devoted to different enterprises, there once was relative equilibrium between the market's provisions in the economy, the state's attention to governing, and civil society's nurturing of community. Many Americans knew that being engaged in each of these enterprises—the economy, the government, and civil society—was not mutually exclusive. Fulfilling a vocation and putting food on the table, defending and benefiting from the laws of the land, and giving to and taking from institutionally bound, civil relationships were collectively workable.

One could, for instance, become accomplished in a craft, participate in public service, be an active church deacon and still have time for family and neighbors. These were compatible and even reciprocally reinforcing activities. Time moved more slowly and somehow allowed for such substantive connectedness. This kind of balance represented a fulfillment of the ideals that guided society and of the hopes that Americans attached to their daily lives. The way they lived and the functioning of the main institutions they encountered were in this sense consistent with what they believed.

Of course, social life is always messy, and the short history of the United States has been filled with disruptive social change and severe strife. Indeed, unresolved conflict was a part of the precarious balance from the beginning and contributed in no small part to how it was so thoroughly disrupted in the 1960s. So, this sense of balance should not be understood as stasis or consensus in all things. Rather, these three kinds of institutions—economic, political, and civil—were each strong enough to hold the others in check, so that not any single category had its internal logic negated by the intrusion of the other kinds. In that sense, a sort of institutional parity existed that kept the change, conflict, and logic of each kind of institution—powerful forces all—from undermining the order and meaning most Americans felt in their lives.

THE DECLINE OF COUNTERBALANCING INSTITUTIONS

As evident in the account of U.S. history in the previous chapter, three forces converged in the 1960s to conclusively destabilize this balance, which has led to the moral crisis we now face. The most fundamental factor was the logic of the market itself, which is inherently expansive. As Karl Marx and many others have noted, the market always seeks to spread its influence. Entrepreneurs, inventers, and research and design departments aspire to create innovative products that others will buy. Merchants and managers seek new settings, new people, new desires—that is, new markets—that will allow them to sell more products. Shoppers hope to find services that will accommodate unmet needs, higher quality products, and special bargains. Those who invest in markets—stock brokers, financial advisors, boards of directors, shareholders—hope there will be lots of buying and selling in general. These various incentives have contributed over time to increasingly widespread economic transactions. This expansion of markets within and beyond the United States contributes to increasing wealth but also poses a continuing threat to other institutions, two patterns that gained momentum in the late twentieth century.

The second factor that helped destabilize institutional balance was the gap between our nation's stated ideals of equality and democracy and the reality of injustice and exclusion, or what the Swedish social scientist Gunnar Myrdal described as "an American dilemma."[5] A contradiction since the founding, the special freedoms of the republic were never equally available to people of color, women, and other marginalized groups. This inconsistency became more conspicuous after World War II, both in terms of Myrdal's focus of race, as well as other strata, and led to heightened tension during the 1950s and the unrest that followed. More equality has been realized here than in most other societies, but much more is promised, too.

The third factor, which was activated to some extent by that dissonance, was the diminished credibility of authority produced by the turmoil of the sixties. Unequal access to the American Dream, unrealized ideals of political inclusiveness, and the institutional failures of the era all contributed to a new level of distrust in a wide range of social institutions. At the same time, that is, during the fifties and sixties, the market surged, generating more wealth and more leverage as a central force in American society. Since the early seventies, the influence of countervailing institutions in government and civil society has deteriorated.

This is true of a large range of organizations, voluntary associations, and small groups.[6] The most serious effects related to the spread of market logic, though, involve just a few major institutions, including religion, organized labor, media, education, and government, each of which has a special character that has at times enabled it to serve this valuable counterbalancing function.

The most important organizations in civil society, including each of these countervailing institutions, serve two functions that offset market logic. They (a) create internal community among members or participants and (b) advance an agenda beneficial to society that is separate from the economy. In different circumstances, one of the functions may be more forcefully operative than the other. But the most important parts of civil society, including these five institutions (counting government) serve both tasks.

The weakening of these institutions has resulted in large measure from the broad historical forces described above, including most importantly the slipping credibility of institutional authority in general. In each case, there have also been specific factors that contributed to the deterioration, which I discuss briefly below.[7]

RELIGION

Religion is one of the most vibrant sources of psychological renewal and transformative imagination.[8] While the United States is the most religious society in the West, the way we practice religion is largely compartmentalized.[9] Most analysts now believe that religious organizations have not declined in activity or numbers the way many scholars previously claimed.[10] But some still maintain involvement in religious activities has fallen by 25 to 50 percent over the last several decades.[11] In any case, the real development is not quantitative (i.e., shrinking numbers) but qualitative (i.e., shrinking influence on public life). Those who actively participate in religion do tend to give and volunteer a bit more.[12] Both the charity and volunteerism of religiously active people, however, tend to focus on religious organizations.[13] Among those who volunteer, the more one attends church, the more one is likely to serve church organizations and the less one is likely to volunteer in nonreligious organizations. All things being equal, it appears religiously active people are less tolerant and pluralistic in their attitudes toward other groups.[14]

In general, the influence of religion on economic values is quite limited, allowing most people of faith to retain conventional materialist sensibilities.[15] A lot of folks are very comfortable worshipping earnestly on Sunday and then returning to the grind on Monday morning without ever thinking about what they encountered in church. More broadly, the public engagement of religious institutions has been declining, especially among liberal traditions.[16]

The most potent religious influence in terms of current moral order clearly emanates from conservative traditions. The main focus appears to be abortion and homosexuality. Moreover, key conservative religious leaders have argued that the goals of capitalism are aligned with the teachings of scripture.[17] Regardless, the political coalition that fundamentalist and evangelical Christians share with free-market advocates in the Republican Party seems to have muted any sustained critique of market logic coming out of their churches. With respect to economic issues overall, the impact of religious communities on economic institutions remains subdued at best.

UNIONS

Organized labor is another civil institution that has historically played a vital role in balancing the forces of capitalism. The steady, long-term decline of the labor movement has been well documented.[18] The need for an organizational apparatus to represent the interests of workers became glaringly urgent during the Gilded Age.

From the founding of the American Federation of Labor in 1886, during the emergence of the Congress of Industrial Organizations in 1936 and up to the merger of the AFL and CIO in 1955, the deepening leverage wielded by union officialdom served this purpose and broader goals of balancing the polity. Unions also provided the organizational networks in industrial centers for spirited community life, replete with picnics, dances, sporting events, and so on. In 1960, the AFL-CIO represented a third of all American workers.

By the late nineties, however, that proportion had fallen below 15 percent.[19] A number of factors contributed to this decrease, including economic restructuring involving globalization and the shift away from manufacturing, intra-worker strife and factionalism, successful counter-offensives on the part of employers, and the growing affluence of many workers in the core unions.[20]

The implications of this decline encompass not just a loss of economic leverage for workers or diminished political clout on the part of union leaders, but also expanded influence in general on the part of employers.[21] Large firms increasingly have a free hand to set policies and manipulate politics, a pattern that has been decisive in the increasing concentration of wealth (described in chapter 5). Some observers speculate that the scandals surrounding Enron, Fannie Mae, and other companies represent just the tip of the iceberg, that the culture of corporate excess is much too entrenched for several prosecutions to really fix it.[22]

The continuing involvement of organized labor in government, including millions of dollars of donations devoted to campaigns and lobbying, reflects substantial representation of workers' interests in the political process. Nevertheless, the overwhelming trend over the last half-century is a dramatic shift in the balance of power favoring capital over labor.[23]

MEDIA

Another major institution (or cluster of institutions) that has great capacity for providing moral ballast in society is the media. The press has been heroic in previous decades in exposing corruption, greed, and waste. For example, muckraking journalism and fiction such as *The Jungle* were enormously important in reining in the excesses of the Gilded Age and bringing about a period of reform. While individual journalists have labored diligently ever since, the overall efficacy of the press is more complicated.

The explosion of different forms of media, especially electronic means of communication, is surely one of the most dramatic developments in recent history. The new "torrent of images and sounds"[24] shapes how we think, the values we espouse, and the ways we live.[25] "Image is everything!" Andre Agassi declared in advertisements for Canon cameras. Well, maybe not everything, but image does command more attention than ever before.

We spend increasing time and energy paying attention to information from afar, mediated by advertisers, political strategists, stylists, designers, actors, and other "imagologues," compared to the material circumstances or people immediately around us.[26] As information is channeled in multiple directions, though, there appear to be two main, contrasting trends.

The growth of different forms of media has facilitated a kind of opening up, as if all the dams holding back vast pools of information were knocked down around the same time so that the voluminous data could rush forward and flow throughout the world. More transparency, greater numbers of people interacting across wider distances, access to systematically organized facts all serve noble goals of enlightenment, democracy, and equality. In terms of news and information on history, culture, politics, art, health, food, and other topics, there is an enormous range of outlets and perspectives available to almost everyone.

Compared to the 120,000 entries of Encyclopedia Britannica, the icon of expert-based knowledge, Wikipedia, which is continuously built online primarily by lay people, had over a million entries at the same time in 2006.[27] By 2010, it reported 3.2 million entries in English. Neither shyness, isolation, nor poverty blocks access to knowledge and the resulting power that accompanies it. Certainly the "blogosphere" provides new opportunities for broad-based public discourse and community of a sort. Preliminary research suggests that the Internet can extend social networks in very productive ways.[28]

But all of this interaction and transparency has yielded limited results when it really counts, as the failures of the press to expose the flawed analyses and policies behind the Iraq war and the economic recession demonstrate. In addition, while the new access facilitates inclusive discourse, it appears to complement another disturbing pattern— the fundamental loss of literacy. After spreading for decades, anti-intellectualism has been further exacerbated by the way the modern media infantilizes consumers.[29] The dumbing down of American culture contributes to a basic loss of memory, knowledge, and perspective.[30]

This slide is likely related to the other major trend unfolding at the same time, expanding oligopoly. Five media conglomerates—Time Warner, Disney, Murdoch, Viacom, and Bertelsmann—control the vast majority of the 178,000 outlets of "information industries." The annual expenditures of $286 billion paid for mass media advertising and the $800 billion Americans spent on media products during the early years of the new millennium went mainly to these companies.[31] There is now some question as to how involved corporations are in manipulating information on Wikipedia and various blogs, surely a portent of things to come as big companies seek to gain control over the decentered discourse of the Web.[32]

The astonishing accomplishments of advanced technology as well as the expansive range and complexity of communication facilitated by these organizations constitute a modern marvel. The overarching control of such concentrated power, however, enables some important boundaries. That is, there are at least two messages that are rarely conveyed with any force: turn off this machine; stop spending money. In other words, the mainstream media, not surprisingly, promotes its own expansion, and is deeply enmeshed with the marketing apparatus of capitalism.[33]

As the media empire spreads, so does marketing, always pushing, pressing into previously private places. Now we can even get information about products on eggs (themselves), in the bottom of urinals, on airplane motion-sickness bags, in the bottom of security bins used at airport checkpoints, or anywhere you are plugged in.[34] Who would have thought even a few years ago that huddling pro football players or winning jockeys would accept a microphone stuck in their faces just before or after their key competitive moment? That families would invite unsupervised encounters with advertisers into their young children's bedrooms by way of the computer?

The themes that are effectively transmitted in the new media, Todd Gitlin shows, include celebrity worship, paranoia, and "disposable feelings," sensibilities that fit nicely with capitalistic activity.[35] These patterns partly represent a shift away from print media (which tends to foster social capital) and toward TV (which does not).[36] In short, while there is much to celebrate in the development of modern media, there is no question that this cluster of institutions does little to balance the influence of market logic in our lives.

EDUCATION

Education has always been a double-edged sword, at once cultivating new generations to take their places in the American stratification system while at the same time providing the means for subverting such arrangements. Numerous exceptions notwithstanding, though, the former trend remains much stronger. A person born into a family in an affluent neighborhood can count on better schools. An average student at a better school can more easily gain admission to college. Graduates of more prestigious colleges are welcomed through more open doors after school.[37] This is partly how class structure works. The access that is available to lower-class students nevertheless enables significant mobility that is distinctive in the United States.[38]

In primary and secondary education, the main achievements in this regard have been more access for a much broader range of students, inviting them into more diverse occupational trajectories. As important and hopeful as this trend is, that portion of the educational system functions in tandem with the large social structures of our society, including the market. And, at any rate, access to college in particular remains disproportionately available to historically privileged groups.[39]

Moreover, the decline of basic proficiency in terms of literacy, history, and civics in primary and secondary education is a national scandal.[40] Beyond not knowing the dates of the Civil War, the primary author of the Declaration of Independence, or the main conclusion of *Brown v. Board of Education*, American students are being rapidly outpaced in basic skills by kids throughout Europe and Asia.[41] While the main factors behind this problem remain a subject of intense debate, there is little question that the educational system itself is implicated.[42] In any case, it is easy to see how a poorly educated citizenry can be manipulated by marketing.[43]

Higher education is something of a different story. The academy in particular has the capacity to be a counterbalancing institutional force, fostering imagination, civic sensibility, and expertise that can resist stupefying marketing or the "tyranny of the bottom line."[44] Despite the regular news stories portraying the subversive indoctrination of left-leaning political correctness, however, there appears to be little substantive institutional forcefulness on the broader public stage.[45]

Like religion, educational institutions have been effective in formulating alternative images of how social life could be arranged. Informed by extensive, sophisticated analyses, imagination does thrive in the academy. But, like religion, such vision appears limited in its effects on the choices people actually make in their economic lives, the priorities they set, how hard they work, what they buy, and so on.[46]

In reflecting on twenty years of experience in academia, I think there are several reasons for such limitations. First, as befits intellectual endeavors, we are much better at analysis and argument than we are at practice and application. Scholars generate the most carefully thought-out ideas but, at least in this generation, are unschooled in the organizational challenges of actually effecting change. This is a bigger problem now that American life is so privatized and enshrouded in the media torrent. The blaring chatter of "imagologues" has drowned out the more faint voice of genuine experts.

Academic research also tends to be specialized. Partly that is justified by how much is now known and how complex the foundations of knowledge are in any given area. Specialization to some extent reflects a necessary division of labor.

An exacerbating problem, though, is that we in the academy relish the obscure, the esoteric and, sometimes, the inane. "Professionals write for other professionals," Alan Wolfe laments.[47] One problem, of course, is that almost all great ideas in human history were at one time obscure, esoteric, and even inane in some sense. Still, it is far from clear whether most scholars think at all about the actual impact of their research in the broader world.

To make matters worse, those administrative officials charged with guiding academic institutions forward, and with thinking institutionally, feel captive to the sovereignty of consumers, further curtailing the active engagement of the academy in public life. The widespread use of underpaid labor to teach students and the full-throttled commitment to big-time sports so common at major universities also reflect the submission to market logic. Like religion, the labor movement, and the media, the academy's contribution to balancing market logic, which has at times been significant, is now quite weak.

GOVERNMENT

Though usually not considered part of civil society per se, government is another even more significant institution that has occasionally served a counterbalancing role. The state has the power to fundamentally alter the operation and leverage of other institutions, including the market. During the Great Depression, for example, the Roosevelt administration directly confronted the market, and, in some sense, rescued it from itself. The state in a capitalist society seeks to protect order and maintain business confidence, which makes it an inherently conservative organization. The only time it departs from such priorities is during a major crisis, especially when business confidence has already collapsed (as in the Great Depression), and other institutions (e.g., unions, churches) pressure government to take action.[48] So, while government has great capacity for confronting the market, as it did in the 1930s, it is generally not likely to use it. The extent of government's exertion against market forces in the current economic crisis is hotly debated, but there appears to be little systemic adjustment (such as addressing the problems of deregulation) relative to the underlying problems (see chapter 3).

More broadly, the state's incentives for serving the interests of capital are well established. State managers and corporate leaders overlap a great deal in their backgrounds and education, and in the organizations with which they are associated. In fact, they are often the same people.[49] Plus, elected officials are dependent on corporations for campaign finance and economic stability. In 2008, $5.3 billion was spent on the presidential election alone.[50] Needless to say, a large majority of those funds were derived from donations from businesses. "Rare is the politician," Robert Kuttner notes, "who will not take a phone call from a larger donor or fund-raiser."[51]

The increasing power of multinational corporations, the weakening of the labor movement, and the concomitant shrinking of key elements in the federal government have only strengthened this alliance in favor of corporate influence.[52] The exorbitant amounts of money now flowing into Democratic and Republican campaigns alike, and the "campaign finance reform" everyone recognized as lip service even before *Citizens United v. Federal Election Commission*, seem to reflect new resignation; this is how it is.[53] Even dedicated state managers sincerely committed to government's great promise are confronted by problems of such scale and complexity, there is little they can do to check the overwhelming momentum of market forces. The result of this shift has been, basically since the 1970s, an extensive pattern of deregulation, increasingly regressive taxation, expanding privatization of institutions, a related deterioration of public infrastructure, and growing inequality.[54]

The other vital role that government can help facilitate in civil society is fostering a buy-in on the part of citizens. By symbolically communicating the value of democracy and substantively delivering returns for working within the system, government has a deep capacity for creating and re-creating the largest and most important form of community, that is, society.[55] Needless to say, our government has for some time failed magnificently in this role. In addition to ceding control of vast portions of the public good to the market, government officials across the political spectrum have made their own mistakes that contribute to cynicism and distrust.[56]

CONCLUSION

As beneficial as the healthy functioning of these institutions has at times been for society, it is important to acknowledge their ugly side and the potently destructive possibilities that extend from it. Each of these institutions has in certain historical moments also served as a destructive force that is as morally corrosive as (and separate from) unbridled market logic.

The tight community nurtured in religion often results in hostility to the "other." For instance, mainstream Christian churches, Protestant and Catholic, have been entangled in anti-Semitic and racist practices. Labor unions have at times served the interests of white men to the exclusion of other workers, maintained criminal ties with the mob, and contributed to inordinately inefficient practices. Higher education and academia in particular have enabled noncompetitive privilege for well-to-do families. Professors sometimes engage in the most cynical kinds of careerism at the expense of educational priorities. The media has often turned a blind eye to injustice or incompetence. Perhaps the antics of Joseph McCarthy constitute the most famous example, but the coverage of what transpired before the Iraq war and the economic crisis also comes to mind. And of course American government has enslaved people, disenfranchised citizens, toppled democratically elected governments, and betrayed its own ideals on numerous occasions. None of these institutions offers a silver bullet, a pure, simple, conclusive resolution for the problems of our society. The internal logic of each one carries particular risks for corruption and immorality.

On the other hand, when operating with internal integrity and properly embedded in and offset by the structure of other social institutions, these counterbalancing forces have provided vital sources of perspective, accountability, and functionality in society. In their best moments, each of these institutions has engendered a conservative kind of root-edness that facilitated communal memory *and* a progressive sense of hopeful possibility that seeks society's improvement.

The prophetic traditions of Judeo-Christian theology, the engaged activism of labor unionism, the accountability facilitated by public discourse in journalism, the empowerment and innovation enabled through education, and the fair application of rational law have each served a constructive role in American society. Precisely because of the capacity of each one of these institutions to foster social solidarity and fulfill a valuable noneconomic objective, they have been effective in containing market logic and providing moral ballast.

They have, at different times, brought people together, imbued them with a meaningful identity and purpose, and helped them personally and collectively resist the temptations of market culture. That singular accomplishment of these institutions gives them special value and, given that they are now faltering, helps clarify why things are unfolding in our society the way they are.

Once we allowed the disintegration of our *moral hardware*, of the once vital countervailing institutions, our ability as individuals to make hard, wise decisions for the greater good—that is, our *moral soft-ware*—became largely unworkable.[57] We lost the contexts in which the language of virtue could be grasped and spoken. As a consequence, "American values" and the ideology of the market have become one and the same. We have no buffer for resisting the capitalist goals of profit, efficiency, and technological innovation.

That includes the places where we work, our homes, our com-munities, and numerous other social settings. In this new culture our treasured morals derived from honorable traditions of philosophy and common sense have devolved into themes consistent with this logic. The old vocabulary is distorted with new grammar and interpretation. Hence the "freedom" to consume, the "equality" of competition, the amazing efficiency of our "productivity," the insatiable craving for "prosperity," all in support of the increasingly strained narrative of "progress." If American ideals have changed beyond recognition due to the weaken-ing of these institutions, then what is the result? That is the topic of the next three chapters.

5

ECONOMIC LIFE:
WINNING THE RAT RACE

You have to be popular, you have to be in style—in order to be popular you have to be in style, so to achieve popularity you have to have a lot of clothes, a lot of shoes. My parents used to give me the money, but they saw how I got out of hand with my spending, so I had to get a job and pay for everything myself. Sometimes it can go close to about $700, $800 a month, just on clothes.

—Sean Michael (age seventeen)[1]

Each individual's biography must be understood in the context of society's history.[2] It would have helped if this basic sociological insight had been on my mind recently when my wife's Italian American family gathered for a holiday meal. As usual, women from three generations had prepared a large spread of baked ziti, meatballs, broccoli rabe, and more traditional American fare, way more than our number could ever eat. After much talk about the food and family, a lively conversation unfolded about "success."

My wife's cousin Tony was chiding the wise patriarch, Enzo, and other senior members of the family. "If you didn't want all of us to be successful, why did you push us so hard?" The older folks grew tense and mostly looked down at their dessert. "And why do you always say things like, 'So and so has done really well for himself, he and his family

have a beautiful home on the Main Line'? Yet, at the same time, you dis-
approve of anyone you judge to be too greedy or selfish." The approval
of someone's new home and the lament about greed had both been ut-
tered when the meal began. "It's hypocritical to celebrate ambition and
affluence but criticize those who make it."

When I heard Tony admonishing his relatives, it sounded self-
serving. Always carefully groomed and dressed, Tony is the kind of guy
who wants you to see his Mercedes and his swagger in the hopes of
clarifying beyond any doubt that *he* has made it. The exorbitant cost of
any item he has recently bought somehow emerges in every conversation. That night, he was rationalizing his pursuit of status and stuff, I
thought. But the usually outspoken Enzo and the other exasperated
elders voiced no response to his charge. He just doesn't get it, their
brooding faces suggested. Upon reflection, I have come to recognize
that this intergenerational dispute over what a good life is reflects a
fundamental shift in American culture. Tony's materialism is a sign of
the times and his incomprehension is understandable. His biography
reflects our history. And his question is therefore a fair one. Why are
we all working so hard?

Another cousin at the family gathering, Lila, shared her anxiety about
the mounting pressures she feels in balancing the significant demands
of her job as a professional with those of raising two small children. As
she considered leaving her vocation in favor of full-time motherhood
her mother was incredulous. She exclaimed to her daughter, "Honey,
everyone hates their job." Whether we personally live it or recognize it
from a distance, *Dilbert* and *The Office* seem to convey something very
familiar and real about modern work.

That same evening Uncle Bill reported having trouble with his teenage daughter, who is terribly sleep-deprived. She responds at all hours
to e-mails and cell phone calls she receives nightly and then, not surprisingly, "wakes up" not fully rested. As parents spend long hours in jobs
they don't like, buy cell phones, iPods, and other expensive toys for children as well as new kitchens and new cars for themselves, it seems that
some basic sense of proportionality is lacking in many people's lives.

There is no question that the market economy is the most productive economic system humans have devised. And there is no question
that the United States has pushed the farthest in its combination of

scale, technology, and productivity—an accomplishment only mildly diminished by the recent economic collapse. Ours is the richest, most capitalistic society in human history. America's wealth is recognized throughout the world and admired by many. It is in large measure what draws a constant stream of immigrants across our borders each year, and why even discontented Americans do not wish to live elsewhere. And it is partly what motivates the emulation of our economic policies in many countries. In addition to the leverage wielded through political and economic means, the storied American way of life generates a kind of cultural gravity.

At home, though, greed, waste, poverty, inequality, or corruption routinely sparks a sense of outrage or at least regret. Unhealthy products, degrading marketing, distasteful popular culture, and violent images are constantly presented to us. And yet, sometimes we like to indulge, "nice things" are appealing, choice matters, and we would not have our freedoms constrained by unworkable solutions for curtailing these problems. That is, we know something is wrong but are not sure what to do about it. This was true even before the economic crisis began in the fall of 2008.

In the most prosperous society in the world, we spend inordinate time and energy on economic activity. For most Americans, even during a recession, it is not about survival but extravagant expectations that motivate exorbitant levels of producing and consuming. This preoccupation draws us away from other important activities in life, such as those revolving around family and community. Worse yet, the distribution of resources is persistently unequal. Even in the context of this affluence many people live in poverty. There is, in short, something fundamentally wrong in all three phases of economic life in the United States: production, distribution, and consumption.

Market logic plays an expanding role in the daily decisions we make in three ways. First, by pushing us to be more aggressive when thinking about economic choices. That is, when we are working or consuming, we commit more intensely to market logic relative to other ethics.

Second, we spend more of our time and energy actively engaged in or thinking about economic behavior, at the job or while shopping. We are mentally at work even when we are physically not there. Obviously, such preoccupation is prevalent in the context of increasing foreclosures, layoffs, and salary freezes. But plenty of evidence suggests this behavior was widespread even before the recent recession. Indeed, risky, profit-oriented economic choices—on the part of corporate executives and consumers—contributed in a big way to the recession occurring in the first place.[3]

And third, this kind of logic is more common in other parts of our lives generally not thought of as involving economic goods. This applies to family life and civic life as outlined in other chapters and various other social contexts (e.g., sports, arts, hobbies, medicine, etc.). So, for example, rational organization and materialism are prevalent themes in American households, and achievement and competition are standard aspects of many pastimes. These effects of seeping market logic account in part for the frustration and bewilderment expressed among my in-laws that evening. Below I illuminate these connections further by examining the particular problems of production, distribution, and consumption in our economy. Throughout this discussion of broad economic patterns, an underlying theme is the contribution individual choices make to these problems.

PRODUCTION AND PRODUCTIVITY

Endowed with abundant natural resources and advantageously positioned in the developing world economy over two centuries ago, the United States was at its founding well situated to become a powerful nation.[4] Alexis de Tocqueville, Max Weber, and many other observers have recorded the unusual industriousness of Americans. Early on, the ideals of freedom and progress and the reality of opportunity available to many Americans made diligence and hard work pay off. Immigrants arriving in search of such possibilities came with big ambitions and met real challenges. Success yielded huge gains and failure was very costly. Laborers during the eighteenth and nineteenth centuries, both in agriculture and industry, endured great hardship. After industrialization revolutionized the economy and contributed to the rise of new class groups, the work ethic persisted.[5]

A momentous turning point in the twentieth century for laborers was World War II. Most Americans felt compelled to chip in and work extra hard in the war effort. Between 1940 and 1944, the average workweek in manufacturing increased seven hours. When the war ended, many workers needed to and were expected by employers to continue working long hours to earn the take-home pay to which they had grown accustomed.[6]

The spread of consumer culture in the fifties motivated long hours, too. New opportunities to make money, novel products, and an expanding sense of the household and all its appropriate accoutrements kept the productive incentives in motion. In *The Overworked American*, Juliet B. Schor reports that Americans doubled their productivity over a period of fifty years, increasing it every year between 1948 and 1992 except for five.

By 1987, the average American in the labor force worked 163 hours more each year compared to the time at work in 1969. In recent decades employees have also sacrificed paid leave time.[7] Today we spend more time at work than workers in most any other affluent nation.[8]

Deindustrialization and shrinking U.S. competitiveness in global markets led to the abrupt slowing of economic growth in the early seventies.[9] Americans needed to work harder than they had in some years to maintain their quality of life. Even then, though, they could have retained the standard of living known in previous decades without ongoing increases in work hours, a tradeoff few were willing to make. With only minor fluctuation, GDP per capita has been rising since the 1940s and is now near $47,000, the highest in the world.[10]

Flush toilets, electric refrigerators, dishwashers—luxuries enjoyed by a small minority of the world population—have all become normal in middle-class households. Obviously, the percentage of Americans who regard many such items as "necessities" has increased a great deal. Since 1996, at least 20 percent more Americans now think of items like clothes dryers, air conditioners, microwaves, computers, and cell phones in this way too.[11]

The variety of what is available is also extraordinary. In 1998, there were 11,037 new food products alone.[12] One can sense this trend, growth so rapid the selections change from one shopping trip to the next. Between 1986 and 2004, there was more than a 60 percent increase in the number of shopping centers in the United States, now totaling upwards of 46,000.[13] We are producing a lot.

There are several good reasons to work really hard. The most fundamental is practical. Putting food on the table matters. Getting it done
is satisfying, even if the work is not inherently meaningful. A job also
provides structure in which a person can develop an identity and meaningful relationships. Whether to employers, employees, coworkers, colleagues, or customers, a productive person is usually connected. Being
a part of an enterprise can be rewarding, which ties in to another factor.
The work itself might be fulfilling. A person may like what she does.

Certainly a lot of Americans work for some or all of these reasons.[14]
The problem, however, is how many people work so hard for no such
reason.[15] Income is clearly the main motivation for most members of
the U.S. workforce, as it is in most countries.[16] But we enjoy a higher
standard of living *and* work harder than people in most other industrialized nations.

For more than forty years, Americans have been feeling increasingly
rushed.[17] During that same period, they felt more and more unhappy
at work. From 1972 to 1994 the proportion of Americans who felt "very
satisfied with their jobs" dropped from 50 percent to 44.[18] Overt rudeness in the workplace is on the rise.[19] Despite the superficial emphasis
on cooperative teamwork, many in the workforce think of relationships
at the job as instrumental or utilitarian, rather than substantively communal or nurturing.[20]

The social prestige and affirmation that accompanies certain occupations, positions, and achievements is another factor that sometimes
compels Americans to work hard.[21] The compulsion to make money
induced by the ever-present marketing system is complemented by
continual celebration of those at the top of their game. As Vince Lom-
bardi famously said, "Winning isn't everything. It's the only thing."
Or conversely, as Richard Sennett notes, "Failure is the great modern
taboo."[22]

The encompassing role of competition in our culture contributes immensely to this sensibility, which also encourages the intense drive to be
successful at work and in all endeavors.[23] This motivation, along with the
technological fetish of our age, has also fostered a widespread phobia
of wasted time and a related preoccupation with careful scheduling.[24]
In effect, the hallowed American work ethic has evolved into a broad
ambition to be productive and efficient in all things. For instance, many

now take for granted a competitive spirit in parenting, the "commercialization of intimate life," and a sense that even leisure should involve achievement.[25]

When our productive drive leads us to ignore other important aspects of life, like child rearing or civic engagement, not to mention reflection, meditation, or prayer, it becomes counterproductive. And there is clear evidence that for many of us, this is exactly what is happening. A great proportion of Americans are themselves disappointed about how the excessive amount of energy spent at work detracts from quality time with family and friends.[26] And what time is spent with people who matter to us is increasingly shaped by the organizational logic of the private sector (a topic discussed further in chapter 7).[27] In one large study, the main wish children expressed in terms of how their families' lives could be different was for their parents to be less stressed and less tired.[28]

All of this suggests that the part of economic life devoted to production is out of whack. Some spend an inordinate amount of time doing work they find unfulfilling to generate stuff they don't need. Others persistently neglect what they value most, and know they are doing it. The addictions to work itself, to the things we can acquire through work for pay, and to the status of being highly productive, are directly caused by the widespread embrace of market logic.

DISTRIBUTION AND MOBILITY

Given how hard so many people are working, an obvious question is, what does it get you? For society as a whole, the answer is a lot. For individuals, of course, the answer is it depends. The way resources are distributed in American society is more fluid than in almost any other nation. Compared to other industrial societies, there is more mobility here, more capacity for getting rich and greater vulnerability to ending up poor.[29] It is possible to grow up in a lower-class family, do well in school, and land a high-paying job.[30] It is also possible to get laid off, as more than 30 million Americans have since 1984, and face a downward spiral of declining prospects.[31]

Class structure is more complicated than many critics have claimed but it does exist. There are not simply two or three classes but rather a range of class positions shaped by several factors. Most scholars who study economic inequality emphasize some combination of the ownership of wealth, particular skills, and related credentials, and the prerogatives of supervision and management in shaping the systematic distribution of resources.[32] There are now many more white-collar jobs, and multiple strata, we might think of as middle class. For example, some 43 percent of the workforce now hold office jobs.[33]

Despite this fluidity and complexity, there is still an extremely unequal distribution of resources not based on individual merit. Just by knowing a person's class position, we can accurately predict a lot about how his life will unfold. As in other countries, even liberal democracies, the real wealth does not shift that much. Most of the families with the majority of the wealth keep it across generations.[34] In 2001, the richest 10 percent of American households held some 70 percent of all wealth, and the top 1 percent held 33 percent.

Only 31 percent of the richest individuals ranked in the "Forbes 400" did not inherit significant interests, meaning most people on the list did not generate their own riches.[35] The twenty richest Americans include ten individuals from three different families.[36] And the top marginal income tax rate is historically low at 35 percent.[37]

The enormous pay of CEOs, which averaged as much as 501 times more than that of workers in recent years, suggests something other than merit.[38] As John Kenneth Galbraith mused three decades ago, "The salary of the chief executive of the large corporation is not a market award for achievement. It is frequently in the nature of a warm personal gesture by the individual to himself."[39] It is now well established that the huge compensation packages of CEOs are divvied out without much consideration for performance.[40]

There is growing concern as to how systematic profiting from fraudulent stock sales is among top executives. Between 2005 and 2007 some 250 companies came under suspicion for illegally rewarding their executives and directors.[41] One of *Fortune* magazine's "four investment giants of the twentieth century," John C. Bogle chronicles how such practices became widespread in *The Battle for the Soul of Capitalism*.[42] We also know that such practices contributed significantly to the recession of 2008.[43]

Given such developments, it is no surprise that economic inequality in the United States continues to intensify.[44] In the last twenty-five years, the ranks of American billionaires swelled from thirteen to over four hundred.[45] The richest 1 percent of households increased its share of total wealth from less than a quarter to roughly a third. During that time, income distribution has become spread more unevenly, with the bottom fifth of the population actually taking home less real income and the top fifth gaining more than 50 percent. If the growth in economic productivity between 1973 and 1998 had been passed on to workers, one estimate suggests, their average hourly wage in 1998 would have been $18.10 instead of $12.77.[46] More recently, between 1995 and 2006, the growth of employee productivity outpaced increases in real wages by 340 percent.[47]

Despite a period of collective prosperity, a great many people lost out. Conservative estimates indicate that in 2006, before the recent recession, at least 13 percent of Americans, roughly 37 million, were poor.[48] This includes countless workers in various industries (e.g., construction, garment factories, nursing homes, agriculture, poultry farms, and day labor) whose employers engage in "wage theft," violating wage and hour laws and compensating workers less than they deserve.[49]

Another huge factor in this system is the utilization of foreign labor. American-dominated multinational corporations have shifted the bulk of production to low-wage regions throughout the world. Foreign workers constitute an important part of the producing class in the American economy and thereby reflect another aspect of the uneven distribution associated with it.[50]

Even champions of orthodox free market capitalism are starting to wonder. In a column lauding Milton Friedman's accomplishments, *New York Times* columnist David Brooks offered this lament: "His death is sad, too, because classical economics is under its greatest threat in a generation. Growing evidence suggests average workers are not seeing the benefits of their productivity gains—that the market is broken and requires heavy government correction."[51] Faith in the market's capacity to distribute resources fairly is being undermined by three decades of steadily increasing inequality, and lately, the recent economic crisis.

American class structure makes for more inequality and unnecessary poverty than that of almost any other industrialized nation. Education, employment, housing, and taxation laws are all implicated in this system.[52] These arrangements represent large, systemic powers that are not easily confronted by individuals. The main role most Americans play in such dynamics is to surrender to them fully. We support candidates, policies, and laws that embrace this injustice. Only some of us benefit directly. Ultimately, however, this is an enormously important problem that bears greatly on the future of our moral predicament. And there are costs here for all of us to pay.[53]

Unequal access to education, medicine, or job opportunities have broad, expensive implications. The United States spends more per capita on health care and incarceration, for example, than any other industrialized nation.[54] The main victims of unequal distribution of resources, however, are primarily a poor segment of the population, the "have-nots," rather than the majority of Americans. Sadly, this is an old, deep stain on the moral fabric of our society. A broader portion of Americans in lower-middle-class strata are not proportionately rewarded for their efforts and struggle to make ends meet.

CONSUMPTION AND MORE CONSUMPTION

A major factor in the patterns of persistent hard work and inequality is consumption, the third main component of the economic system. Most people know that unbridled greed is bad, that it erodes character, relationships, and resources. The tricky part, though, is how we justify materialism to ourselves. I work hard, so I deserve this. I want my children to have more than I did. Everybody has one. I need it. We work hard to buy nice things, for ourselves and for our loved ones, and for others to see. The nice things become *very* nice things and require even more hard work. Then we compensate for not being present with more nice things. And as a reward to ourselves for such sacrifices, we need . . . nice things.[55]

Definitions of "the good life" or even basic "necessities" are expanding.[56] In addition to the new products mentioned above that have become normal, high-end items like high-definition TVs, playground equipment, professional kitchens, wine collections, and lots of other "luxuries" have all become common as well.[57] Consumer spending as a share of GDP hovered near 60 percent from the end of WWII up through 1980. After that it starting rising, up past 70 percent by 2008.[58]

So-called working-class millionaires who have $2 or $3 million no longer feel privileged. People like Hal Steeger in Silicon Valley feel they just don't have enough. "I know people looking in from the outside will ask why someone like me keeps working so hard. . . . But a few million doesn't go as far as it used to. Maybe in the '70s, a few million bucks meant 'Lifestyles of the Rich and Famous,' or Richie Rich living in a big house with a butler. But not anymore."[59]

The absurdly brazen consumer items like the six-and-a-half-foot Kalamazoo barbeque grill ($11,290) does not really reflect the indulgence of regular people. Top-shelf premium grills, which begin around $2,000 and peak with the Talos Outdoor Cooking Suite, priced at $35,000, accounted for only 3 to 4 percent of the 14.5 million grills sold in recent years.[60] They do, however, reveal where the parameters of consumerism have shifted to. Buying a $1,000 grill is now, by definition, not excessive.

Nor is a $40,000 car (compared to a Porsche) or a $100 haircut (compared to a visit to a Jonathan Antin salon) in such "expenditure cascades."[61] Even during a recession, many do not blink at a $10 martini, a $4 latte, or a $1.50 bottle of water.

In their book *Mass Affluence*, marketing consultants Paul Nunes and Brian Johnson offer advice on how to get the "the Underspent American" to buy more.

> The new focus on the care and feeding of oneself will be another significant opportunity. Characterized by Robert Putnam in the best-seller *Bowling Alone*, Americans have moved away from traditional social and civic interactions to more individual pursuits and activities. The moneyed masses have taken cocooning to heart and are actively grabbing onto once-shared facilities and making them their own. Evidence of this trend can be seen in the creation of sumptuous spa baths and media rooms in homes with relatively few occupants to enjoy them. . . . Consider the sale of children's playground equipment, in which a few swings and a clubhouse from companies like ChildLife and Rainbow Play Systems can start at $3,000 and quickly move in to five figures. . . . Where can this trend lead? Companies must search the ranks of shared enjoyments and consider what can and will be moved figuratively and literally in-house.[62]

Despite all the material improvements in Americans' lives, Schor esti-mated a decade ago, over half the population felt they could not afford everything they "really need." This included 17 percent of those with household incomes over $100,000.[63] If our practices related to distribu-tion and production are problematic, consumption patterns are disas-trous. Going into debt or missing out on proper nutrition, two routine results of this problem, may be devastating for poor people, shaping their lives in unalterably bad ways. But it is clear that there are also extremely unfortunate results of consumption norms for a large portion of the population as a whole. In other words, some of the most clearly destructive elements of our economic life are manifest precisely where the market flourishes, that is, where it facilitates "success."

The media has a big role in cultivating such distorted ideals and the realistic expectations extending from them. *Fortune* magazine's annual edition detailing the numbers for the Fortune 500 also has a section advertising upscale "indulgences," which includes a bunch of ways to spend $500.[64] You can drink a cocktail at the Paris Ritz made with 1834 cognac, spend fifty minutes with a top divorce lawyer, get a shot of Bo-tox, or buy a water buffalo for a "needy family overseas."

The bases of the astounding success of the top firms and the need to get away from it all, portrayed together in the same pages, and awk-wardly bundled with the thoughts of settling your divorce and doing a good deed, are revealing. Success costs something more than hard work. That same issue of *Fortune* reports that the top three marketing firms in 2005 (Omnicom Group, Interpublic Group, and Vertis), together generated some $18,366,000,000 in revenues. A large part of that effort involved television.

There is little doubt that the persistent projection of television into Americans' lives has profound influence on how we think, feel and live.[65] It shapes our psychological and physical health, our political and moral views, our consumption habits, and our cultural sensibilities in general. Overall, Americans are averaging about fifteen hours of television a week.[66] Despite this commitment and the desire to find a few extra min-utes for *more* TV, people are increasingly unhappy with television.[67]

For many Americans, popular shows like *The Apprentice*, *American Idol*, or *America's Next Top Model* appear to be a kind of "guilty plea-sure," recognized as formulaic and vapid, but thought of as liberating or fun. There are now various "reality" shows with ongoing elimination of the "competitors," each of which involves corporate management, homemaking, cooking, baking, dating, losing weight, modeling, hair styling, fashion design, dancing, comedy, football, rodeo, professional wrestling, "ultimate fighter" competition, or talent in general. Behind the poignant judgment of personal efficacy the performers seem to feel, the amusing drama is a game. It becomes easy to imagine that everything is a contest or that competition makes anything more interesting.

The old tradition of shows about winning a lot of money quickly also continues in new programs such as *Deal or No Deal*, *The Weakest Link*, or *Who Wants to Be a Millionaire?* Surely, the attraction to competition, money, and celebrity in our culture draws us to these programs. By the same token, these shows teach us that such values are somehow normal, that it is reasonable to focus on short-term gratification, being "first in line," and other childish sensibilities.[68]

What goes on between shows is also significant. We have invited marketers, and many others making uninterrogated claims about what is important, right into our living rooms. According to one estimate, American children see 30,000 advertisements by the time they reach first grade. In 1994, they spent an average of 21.5 hours a week watching TV.[69] It appears that that number has been declining, but almost two-thirds of kids still report watching TV every day, allotting more time to it than any other activity except for sleeping and school.[70]

Kids prefer shopping above most every other leisure activity. Some 93 percent of teenage girls ranked it number one in a 1987 survey, a preoccupation that appears to be spreading for both boys and girls.[71] As a sixteen-year-old from Los Angeles interviewed by Lauren Greenfield of the *New York Times* suggests, spending exorbitant amounts of money starts early and becomes sort of normal. "For our prom we all got picked up in a big Hummer limo, and I think it was $100 a person. So we all get into this big limo and go out to dinner. We all spend, like, $50 there. Then we go to the after-prom, which is $40. We're just throwing money at everyone."[72] One estimate indicates that in 1999 children aged six to nineteen years influenced $485 billion in purchase decisions.[73] But of course children do not create the culture of consumption themselves; they are socialized into it by adults.[74]

There are some things money can't buy, but not many, as MasterCard has so persuasively suggested. When we routinely communicate the most precious messages of intimacy through extravagant gifts, the portion of our emotional lives no longer subject to commercialization is small indeed.[75] From $2 billion in 1950, expenditures on advertisements grew to $250 billion in 2000.[76] More broadly, it is through TV that young and old find out we are excessively fat, wrinkled, and smelly, and insufficiently neat, efficient, and hygienic. We are unappealingly and unnecessarily ordinary. The right products would render us informed, cosmopolitan, classy. We could be cool, we could belong, we could be loved.

In his book, *Total Access*, bestselling author Regis McKenna explains a key opportunity in marketing. "Instead of 'I need' being the motivating consumer factor, the power of television as a marketing tool spawned the 'I want' factor."[77] Actually, it is the conflation of needing and wanting that is so problematic. Whatever message the media sends, someone on the receiving end has to accept it if a transaction is going to occur. "By the 1990s, bloated icons of affluence proliferated: the gargantuan pseudo-military vehicle, the 10,000-square-foot hacienda," Jackson Lears observes. "A bigger standard package of household goods demanded deeper debt and accelerated the pace of the consumer treadmill. No one wanted to look like a 'loser.'"[78]

The alluring quick fix of materialism has also contributed to increased rates of gambling, which has been facilitated through the total access of the Internet.[79] If super–role models, like Michael Jordan, or education officials, like William Bennett, can reveal their extensive gambling habits, without these roles being noticeably altered, gaming must be okay. For a lot of ordinary people, however, there are real risks. Debt is an old tradition deeply embedded in the American Dream, but it has reached alarming levels in recent years and culminated disastrously during the recent recession.[80] The heightened tolerance for debt is surely also part of the story behind our anxiety and productive frenzy.

THE CARE AND FEEDING OF ONESELF

The abundance and diversity of products and services we enjoy of course contribute to a very comfortable way of life, but in addition to necessitating hard work and debt, a lot of what we consume is simply bad for us. Marion Nestle points out in *Food Politics*, for instance, that in spite of all the advances in public health during the last century, a number of leading medical problems—coronary heart disease, cancer, diabetes, stroke, and liver cirrhosis—extend from poor dietary choices. We could be healthier if we made different choices and, in many cases, we know better.[81] On this issue it is not so much that we are losing ground, for the most part, as the fact that things are not improving as quickly as we might expect.

A growing body of research now recognizes the relationship between idealized, marketed images of women and the dissatisfaction and shame women feel about their bodies. There is a documented connection to eating disorders and other psychological difficulties.[82] As destructive as such images are, we buy them.[83] It is no secret that numerous products marketed to women, such as tanning salons and high heels, are both unhealthy and very popular.

As much as they do consume, women routinely buy more than they can use—according to one estimate, the average American woman owns more than $600 of clothing she has not worn in the last year.[84] All of this craziness around unrealistic notions of attractiveness is now wrapped around masculinity too. Proliferating demand for fitness programs, exercise equipment, expensive haircuts, and hair loss treatment suggests more inclusive beauty myths.

The problems associated with diet and our confusion about body image—and the marketing that exacerbates them—run in other directions as well. During the last two decades, obesity has risen by about 50 percent. It is worse here than in most any other industrialized country.[85] Almost a third of U.S. adults, more than 60 million people, are obese. Another third is overweight. Since 1980 the number of young people who are overweight has tripled. That now includes 16 percent of those aged six to nineteen years.[86] As Michael Gard and Jan Wright explain in *The Obesity Epidemic*, the conversation about obesity is muddied by various political agendas but there is little question that we have a serious problem.[87]

The U.S. population consumes an average of twelve ounces of carbonated soft drinks per person per day.[88] With 12,804 stores in the United States, McDonald's had over $19.5 billion in sales during 2000.[89]

The impact of *what* we eat seems clear; what has been less well documented but also appears damaging is *how* we eat. The speed of fast food surely works against healthy digestion and sane social exchange.[90] Moreover, immoderate consumption goes hand in hand with waste. According to one study, 14 percent of household garbage consists of good, unwrapped, not out-of-date food, which contributes to some $100 billion of wasted food in the United States every year.[91]

From the late 1970s, abuse of drugs and alcohol declined steadily for about two decades and then began increasing modestly.[92] The direct effects of such addiction are pretty familiar, but the indirect effects are significant too. The total costs to society of alcohol abuse for the year 1998 has been estimated to be $184 billion. Again, a lot of people and powerful interests have a stake in this issue. According to the Center for Science in the Public Interest, Americans consumed upwards of twenty-seven gallons of beer per capita in 2000.[93]

Another detrimental mania in the United States has been petroleum. "America is addicted to oil," lamented President Bush in his 2006 State of the Union address. That year, more than three-fourths of all Americans drove to work alone. Only about 11 percent of commuters drove with someone else, and just about 5 percent took public transportation.[94] We use about 20 million barrels each day, or one fourth of all the oil consumed in the world, three times more than the next biggest consumer, China.[95] In 2005 Exxon-Mobile was the most profitable company in the world with over $36 billion in profits.[96]

Due to direct and indirect costs, most Americans who are not oil barons think we would be better off if we used less. The United States produces upwards of twenty tons of carbon dioxide per inhabitant each year, more than any other country.[97] Three quarters of respondents in one poll fear supply will not keep up with global demand.[98] And the best evidence suggests they are correct. Aside from the implications for the environment, which appear to be significant, one conservative estimate indicates that current use rates will lead us to exhaust global oil supplies within thirty-five years.[99] Needless to say, the implications for the global economy would be catastrophic.

If oil has driven us in a previous era, the next age will center on digital power. Alongside the amazing achievements facilitated by this incredible technology, some unsettling implications of this addiction are adding up too. Sales of home computers and software went from $28.7 billion in 1998 to $34.3 billion in 2000. Nearly two-thirds of households with children bought a computer that year compared to 41 percent in those without.[100] Recent data suggest that 82 percent of kids go online by the seventh grade.[101] Given how critical competence with computers is in the information age, there are of course real rewards attached to such access. But we are starting to see costs too.

Inordinate rates of sleep deprivation among youth are largely due to their bedrooms being too "wired." They pay attention to televisions, cell phones, computers, and video games at night when they should be asleep. As with Uncle Bill's daughter mentioned at the beginning of this chapter, the result for young people is trouble waking up in the morning, being late for school, and falling asleep during the day.[102] One study found that 39 percent of children have four or more electronic items in their bedrooms. The kids who do were twice as likely to fall asleep in school.[103]

With more items available to them, children and youths are doing more things at once. A recent survey of Americans ages eight to eighteen shows that the time spent using such technology is holding steady at 6.5 hours a day. But kids are now cramming in more media exposure, 8.5 hours according to this study, through "media multitasking."[104] At the gym where I exercise, young people come in routinely and turn on the TV and their iPods at the same time before they get on the treadmill. You can also see teenagers frequently having conversations with one another while music (so loud you can hear it across the room) continues to play in to their earphones. According to mounting research, the constant encounter of e-mail, texts, and phone messages has significantly deleterious effects on concentration and memory, even more than marijuana.[105] It is also an increasingly significant factor in traffic accidents.[106]

Another issue related to this use of technology is our concern about efficiency and time. In *Queuing and Waiting*, Barry Schwartz shows how the societal shift toward mass consumption of goods and especially services has contributed to the scarcity of time.[107] We have to spend time figuring out what to buy or waiting for an appointment for service, burdens previous generations rarely encountered.[108] A good example of this is surely the increasing number of hours during which we are learning about new computer technology, purchasing and setting it up, figuring out how it works, and then using it. Of course there are huge gains in efficiency, but there are also significant costs (e.g., money, energy, and time) in addition to the impact on social capital (detailed in chapter 6).

Beyond the inherently deleterious effects of products we buy, researchers in various fields have documented the harmful impact of extreme consumerism in general. The number of choices we face, the way we think about what we do not have, the elusive contentment of seeking more, and the ample time spent shopping that is not used for more fulfilling endeavors—all part of the experience of modern consumerism—wear us down.[109]

Children who buy into the materialism face serious risks, including low self-esteem, higher rates of personality disorders, and hazardous behavioral patterns such as drinking, smoking, and illegal use of drugs. They are more likely to do poorly in school, jobs, and extracurricular activities. More broadly, prioritizing financial success over friendship and community diminishes psychological adjustment. Such goals are also strongly correlated with various measures of well-being and quality of life.[110]

Again, the point here is the issue of proportionality. Most people agree that makeup, beer, hamburgers, cars, or laptops are not inherently evil. For a lot of us, these items offer a chance for joy, fun, or at least bearing the burdens of life. And of course the same goes for choice and abundance in general. The question is when is enough too much? As tricky as it is to answer such a question with any specificity, it is not hard to see by our own historical standards, in comparison to other similar societies, and in relation to the key values that hold our nation together and nurture what is most lasting and good in our society, we are in fact consuming too much.

CONCLUSION

A substantial portion of our time devoted to work is unfulfilling. We allow unnecessary levels of inequality and poverty. And our consumption habits include unhealthy and wasteful patterns, many of which we ourselves recognize as problematic. The urgent need to produce and achieve, both in our jobs and in other parts of our lives contributes to the neglect of organic social interaction. The concern with competition at all costs fosters dramatically unequal distribution of economic resources. Those marginalized by such inequality suffer in terms of inferior medicine, education, housing conditions, and other resources. Those on the winning side of such competition suffer in other ways, including, most importantly, accepting the illusion of happiness through materialism.

In short, the internal circumstances of American economic life—in terms of production, distribution, and consumption—are messed up. Most of these problems were well established before the recent economic collapse. Indeed, the economic crisis might be obscuring the ongoing moral crisis that preceded it.

It seems clear most people want to live good, moral, fulfilling lives. Certainly this aspiration applies to my wife's entire family. Throughout his life Grandpa Enzo conscientiously sought to realize such goals and instill them in his children. As we collectively slip toward a culture that embraces greed, selfishness, and waste, however, such hopes seem more elusive. We are literally driving ourselves crazy. We have together let the goals and means of the market—efficiency, marketing, consumerism, and profit—become central guideposts around which we organize our lives.

But the new rules do not serve us well. There is evidence of this in the ambition and petulance of cousin Tony. Why are his values in question when he is playing by the rules? And it is manifest in Lila's dilemma. Why is it so hard to be an accomplished professional and a good mother? Because our new normative expectations of "success" are ultimately incompatible with meaningful relationships and the best of what Enzo hoped for in a previous era.

There are powerful forces at work contributing to the circumstances of our economic sphere, including the laws, rules, and norms associated with Wall Street, Madison Avenue, the Federal Reserve, different parts of government, and so on. The focus here, however, is the choices that regular Americans make in relation to these issues, choices that are affected by large structural factors but that are ultimately under the control of individual people. The point is that among the most serious symptoms of our current moral crisis are the normative economic practices in terms of how hard we work, the inequality we allow, and the ways we consume.

The reduction of "success" to working and consuming a lot contributes to the marginalization of other principles that have historically been central to our way of life. Hence the corruption of "progress," "liberty," "prosperity," and other American ideals. In undermining the genuine promise of these values, the dysfunctional economic life of America is a big part of our moral crisis.

6

CIVIC LIFE: COOL iPODS, ROLLING STOPS, AND FIGHTING DADS

[T]he only thing that really matters in life are your relationships to other people.

—George Vaillant[1]

We rush everywhere, coasting past stop signs, compromising the safety of ourselves and others nearby, in the hope of saving a few minutes. We speak on cell phones, louder and longer than we know we should, disregarding the impact on those around us. Sometimes we do both at the same time. And sometimes we get annoyed with others for the very same behavior. Why? The answer involves a weakening sense of the collective good to which we are beholden.

In all societies, community is central to moral stability and individual sanity. As a network of people who share meaningful symbols by way of common language, memory and responsiveness, members of a community are *social* in the deepest sense.[2] The main institutions that foster community in modern society, which constitute what is often called civil society, have a rich, old history in our country. Distinct from the state and the market, civil society encompasses the structural incentives and cultural norms of public life that engender social solidarity.[3] This includes great institutions of society like religion, education, and media, as well as more parochial associations and semi-structured social movements.

From the nation's beginnings, Americans have been deeply committed to voluntary organizations that serve the common good and foster virtue. Whether it was the YMCA, the Elks, Oxfam, or other civic organizations, such groups have facilitated active and informed participation in politics and public life. They have integrated substantive concerns of ordinary citizens into political discourse and policy. And they have socialized generations of Americans with a civic sensibility that transcends narrow self-interest.[4] Here I examine the state of civic life in America today, the respective implications for social collectives and individuals, and how these patterns are linked to market forces.

AMERICAN COMMUNITY IN TRANSITION

The concern with community decline is now part of a long tradition of social theory coming to terms with modernization.[5] In some sense each generation has to wrestle with the part of such transformation that defines its era. Even with such recognition, the challenges of our time appear especially poignant and portentous.

Amid many appealing and hopeful signs, we may not notice, hidden in plain view, that American civil society is suffering from a kind of "moral malnutrition."[6] There is more activity than ever before in human history. Americans are busy in productive and public ways. We are in some sense more social—that is, in a quantitative sense, in terms of the number of people with whom we interact. But we are less social in another, qualitative sense. The networks of relationships are in many cases thin or superficial.[7]

A recent advertisement for cell phones that download music shows a teenager bowling with friends while listening to his MP3 player. He is part of the group but independent at the same time, shut off from the others by way of earphones. This guy is having fun. He is his own man, at ease, chillin'. Sufficiently cheap for many to buy, but cool and expensive enough to be special, the iPod is an emblem of our time. There is always a better, smaller, cooler one to get. And it attaches a person to music and information, a broader world in some sense. All appealing aspects of this wildly popular gadget.

This technologically enabled separateness was not exactly what Robert Putnam meant in the title of his seminal work *Bowling Alone*. But the current crisis of community encompasses this type of social atomization and a number of other related patterns. As he enters public space, the iPod user becomes less, not more, sensitive to perceptions and needs of others around him.

Putnam documents the decline of various kinds of social engagement over recent decades, including bowling leagues, as well as PTA, family meals, card games, religious activity, political participation, union membership, community projects, entertaining at home, informal visiting, and the like. The decline of community, or "social capital," does not mean people are not engaged in productive activity.[8] As noted in the last chapter, we are spending more time at work. But the time devoted to work is not our own insofar as it belongs in some way to the employer. And the relationships developed there are often instrumental or utilitarian and not conducive to durable community.

Due in large part to our commitment to work and despite all our technological innovations, Americans feel increasingly crunched for time.[9] The way we use the scarce time left over, "down time," seems not to foster meaningful relationships either. It involves much greater use of new technological modes of communication and entertainment (think of television, e-mail, cell phones, and videogames as well as MP3 players) and a general commitment to efficiency. Recreation is pressed into smaller, fragmented time slots.[10] And even "leisure" time is often devoted to something "productive."[11] Those people who use the bulk of their free time for TV, a widespread pattern over the last three decades, are certainly less engaged in civic associations.[12]

This temporal fragmentation inhibits ongoing dialogue too. We spend a lot of time "listening," receiving information in the contexts of TV, the radio, the Internet, automated messages, and even live settings like sports events, museums, and so on. And we spend a lot of time "talking," expressing our thoughts through letters to the editor, campaign signs in our yards, holiday decorations, blogs, honking our horns, and so on. The problem is how much of this listening and talking do not involve the same parties; the people we are listening to are not the ones we are talking to.

In effect, there is not enough sustained discourse. This has always been the key for children and parents, spouses, neighbors, teachers and students, employers and employees, coworkers, clergy and congregants, political adversaries, or, in short, every kind of important relationship. Without it, we are lost.

We see in these patterns both some of the changed American values—in this case, "progress," "freedom," "productivity," and "authority"—as well as market principles of efficiency, and techno-logical innovation. Increasingly skeptical of institutional authority, individuals organize their connections to others through fragmented, distant interactions on their own terms.

PRESENT OR CONNECTED

These trends reflect a growing sense of our social disconnection, or at least connecting at a distance. The people who use electronic communication—three-quarters of adults use the Internet and about two-thirds use cell phones[13]—might interact with hundreds of people during the day, but the number of *substantive* face-to-face conversa-tions has declined. In that way, networks of relationships are broader but thinner.[14] The more time people spend on the Internet, the less time they spend with family and friends.[15]

There are, however, also some hopeful possibilities for social in-teraction enabled by innovative computer technology. Some research indicates that the Internet can help people supplement the contact they have with important relations but not replace it.[16] The successful networks maintained this way tend to revolve around individuals rather than households.

Through Internet communication people attend to different issues, including caring for someone with illness, making informed financial decisions, changing jobs, home repairs, and political discourse.[17] The investigators in this research argue that such connectedness serves to strengthen existing relationships built offline but concede that this "net-worked individualism" cannot replace conventional community.

Other research indicates that the Internet provides a useful catalyst for social networks involved in practical applications such as education, workforce development, social activism, political involvement, and local entrepreneurship.[18] Again, the technology works best as a supplement to established social networks. Despite these prospects and all the other wonders enabled by the Internet, many unanswered questions remain about the impact of digital communication on civic life.[19] Will relationships initiated online last? How deep will they go? How will they affect other kinds of relationships? We do not yet know.

As we get more connected to people physically distant, direct physical interaction involves a new kind of aloofness derived from the assertion of personal autonomy. Quoting Bart Simpson, Lynne Truss calls this sensibility "my bubble, my rules."[20] Think of the inattentive person next to you in line distracted by iPod music, the texting driver, or the intrusive cell phone conversations so common in public spaces.

"I have had it 'up to here' with people who conduct loud conversations with their cell phones," one commuter in Minneapolis recently wrote Dear Abby. "I have learned far more than I ever wanted to about medical problems, restraining orders, relationships that are falling apart, etc. I would love to make eye contact and give them 'the look,' but these folks are too absorbed in what they are saying to glance in my direction." More generally, there is a correlation between physical proximity and the "moral intensity" people feel about a given situation.[21] We tend to be more conscientious when we pay attention to the problems nearby.

According to mounting research, the constant encounter of e-mail and text and phone messages greatly inhibits concentration and memory, even more than marijuana.[22] The growing popularity of text messaging in particular makes electronic communication increasingly remote.[23] It might be said we are well connected but hardly present. Among the many implications of this dramatic trend is the declining ability for friends and family to easily offer assistance and support when they are not geographically close.[24] And, again, this raises the question of the significance of the "relationships" we have online by way of MySpace, Facebook, or blogs, which appear to be more ephemeral or disposable.[25]

In other ways, though, we are present but not connected. Whereas live attendance at spectator sports has essentially doubled since the sixties, we are *participating* in sports less.[26] Consider the public displays of festivity and "tradition" demonstrated in Halloween, Thanksgiving, Christmas, and Easter decorations so common in suburban neighborhoods. Neighbors can say something to the world about their values without ever speaking to one another. In making demands on waiters, walking inordinately slowly across a street while traffic waits, or offering intimate confessions (to talk radio, talk shows, newspapers, or blogs), the pursuit of attention seems ubiquitous.[27]

"Between 1986 and 1998," Putnam documents, "while churchgoing was falling by 10 percent, museum-going was up by 10 percent; while home entertaining was down by a quarter, movie-going was up by a quarter; and while club meeting attendance was down by a third, pop/rock concert attendance was up by a third."[28] All of this free activity is less encumbered by the boundaries of relationships.

We want to be busy, we hunger to see and be seen. Needless to say, though, to exhibit or observe, even in a crowd, is not the same thing as substantive, sustained interaction. Another poignant sign of the times is the quasi-social phenomenon of *silent* raves," which recently became popular in big cities for a while. The young people, who get together with iPods and dance while privately listening to their own music, do not have to hear others or their music.

Alongside these patterns, there is evidence to suggest that we are expending substantial, perhaps increasing, energy in the service of others. Voluntarism has increased a lot since the seventies.[29] The efforts are intermittent, though, and those oriented toward community projects in particular have decreased significantly.[30] We actually discuss local problems with our neighbors less and less.[31]

Some research suggests that 75 million American adults were regularly active during the 1990s in small support groups oriented toward Bible study, twelve-step programs, self-help groups, book discussion clubs, hobbies, or coping with illness.[32] These supportive activities appear to generate more "bonding" social capital, networks that are inward-looking, as opposed to externally directed "bridging" capital, which cultivates broader identities.[33] In contrast to the nationally oriented agendas of American civic organizations in the eighteenth and nineteenth centuries, these connections remain very personal and localized. That is, they tend not to speak to public life per se.

Moreover, these groups are not alleviating the growing trend of isolation. Twenty years ago the most common number of confidants each American had is estimated to have been three. Such partners play a key role in emotional support, problem-solving, and so on. Today, that number is zero. Almost half the population, recent research suggests, essentially has no network of counseling support.[34]

It is true that quite a few civic and political associations that are explicitly geared toward public life have been thriving in recent years. People continue to trust certain civic institutions, such as those associated with religion and education.[35] The civic institutions that are growing in number, however, tend to involve hired professionals that facilitate advocacy rather than grassroots members. Such parties become players in national politics, injecting substantive agendas into political discourse and policy. But they usually do not engender strong social ties historically found in neighborhoods or protest groups.[36]

"Between 1958 and 1998, the number of American national associations grew by some 253 percent overall, and almost all of this proliferation came between 1969 and 1990."[37] Theda Skocpol estimates, however, that close to half of these organizations have no members at all and about a quarter have fewer than a thousand members. Part of the issue here has to do with increasingly well-educated, sophisticated experts who understand how to successfully focus advocacy efforts. The upshot is efficacy in pressing the pertinent agenda, but ignoring or even alienating masses of people uninterested in the "special interests" of Washington.

So, the news is not all bad. There is substantial attention devoted to addressing society's ills, mostly through the efforts of professional organizations with highly skilled staffs. And nurturing community groups continue to draw people to one another by organizing around specific needs for care and support. The problem is that these two sets of activities do not overlap enough. That is, a small number of people think about the big picture and a large number of people think about particular issues. In this way, we ignore one of the fundamental insights of sociology mentioned in the last chapter: "Neither the life of an individual nor the history of a society can be understood without understanding both."[38]

In terms of the pervasive moral uncertainty of modern society, this disconnection is very problematic. The dilemma is that as society becomes more complex, and thereby more overwhelming to comprehend, the more imperative sorting out moral problems involving large numbers of people is. The harder it gets, the more important it is. That is because larger numbers people are connected through the political, economic, and technological systems to which we are each beholden. For instance, alarming global warming, volatile international markets, and an active nuclear black market are just some of the problems that we know about.

THE COSTS OF COMMUNITY DECLINE FOR THE COLLECTIVE

The problem of community in terms of the moral crisis is two-fold. One side challenges the group and the other confronts the individual. From the perspective of society writ large, the continuing decline of community decreases the capacity for the development of public goods. This includes collective solutions to problems that involve diverse interests. Whether it is environmental challenges, economic development, or energy sources, groups that do not have active, informed, democratic processes end up with outcomes harmful to many and advantageous to few.[39] Suburban sprawl comes to mind as an example of creeping degradation that many lament but few resist.[40] On a smaller scale, consider the common dynamics in an office when tension and dispute become the norm in all relations.[41]

As the institutional contexts in which civil society is maintained wither, the tools and practices learned in those settings deteriorate as well. Such tools and practices are themselves public goods. For instance, problem-solving, conflict resolution, or compliance with ethical norms, all invaluable skills and sensibilities for functional democracy, are becoming scarcer.[42] Some of the most basic public goods, like civility and trust, constitute the building blocks for all others.

PLEASE, THANK YOU, EXCUSE ME

"Of all the forms of rudeness," Lynn Truss complains, "the hardest for a lot of people to understand is the offense against *everybody*."[43] In one study of metropolitan New York intersections between 1979 and 1996, researchers found that the proportion of drivers who came to a full stop dropped from about 37 percent to 1 percent, a trend generally found in traffic intersections across the country.[44] Overt expressions of anger directed at other drivers or "road rage" is on the rise. According to one estimate, it contributed to some 28,000 deaths per year in the late nineties.[45] Electronic multitasking (e.g., texting and talking on cell phones) is rapidly becoming a significant factor in traffic accidents—a pattern many cell phone users themselves recognize.[46] In a Public Agenda study, 58 percent of respondents said they "often encounter reckless and aggressive drivers on the road," 64 percent think the problem is getting worse, and 35 percent admit they themselves are part of the problem![47]

Beyond tailgating and horn-honking, we are rude to one another in numerous other contexts. Americans are increasingly disappointed with the customer service they receive. In the Public Agenda study, almost half the respondents reported having walked out of a store because of poor service. It also revealed that four out of ten respondents again "admitted that they were partly responsible for the growing lack of courtesy in America."[48]

An Associated Press poll found that almost 70 percent of respondents believe people are ruder than they were two or three decades ago.[49] Eighty-two percent of Americans "report being irritated at least occasionally by loud and annoying cell users who conduct their calls in public places." This group includes 86 percent of cell phone users themselves.[50]

The inclination to be rude in the workplace in general has become so pervasive that it compromises most every goal of the setting, including motivation, performance, creativity, helpfulness, and turnover.[51] Ten percent of people encounter rude behavior at work once a day, one study indicates, and 20 percent feel they are targets of incivility once a week. Almost 90 percent of respondents in one study think lack of respect is a serious problem. Sixty percent of them believe it is getting worse.[52]

This epidemic of incivility plagues many other settings too.[53] We see it at the daycare center, on the airplane, in the doctor's office, and of course, on television. There have always been situations in which contentiousness and confrontation were expected. An aggressive cross-examination in court, a scathing political speech critiquing an opponent, or trash talk in sports, for instance, have been familiar elements of public rhetoric for some time. But now harsh criticism on "talk shows," brow-beating commentary by pundits, or litigious threats by customers have reached new levels of shrillness—and normalcy.

In explaining his invitation for al Qaeda to attack San Francisco, the most influential figure on cable TV, Bill O'Reilly, illustrated just this point.

> Well, you would have thought I suggested blowing up the Coit Tower! Wait a minute, isn't that what I did? Uh-oh. Actually, this is standard talk-radio stuff, intentionally using hyperbole to make a point. In its reporting on the incident, even the far-left *San Francisco Chronicle* reasonably pointed that out. Surely, we all know that people listen to talk radio to be entertained as well as informed.[54]

Some commentators attribute the spread of rudeness to egalitarianism, an argument that contains a grain of truth.[55] Certainly there are some historic linkages between manners and class structure, patriarchal chivalry and racial segregation.[56] Decorum provided a guide for boundaries, for separating the fine from the common, the strong from the fragile, the pure from the unclean. Over time the ideals of hierarchy eroded along with the ideals of etiquette. Given how vile and unjust such codes were, for the most part, we can rejoice in the demise of both kinds of ideals, but only those of etiquette in so far as they are related. The more relevant factor behind spreading rudeness, though sometimes misnamed egalitarianism, is actually entitlement, or more accurately, the sense of self-entitlement.

This widespread sensibility, which transcends underprivileged groups and may even be more intense among people who have not been historically marginalized, reflects a kind of self-absorption. Unlike "booing the judges," as Truss describes the lack of respect afforded to persons of a certain station—which is more closely related to egalitarianism—the incidence of generic rudeness rooted in entitlement has other bases. Specifically, this expectation is cultivated by way of aggressive, relentless marketing. You deserve more, more than you have, more than you need, more than others; you are entitled to it. Hardly an egalitarian message, this perversion of the American Dream is now dispersed throughout the atmosphere of public life.

Unable to avoid breathing it in, we are, not surprisingly, expectant. A lot is never enough. With an itch we can't scratch, the unfulfilled expectation makes us, well, rude. The main chance we have for ingesting less of the message of entitlement is the compelling pull of meaningful relationships, which demand our attention and help screen out the poisoning allure of marketing.

"Please, thank you, excuse me, sorry—little words, but how much they mean."[57] Such reassuring flags of goodwill communicate that, "I recognize there are some rules we are expected to follow, I plan to play by them, you can trust me that way." It is easy to recognize the links between small acts of decency and the widespread resentfulness, distrust, fear, and compounding rudeness resulting from their disappearance.

One of the most important collective goods related to rudeness is social trust. In recent years, there are signs that social trust has stabilized to some extent. As noted above, Americans evince trust toward specific institutions such as religion and education.[58] The common threat of international terrorists has at times been unifying.[59] And young people in the "Millennial Generation" trust social authority much more than their forerunners.[60] But the overwhelming, long-term trend since the 1970s is pervasive loss of trust.[61] This is especially true for how Americans feel about other individuals in general.[62]

In settings with substantial social capital, where trust is assumed and accountability is thereby enabled, parents recognize other parents' authority to monitor children in the neighborhood, and so children do, too. People are less rude and less violent in such an environment. They talk, they listen, they debate, they gain greater mutual understanding.[63] Without trust, life spins out of control.

In 2006, Darrick Shelton got upset during a football game his seven-year-old son was playing near O'Fallon, Missouri. Shelton and his brother Garrick began cursing when the referee made a call they did not like. After a coach asked them to calm down and they became belligerent, an off-duty sheriff's deputy shot Garrick with a Taser and then the Shelton brothers were both arrested.[64] Maybe this kind of trouble should be no surprise in light of the hyper-competitiveness that permeates American sports. But the escalating level of conflict in such settings is somehow still shocking.

While watching their sons and some other twelve- and thirteen-year-olds play pick-up hockey in Reading, Massachusetts, in 2000, Thomas Junta and Michael Costin had a disagreement about the game. Afterwards, Junta fatally beat Costin.

> Bob Still, a spokesman for the National Association of Sports Officials, which represents 19,000 umpires and referees in professional as well as high school and youth sports, said his organization had seen a sharp increase in reports of violence by parents at sports events in the last three or four years. "We get two or three reports of this kind of behavior a week," Mr. Still said in an interview from his group's headquarters in Racine, Wis. "There is definitely a trend." Last week, Mr. Still said, he received a report that a coach, the father of a player, had broken the jaw of a 13-year-old umpire at a Little League game in Davie, Fla., because he did not like a call. And last year a mother in Virginia slapped a 14-year-old official and knocked him to the ground because she disagreed with a call during a soccer game, Mr. Still said.[65]

This sort of aggression should not be mistaken for widespread violent crime, which has been successfully curtailed. The overwhelming trend in crime rates in most categories is a precipitous decline for the last decade.[66] For a host of reasons, criminologists, policymakers, and other professionals in criminal justice have been very effective on this front. In some cases, though, like conflict around youth sports, these two manifestations of hostility—violence and rudeness—are only separated by way of the thin line of physical expression. The rude guy who takes a swing becomes the violent man. What is interesting about violence associated with youth sports is how out of place it is. It contradicts the spirit of the setting, and goes against the general pattern of crime rates. Given the loss of social trust, such behavior is more in line with how people *feel* about public life. It resonates with the anxiety they have, with the fear that is marketed to them, and with the images of random violence shown on *Cops* and elsewhere.[67] And it becomes part of the ongoing cascade of damaging social interactions like those depicted in the film *Crash*.

While our nation may be safer than it was ten years ago, at least in terms of domestic crime, the social ties that facilitate trust have thinned as the civil institutions that maintained them have weakened. Once the vitality of civic life, and the engagement with public issues and in public spaces, begins to dissipate, the momentum is not easy to stop.[68] Atomized individuals have no avenue for resisting a tragedy of the commons such as suburban sprawl, degraded environments, or cynicism in politics.

THE COSTS OF COMMUNITY DECLINE
FOR THE INDIVIDUAL

The other significant implication of weakening communities is the effect on individuals. However much we resent peer pressure or try to elude social control, each of us needs the group. And the institutions that we construct together then define the parameters and character of the choices we make as individuals. Despite the overblown claims of biological or cultural determinism we continue to hear, scholars have clearly established that nature and nurture are both important.

We are genetically endowed with different propensities (which vary by age, sex, race, and numerous other variables) that create probabilistic patterns of behavior, which are then mediated by situational contexts. Certain aspects of brain structure make some probabilities so strong, such as those for schizophrenia or Huntington Disease, that environment has little influence over their manifestation. As powerful as genetic configurations can be, though, current research suggests they account for only about half of the variation of psychological traits. The other half of the variation is shaped by external factors, including cultural forces.[69] And some externally derived factors are so powerful as to guarantee certain physiological and psychological consequences, such as malnutrition or physical abuse, for example.

The vast majority of the effects of nature and nurture, however, are highly probabilistic and interactive.[70] It is thus not unreasonable to think of humans as being at once selfish and altruistic. Which of these impulses are expressed overtly is to a large extent shaped by surrounding conditions such as social life.[71] "A person is a personality because he belongs to a community," George Herbert Mead suggested, "one has to be a member of a community to be a self."[72]

The loss of community means that as less is asked of each of us, less is given. Then the social support of the community that is offered to individuals in return for such commitment is not awarded.[73] In the absence of being bound in meaningful relationships, the result is a widespread loss of self-esteem. The impact of that pattern is, among other things, fear.[74] There is plenty to fear and worry about in our world. But the loss of meaning makes coping with such dangers increasingly difficult, even for those without a genetic predisposition toward anxiety.[75]

Peter C. Whybrow, professor of psychiatry and bio-behavioral science and the director of the Neuropsychiatric Institute at UCLA, has documented the significantly increased incidence of manic-depressive illness and anxiety disorders.[76] "From the character of the struggles that my patients report; from the subject matter of newspaper and magazine articles; from talk shows and the concerns expressed during chance conversations with strangers; and from discussions with colleagues, friends, and family, it is clear to me that many Americans are experiencing a discomfort for which they have little explanation."[77]

The consistent decline in happiness over the last several decades has been paralleled by increasing rates of alienation and depression.[78] Some 26 percent of Americans eighteen and older, which means close to 60 million people, suffer from a mental disorder in a given year. Some 40 million of those cases involve problems with anxiety. While the higher rates occur among adults, half of the illnesses begin among children before they turn fourteen and three-fourths by the age of twenty-four.[79]

It is impossible to know exactly what Eric Harris and Dylan Klebold were thinking before they went on a murderous rampage at Columbine High in the spring of 1999. Tragically, however, this horrific event has become part of a gruesome pattern with familiar essentials.[80] Why?

The various hypotheses about exposure to violence in popular culture, access to weapons, the impact of bullying and social exclusion, inattentive parents, and psychological disorders all have credible elements. One specific sociological view may offer particular insight. Anomie-strain theory contends that society must cultivate in individuals core values and goals, and provide means for attaining those goals.[81] This includes developing the ambition and capacity to get a job, for instance. It also involves the desire for and ability to receive recognition and affirmation.

When such legitimate goals and means are not provided, the frustrated person might seek to fulfill nonlegitimate goals and/or use illicit means. For those young people who are good athletes, charming or "cool," academically successful, religiously devoted, or in other ways embraced by some viable circle of friends that affirms their efforts, society has done its work. For those unable to realize the goals, the "strain" may motivate them to take matters into their own hands.

Along this line of reasoning, perhaps some teenage boys marginalized in most social settings seek to exert their masculinity, an aspiration successfully instilled, through violent means.[82] In the context of extreme competition (in sports, social circles, or academics), this lashing out, even to such a shocking degree, may be a hopeless act of self-assertion.

In any event, there is no question that part of the explanation here lies in the killers' disconnection from meaningful relationships. The absence of social trust has been shown to be associated with high homicide rates.[83] The fraying social fabric of our society is an important context in which these monstrous acts took place. This piece of the story is particularly distressing because it links so many of us, both as unwitting accessories in these grisly incidents, potential victims in numerous other settings, and collaborators in countless less extreme but nevertheless destructive manifestations of community decline.

Life, especially in modern society, imposes so many pressures of stunning complexity and intensity on each of us. Without the buffer provided by meaningful, nurturing, demanding community, any given individual is in trouble.[84] The "overburdened self" may not murder.[85] But he will be lost, unsupported by those who make the challenges bearable and untethered to the norms and strictures that shape a fulfilling and productive life.

The good news in terms of violence in schools is that the dominant trend for the last ten years has been growing safety. The Bureau of Justice Statistics reports that about 5 percent of students nationwide experienced crime in 2006, some 4 percent recording theft and 1 percent having been a victim of violence. These rates represent about half of those recorded in 1992. During 2003, some 7 percent of students reported having been bullied, a rate that has been fairly steady. Twelve percent said that "someone had used hate-related words against them at school."[86] As crime rates in general have been declining since the 1990s, remarkably good news indeed, the persistence of rudeness, bullying, and hateful language is an important countertrend.

CONCLUSION

The state of American civic life is a bit more complex than many critics lamenting its deterioration suggest. Civic institutions continue to increase in number, though without much support from the bottom up, which means few gains in terms of the camaraderie members would share. Local community groups are also strong in number, but with little cosmopolitan vision or long-term mission.

New possibilities for communication and social networks are emerging through innovative digital technology. The impact of those developments appears to be profound, but what we know at this point is mixed. In the context of established networks, e-mail can strengthen relations and help resolve various kinds of problems. The technology serves the old goals of productivity and prosperity, though many Americans still feel like they do not have enough time or money.

More generally, there seems to be a kind of ephemeral or disposable quality to relationships or conversations that occur online. For some people, the Internet may be as isolating as television. And all the technology is clearly wrapped up tightly with extensive consumerism. More importantly, though, how the Internet will bear on civic life in the long run is really not yet understood.

Overall, there appears to be little question that civic life is in trouble and that the social functions it has served—in relation to issues that necessarily involve collective solutions as well as the psychological needs of individuals—are in serious jeopardy. In many ways, our inability to sustain durable, engaged civic relationships reflects circumstances beyond the control we have as individuals. Large numbers of diverse people in an age of powerfully volatile technology makes for complex social problems. The part of this situation that can rightly be thought of in terms of moral disorder, though, involves problematic choices we make, many of them knowingly, that work against community.

"In most surveys Americans put family and friendship, rather than money or material things, at the top of the list when asked what it is they seek in the good life," Peter C. Whybrow notes. "We intuitively under-stand that happiness comes from fellowship, but in our social and po-litical behavior we fail to exercise that understanding. In consequence, community withers all too often in the face of commercial demand."[87] The choices we make in such behavior too often work against our own engagement in community and against the institutions that would pro-tect such solidarity.

Large social institutions such as education, religion, and even govern-ment continue to enjoy a certain degree of confidence and trust, though there are surely some concerning signs on this front. In the context of shrinking social capital, individuals appear to be faring poorly, as indicated by increasing rates of rudeness, distrust, anxiety, and mental illness.

Along with the extensive decline in social capital, we find a parallel spread of individualism. There are countertrends such as lots of vol-untarism, ample public activity, "networked individualism" of Internet communication, and widespread participation in local groups. In most cases, though, the effort tends to be parochial rather than cosmopolitan, short-term rather than long-term, and small rather than large. In this increasingly meager civic life, we can see signs of market logic. Produc-tivity, efficiency, and consumerism all serve the market at the expense of community. That is, the slow, tedious work of building relationships around common concerns cannot compete with our investments in long hours of work, getting things done fast, and more stuff. Communities are in trouble, but closer to home there may be even more cause for concern, which is the topic of the next chapter.

7

FAMILY LIFE:
FRENZY AND ATOMIZATION

Tony Soprano's "family" has issues. Both in terms of his work life, his mob family, and his real family at home. Aside from the fact that most of his close friends are murderers and that he himself murdered his closest friend, there is something oddly resonant with the burdens Tony bears. Indeed, coupled with the violence of life in the mafia, what is remarkable about the Sopranos is how ordinary and familiar their struggles are. Not that everyone has a narcissistic sister, a despondent son, a hateful mother, or a household so painfully tense. But many of their challenges seem emblematic of middle-class family life in our time. Seeking the right college for your daughter, struggling to keep your son focused in school, making time for your spouse, coming to terms with your own loneliness, guilt, and shame, all the while trying to pay the bills on time and meet the demands of work—it is enough to drive you to do something you thought you would never do: therapy!

As the Cleavers, the Bunkers, and the Huxtables taught us about ourselves in other eras, the Sopranos more recently became America's family. If this family, as foreign as it is, rooted in a violent subculture and old-world traditions, faces such challenges, the underlying issues may be fundamental to the experience of American families in general, perhaps even my own. One of the common themes among all the varied forms American families take, so powerfully portrayed on *The Sopranos*, is strong centrifugal pressures that pull us apart and de-center the household. It is not just that following the script for the American Dream—working hard, honoring your parents, making your way, taking care of your loved ones—is somehow contested, it is that the whole idea of a script has disintegrated.

In a previous era, the script provided order. Family members knew something about their expected roles: breadwinning fathers, homemaking mothers, deferential children, and so on. There was more clarity about who they should marry, where they should live, how they should worship, and what work they should do. What we recognize in *The Sopranos* is that the loss of the script is a very good thing and nevertheless extremely problematic. Few of us know about the kinds of problems Tony faces in his mob "family," but a lot of us recognize something familiar about the issues in his home. The old order was brutal and the new openness is terrifying.

In our homes with our families, our most precious hopes of intimate, meaningful relationships are played out. This focal point for ambitious dreams and sacred rituals demarking the stages of life is also the most familiar site of emotional dysfunction and crippling disappointment. Despite regular questions regarding its fundamental viability, we know the family is firmly embedded as a foundational institution of our society.[1] On the other hand, there seems little question that its new forms do not align with particular idealized notions of the past. With these premises in mind, it is no stretch to assert that the institution of family *as we have known it* is crumbling.

In this chapter, I review contemporary patterns and problems surrounding family life. In pondering the main factors behind current challenges, I make the case that established arguments about women working outside the home are clearly relevant but that our ability to ameliorate these challenges would be better served by refocusing our attention onto other forces, namely the compelling pull of efficiency, productivity, and consumerism.

The main facts are well established. Extended family is more distant and the nuclear family is shrinking.[2] There is more uncertainty about roles that different individuals play in a family setting. The identities and related behavior of "mother," "father," and so on, have become less

scripted and more contested. Such unsettled roles make for intense dis-
putes over a range of issues including division of labor, child rearing, education, abortion, and sexuality.[3] And there are real costs associated with
the declining time and energy spent at home, and the ambiguity about
who will do what. The family is increasingly less coherent, less durable,
and less powerful compared to other social institutions. Its traditional
functions of procreation, socialization, and care have diminished.[4]

People who are married may be happier than people who are not,
but half of them are not happy enough to stay married and some large
portion of the rest, about 60 percent now, are not "very happy," either.[5]
Over the last few decades more people are choosing to live alone, at
least two times as many in most age groups.[6] Given the growing number of people who believe divorce is "preferable to maintaining an
unhappy marriage," it is certainly reasonable to expect increasing rates
of divorce.[7] In any case, there can be little doubt that both divorce and
unhappy marriage are deeply troubling, damaging experiences.

There has been a steady increase since the 1960s in the number of
children not living with both parents.[8] Around a third of all births occur
out of wedlock. Some 71 percent of adults feel that a growing number
of children born to unmarried mothers is "a big problem," which plenty
of research confirms.[9] Young people who live with one parent are much
more likely than those with two parents to have trouble with delinquency, child abuse, and emotional problems.[10]

The main factors appear to involve economic resources and parental
conflict. Households headed by women tend to have fewer resources.
And conflict often occurs before, during, and after divorce. In both
cases, the effects on children are very detrimental.[11] But it is also well
established that most conflict within intact families is also quite harmful
to children, in some cases more so than the effects of divorce.[12]

Whether in the context of "traditional" family arrangements or alternative scenarios, children are more and more vulnerable. In 2002, the
federal government documented over twelve million poor children—
nearly 17 percent of all children and almost a third of all Americans living in poverty.[13]

Across socioeconomic circumstances, moreover, there are disturbing patterns. In 1976, cases of maltreatment were reported for about
ten out of a thousand children. Over the next twenty years, that rate

increased by more than 300 percent.[14] Between 1981 and 1988 alone, the proportion of young people receiving professional psychological assistance rose by 80 percent.[15] One in ten children and youths now suffers from a mental disorder.[16]

One of the main forces in play relative to the well-being of children is the time adult family members are willing and able to devote to them. Almost no women with children under the age of one worked outside the home in 1950, whereas half did in 1989.[17] By 2000, about two-thirds of married mothers with children under the age of five were working.[18] As the time women spent at home declined over the decades, men reported modestly increased time devoted to home life, but the overall result appears to be less parental time focused on family care.[19] Given the significant increase in time spent at work outside the home, according to recent estimates for both men and women, this general pattern of declining family care makes perfect sense.[20]

In contrast, however, some research suggests that the amount of time devoted to family life has remained pretty steady during recent decades.[21] To the extent that we are doing more in the same amount of time, the key appears to be multitasking.[22] That is, the *quality* of time we spend together has deteriorated as well. During time that is spent parenting, parents and children alike feel stressed. And everyone feels more rushed a lot of the time.[23] It is also true that children without attentive grandparents serving as supplemental caretakers miss out on certain benefits, a trend that is gaining momentum as contact with extended family thins.[24]

Taken as a whole, this evidence suggests the family is undergoing substantial transformation as a social institution. Not all the trends are bad, but there is surely a great deal of disruption, instability, and psychological distress, and some fundamental question as to whether the family in general can continue to fulfill its traditional social functions. For all the analysis and debate, however, and there has been a lot, we know remarkably little about *why* the family is changing the way it is.[25]

A good deal of research illuminates the particular challenges of low-income families. Enormous attention has been devoted to the effects of divorce. Nevertheless, we know less about the basic pressures that make the family such a fundamentally challenging project. Why do so many families (across socioeconomic status and with diverse configurations) struggle so? Why aren't they happier? What has changed to bring about these circumstances?

THE POSSIBILITIES AND CHALLENGES OF CHANGE

A common interpretation of these developments is to point to women in general for taking up work outside the home and feminists in particular for ostracizing those who don't.[26] Certainly this is a part of the story. Understanding the transformation of family in simplistic terms of irresponsible feminism, however, neglects three important factors: what motivated women to work outside of the home in the first place; other constraining pressures on time and energy spent at home; and the decisions people make about how to use the scarce time left over.

Limited political and property rights, curbed human rights vis-à-vis violence within marriage and in other settings, plus emotional mistreatment, constrained employment opportunities, and a host of other well-documented manifestations of inequality all motivated a desire on the part of women for more independence.[27] The most intimate and immediate setting for different forms of gender inequality has been the family. The modern women's movement helped unravel the ideals of gender roles in the family of the previous era.

The recognition of ongoing obstacles confronting women remains so widespread that the support for the women's movement persists in spite of the pillorying of feminists. In a *New York Times* survey conducted in 1989, two-thirds of women and a majority of men agreed that "the United States continues to need a strong women's movement to push for changes that benefit women."[28] A more recent study conducted at Princeton in 2003 found that 60 percent of women still agreed with that statement. Eighty percent of the respondents said "the women's movement has improved status for women." [29]

In her book *Brave New Families*, Judith Stacey strikes a hopeful note in recognizing the broad possibilities of family attachment in our age.

"The family" is not "here to stay." Nor should we wish it were. The ideological concept of "the family" imposes mythical homogeneity on the diverse means by which people organize their intimate relationships, and consequently distorts and devalues this rich variety of kinship stories. And, along with the class, racial, and heterosexual prejudices it promulgates, this sentimental, fictional plot authorizes gender hierarchy. Because the postmodern family crisis ruptures this seamless modern family "script," it provides a democratic opportunity.[30]

There is plenty of evidence to suggest that the postmodern family can work, whether it is single-parent households, same-sex parents with children, dual income earners, or some version of more conventional scenarios. In each of these arrangements and numerous variants of them, the traditional functions of family can be wholly met.[31] In one study three out of four respondents defined family as "a group of people who love and care for each other."[32] As most people recognize, two parents have always been better for children than one, but one loving caretaker is preferable to persistent conflict or lovelessness.[33]

The promise of unscripted possibilities for loving relationships, brought about in part by the women's movement, is indeed hopeful. But that does not mean we should underestimate the cost of the destabilized family or overestimate the gain of new choices. The burdens of modern life create huge challenges for all families. In this context, the most significant factor shaping the family's transformation and new vulnerability is women working outside the home, a broadened kind of opportunity that is most certainly related to the women's movement.

In the 1950s, many women felt like they had no choice; they were confined to homemaking. Today, many women feel trapped in a new way in being accountable to both homemaking and work outside the home.[34] In *Thinking about the Baby*, Susan Walzer shares this commentary from a mother in upstate New York.

I think it is really conflicting and I think it is really making it hard on women. Actually I think there is no one thing anymore. If being an at-home mother is so good, why is it such a demeaning job to admit that you're a homemaker? But then again, if you're out working and having this great career, then that lessens you as a mother. . . . I think we basically give parents a double-edge sword. Well stay at home and you'll have this great baby but you're not much of a person.[35]

In addition to these burdens for women in particular, there can be little doubt that less time and energy devoted to family care will certainly have deleterious consequences for the entire household.

A STALLED REVOLUTION

This is not the end of the story, however, because there are other factors in play. One of the remarkable patterns in the discourse about family decline is how the focus stays on the family and women's roles in particular. There are in fact other institutions and other roles implicated in this story. The role of men has been conspicuously neglected in the critique of the effects of the women's movement. Whereas women's roles have been dramatically reconfigured during the last fifty years, men's have changed much less. They contribute a bit more in housework and childcare, but not in substantive ways that parallel the expanded work of women outside the home. Arlie Hochschild has termed this partial transformation of family roles a "stalled revolution."[36]

In terms of the coherence of the family, moreover, the centrifugal forces in play have been intense and multifaceted. For women, as noted above, there were substantive reasons to seek more independence. But at the same time, a lot of men were also yearning for more autonomy. Barbara Ehrenreich avers in *The Hearts of Men* that such patterns unfolded in the context of spreading frustration and disappointment among men that undermined commitment to long-term relationships.[37]

During the middle of the twentieth century, a broad range of new possibilities opened up for expressing a kind of masculinity more detached from both the job and marriage. The rebellious spirit of the 1960s drew together notions of manhood, autonomy, and self-expression into a new masculine sensibility. This idea of not conforming, so vividly modeled by defiant youth, took hold among middle-class men and fostered a kind of "flight from commitment" and permanently undermined the conventional breadwinner ethic that had bound hard work to family devotion. It is easy to imagine that the varied ways women and men each sought more independence, albeit for different reasons, sometimes reinforced one another.

This synergy notwithstanding, men and women still understand their family duties in contrasting ways. How men and women care for children, for instance, remains very different.[38] And the accommodations made for those different roles in work settings are effectively quite limited.[39] That is, despite a great deal of rhetoric and even some genuinely flexible policies in some companies, in practice women bear great burdens in trying to carry their normal responsibilities at work while also taking care of the "second shift" at home.[40]

It appears that couples in which the wife works are still more likely to get divorced. Among working couples, however, those in which the men share the work at home are less likely to divorce.[41] Again, the other important connection to the workplace is how much more time everyone is spending there.[42]

The speedup for both men and women is derived from a complex set of pressures, obligations, and choices.[43] Real external factors largely beyond individuals' control, such as employment opportunities and rates of compensation, shape preferences for which jobs can be pursued, and how much time to spend at work, in civic life, enjoying leisure, or at home.[44]

Gross domestic product has been growing fairly steadily since the 1940s.[45] Lower- and middle-income groups, however, have been facing degrees of downward mobility since the 1970s.[46] This trend is reflected in objective evidence of declining real income and in the subjective experience of increasing pessimism about financial stability.[47] It is particularly difficult for those families in the lowest strata, who have taken the biggest hit and are the ones most often chastised for lacking "family values."

Increasing time spent on work for pay is motivated by internal factors as well, such as the need to be "productive" and the desired level of material comfort. Working long hours at the job and spending a lot of money has become a normative way of saying, "I love you."[48] Historically an expression of masculinity, enduring grueling hours at the job is now embraced by women and men alike. The work (for pay) ethic is reinforced by financial and symbolic rewards in that setting, which contrasts the deepening isolation of work at home.[49] Very few young women aspire to be full-time homemakers, less than 1 percent in one large study of first-year college students in 1988.[50]

The discipline of work is also driven by the powerful compulsion of consumption, including the need to "keep up with the Joneses."[51] In general, Juliet B. Schor documents, people buy more expensive versions of products that are socially visible (e.g., makeup) regardless of quality and less expensive versions of those products consumed in private (e.g., toothpaste). The "insidious cycle of work-and-spend" has contributed to material standards that have improved dramatically during the last fifty years.[52]

This combination of women seeking and feeling accountable to more choices in life, men feeling even more professional demands, declining real income for much of the population, increasing expectations about material comforts, and the drive to work more has led to a radically transformed home setting. In the context of these pressures, family members attempt to maintain the social functions historically met there—including raising children and realizing financial security—and fulfill the obligations of gendered identities instilled in them—that is, to be properly "masculine" or "feminine" in credible ways. But such busyness is hard on relationships.

THE NEW FRENZY

This transformation has led to serious trouble. One focal point for the current problems is the way time is allocated. A new sense of frenzy so common among middle-class families today is derived in part from the speedup mentioned above as well as other factors. "Has it been one of those for you, too? One where you sit down and try to gather your thoughts and memories and they all just run together in a swift flow of overscheduled busy-ness? Well, slip your waders on and step in to 2006 as it happened for us!" This was the introduction to a holiday letter sent to our family.

Jim, my friend who wrote this, was always a good letter-writer. His way with words and his family's full life in Morehead City, North Carolina, notwithstanding—he is a pediatrician, his wife, Becky, is a part-time accountant, and they have two sons in grade school—the gist of these lines could have been written by most people I know (including myself) in any recent year.

The allocation of time is intercausally related to how members of a family develop relationships with one another and with others in the community. Relationships lead to support, assistance, and validation, but take time. So, for instance, a young mother would need to spend time getting to know a neighbor who also has children, time she cannot spend doing chores in her own home. But once the relationship is established, she might receive offers to baby-sit, invitations for meals, or basic camaraderie.[53]

Only a network of such relations can provide the social fabric that offers sustainable, meaningful support. The new frenzy has diminished this type of connection as well as the rejuvenating down time within the home among family members.[54] Women in particular are facing a loss of civic connectedness, more so than women in other comparable countries and more so than men in the United States. This is especially true for employed women with children.[55] That Americans have fewer confidants than they did twenty years ago, a point made in the last chapter, constitutes another blow against the community contexts that nurture family.[56]

The concern about scarce time has resulted in an overarching commitment to efficiency, not just at work but now at home too. In the midst of numerous pressures on her time, a young woman named Susan has orchestrated a fluid sense of order for her family in Philadelphia. She and her husband are both full-time engineers. The normal schedule of middle-class children—school, as well as soccer, choir, swimming, art, and so on—keep their two young sons busy, too. For Susan, getting her work done and moving her career forward, managing her home and taking care of her family members, plus the dizzying activities that unfold in a cascading series of events each week, keep the pace hurried.

One key is consistent organization. "I feel like my life is a series of tapes," she says. "I put the 'week night evening' video in to the VCR and press 'play.' Oh, now it is time for a 'weekend-day' tape. And so on. The activities of each tape always play the same way." Each segment is a predictable schedule of routines devoid of any freshness or flexibility. This is the price of order. Everything is getting done. The job is fine, the family is together, and mostly on time.

What is striking about this imagery is how it represents the picture of success for so many middle-class Americans. We aspire to have important, demanding jobs, comfortable, spacious homes and lives rich with engagement and achievement. And of course, for huge numbers of Americans these aspirations are realized.

A student in one of my classes recently asked, "Who controls our time?" Our class pondered this interesting question without clear answers for a while. I am sure Susan would be hard-pressed to identify what factors in her life shape how her time is used. Whoever or whatever does control her time, she surely feels, it is not her.

The best model for this kind of controlled "videotape" routinization is McDonald's, which has fully integrated organizational rationality and related principles with great success. Frederick Taylor, the pioneering author of *The Principles of Scientific Management*, would not be surprised to see a McDonald's in every town across the country and most major cities around the world. Other fast-food restaurants and, for that matter, every major corporation endeavors to be efficient in similar ways.

George Ritzer describes this massive shift toward rationalization as the "McDonaldization" of society, which is manifest not just in fast food and retail but throughout the private sector.[57] This triumph of "fast over slow" is part of a broad, new cultural ethos.[58] Think of Jiffy Lube, drive-through pharmacies and dry cleaners, ATMs, automated customer service, self-service passenger check-in at airports, suburban development, and now the family.

In several studies, Arlie Hochschild has chronicled how the organizational logic of the private sector has encroached upon home life.[59] For starters, as noted above, we spend more time at work. At least as important, though, the time spent at home is increasingly organized along the lines of a job. That is, we plan carefully how much time each activity should take, and what the costs and benefits of that use of time are, and make calculated decisions about when to do what for how long. As much as life at home is organic and unpredictable, it does not just happen. We plan in every possible way. Or at least that is a prominent ideal in American families.

Mr. Taylor might be surprised to see how *social* "Taylorism" is being integrated into home life—an irresistible compulsion many families seem to obey but regret. One study documents parents' presumption that children crave more time with them and the contrasting fact that what children want more is for their parents to be less stressed and less tired when they are with their kids.[60]

As in Taylor's time, the big organizational changes of society are closely related to dramatic technological innovations. Thus, a certain structure that is both organizational and technological shapes the way we use time. The organizational part includes institutionalized activities with relative benefits for participating and costs for not (e.g., employment, "play dates," "travel soccer," applying to college, church choir, etc.). The technological part compels us so powerfully and surrounds us so completely we no longer see it (e.g., watches, calendars, daily planners, cell phones, computers, cars, planes, trains, Blackberries). In this way such structure creates both incentives and opportunities for efficiency. Don't be late, don't be left out, don't be a loser.

This new kind of structure is evident, for example, in the rise of "rent-a-mom" nanny services, companions for the elderly, personal chefs, lawn care, dog walkers, and other opportunities for contracting house-hold responsibilities. There are now even consultants that help executives in organizing their family's needs relative to the specific services they can hire. Family 360, for instance, begins by having an executive and his family members fill out detailed questionnaires on their traditions, hopes, disappointments, and so on.

> The data are then analysed by LeaderWorks, and the results are sent to the executive in a "growth summary" report that presents his family's concerns in the form of bar graphs and pie charts and identifies "focus areas" for such things as "paying special attention to personal feelings," and "solving problems without getting angry."[61]

While most families never go this far, the "culture of outsourcing" appears to be spreading throughout many American households. It is no surprise, consequently, that one of the issues teens are most critical of their parents for is not "knowing what's really going on in my life"—a perennial complaint that may have more credibility than usual.[62]

The urgency of efficiency also contributes to overscheduled children.[63] In some sense, to not be overscheduled is now considered abnormal, as a recent advertising campaign for blood sugar meters suggests.

I'm Maddy and I have Type One diabetes. . . . Well, I have swimming every day, including Saturday mornings, basketball practice Wednesdays and Fridays, piano lessons on Wednesdays. I tutor on Wednesdays and Thursdays. I have the most hectic schedule. Diabetes has taught me that I can be really responsible and watch my body and stay healthy along with all my other activities. Now I am fourteen and I can basically manage everything on my own. . . . There is no reason that my life can't be absolutely normal.[64]

In the last couple decades, the amount of time kids spent playing indoors or watching TV has declined significantly (16 and 23 percent, respectively, during the years 1981 to 1997, according to one source). The kids in this study spent 20 percent more time studying and 27 percent more time in organized sports.[65] The main shift, at least in middle-class families, is toward achievement, a trend that mirrors parents' aspirations and is manifest in lots of different kinds of activities.[66]

For instance, the professionalization of youth sports has required much greater and earlier commitment from any children who want to play. In suburban Atlanta, nine-year-old boys undergo two-day football tryouts, attempt to learn as many as seventy plays, and endure grueling physical costs if they want to be on a team.[67] Needless to say, there are physical effects—sometimes severe or lasting injuries—for kids involved in more frequent and intense sports activities at younger ages.[68] But there are other costs.

The pressures kids feel from their parents to excel academically, athletically, and in other ways have been found to be associated with disproportionate rates of psychological maladjustment.[69] In addition to the problems of kids being too busy or too serious, there is also a question about what they are actually learning when they are spread so thin. A focal point of this issue is mixed media multitasking.[70] Some children who listen to iPods while surfing the net and speaking on their cell phones are able to get very good grades but do not learn as effectively as more focused attention allows.[71]

Not surprisingly, despite all this interaction through electronic media, many young people are entering the work force with inadequate communication skills. According to one study, 34 percent of employers reported dissatisfaction with the communication skills of high school graduates, a problem surely exacerbated by the rapid spread of written messages via electronic media (e.g., e-mailing, instant messaging, texting). Forty-five percent of college graduates entering the workforce say they struggle with public speaking.[72]

The advantages of this new structure have been well documented and internalized by Americans. We get things done. Each of us has the independence to make meaningful decisions about countless choices. Indeed we make a staggering number of decisions about complex issues every day. The rational organization of society helps facilitate our wealth and freedom.

The disadvantages of this structure, however, are less understood. What Max Weber grasped more than a hundred years ago is that this rational organization of life ends up dehumanizing us. The gains in efficiency often seem to end up creating more hurry.[73] The real problem with the primacy of efficiency as a goal, however, is that it negates other ideals. What is produced through the most efficient means is often of low quality. Not just Big Macs, but medical care and banking.[74] Most importantly, relationships do not nurture or endure when they are pursued only within the boundaries of rationality and convenience.[75]

Much of what is pleasing in life and in the family in particular—fun, relaxation, adventure, art, children, love—cannot be organized into predictable, controlled experiences. When we only think about the advantages of efficiency and ignore the disadvantages, we somehow lose control of our own lives. Perhaps Susan, the plaintive mother in Philadelphia, knows somewhere in her heart that saving time makes no sense if you do not control it.

DIGITALLY ENABLED CONNECTION (AND DISCONNECTION)

The sense of urgency and constant multitasking fostered by our unquenchable thirst for efficiency is advanced by the new digital technologies linking us to distant people, remote information, and always, our work. But this connectedness is a ruse. There are other risks associated with separately wired family members whose time engaged with iPods, computers, Game Boys, cell phones, and so on is, for the most part, not time spent together.

According to research carried out by the Pew Internet and Family Life Project, the proportion of American adults using the Internet, about 73 percent or 147 million people in recent years, is increasing rapidly. About 87 percent of children between twelve and seventeen go online.[76] Cell phone users comprise about two-thirds of the population. Among those over eighteen, the younger people are, the more they use both the Internet and cell phones.[77]

Of course the new technology has great appeal. Its many applications facilitate communication, security, practicality, and plain old fun. I wasn't kidnapped, I just missed my train . . . I'm on my way to the E.R.; meet me there . . . I am so glad to hear from you after all these years. . . . We are learning more by way of the incredible information newly available on the Web. Children in particular, who are accustomed to new technology, are more exposed to different cultures, ideas, and people than previous generations. They are in some sense more cosmopolitan, more sophisticated.[78]

But this also contributes to a weakening of the authority adult family members wield in their lives. It is easy to imagine that just as minimal parenting has allowed greater influence of television on the moral development of children, which has been documented, there is a relationship between Internet use and further diminishing of parents' moral influence.[79] The bottom line here is that we have invited a vast range of unfiltered voices into our children's lives by way of computer access.

Moreover, amid the constant images of other people's beauty and accomplishments relentlessly displayed to us in advertisements through different media, we cannot help but attend carefully to the impressions we ourselves give others. And this marketing of the self further undermines authentic relations between persons who might care about one another, a common scenario grotesquely caricatured on so many of the "reality" TV shows.

Certainly it can be enjoyable to watch movies and TV, listen to music, and play video games. However, the entertainment is also undermining the development of problem-solving skills and family coherence.[80] A recent advertisement campaign for Dodge minivans poses a question that is implicit in many commercials: "You know what would be great?" (That is, you know what would make your hectic life better?) The context in one commercial is a crowded school lunchroom and in another a school bus in which the children are wildly out of control. "Having a DVD player wherever you go!"

In one setting, a man who is presumably the school principal pulls from the ceiling a DVD player like the ones in minivans. In the other, the school bus driver does the same thing. In both cases, the children suddenly stop everything and start quietly watching what is on the screen. The calm that follows reflects a kind of quiet relief every parent yearns for sooner or later.

Somehow there is something very realistic about these farcical scenarios. We are now able to plug our kids into new forms of electronic media anywhere. The question is what is lost when we do so? Surely, how we deal with undirected, undisciplined, unstimulated children involves some of the most crucial lessons for children as well as their parents. In those moments we learn about compromise, humility, gratitude, consequences, timing, and context.

Such encounters are critical experiences for shaping our subsequent interactions with employers, neighbors, and the "other," whoever it is to us. Going back to the Dodge minivan ads, what would happen if a school principal put a movie on every time children were out of control? The family that deals with every bit of conflict or chaos by turning to technological distraction whenever possible has bigger problems.

There is no doubt the new technology is logistically very practical. It allows family members to stay more connected in some sense. Children and their parents use electronic means to regularly report to one another. Surely the security and comfort enabled through such contact is very positive, but there is also a downside here. Regular, short conversations from a distance might not be as substantively informative as extended face-to-face conversations. These frequent bursts of contact sometimes reflect apprehension that the ties parents do have with their children are too fragile for time apart.[81] This fretfulness has given rise to "helicopter parents" who hover over their children and are overly involved in their school, work, and social lives.[82]

Such intrusion combined with the special communication enabled by MySpace came to a ghastly conclusion in the story of a thirteen-year-old named Megan Meier. After Megan and a friend who lived on her street had a falling out, Megan got a MySpace account. She was soon contacted by a sixteen-year-old boy named Josh Evans. Handsome, charming, new in town, and home-schooled, Josh sought out Megan's friendship. Eager for companionship herself, Megan chatted regularly online with Josh and over a period of several weeks developed a rapport with him.

In time, though, Josh began questioning Megan, which culminated in the following message. "I don't know if I want to be friends with you anymore because I've heard that you are not very nice to your friends." The next day, after having told her mother how much the messages were troubling her, Megan went to her room and hung herself. Various sources of evidence, including police reports in Dardenne Prairie, near St. Louis, Missouri, where this tragedy took place, indicate that "Josh Evans" never actually existed. He was a fictional persona made up on MySpace.

The parents of the friend with whom Megan had a falling out, Lori and Curt Drew, are alleged to have been actively involved in his creation. Even though they were close enough to take Megan on vacation with them, know she had been medicated for depression, and store furniture for the Meiers, the Drews (at least) enabled this psychological harassment.[83] The new technologies are dangerous weapons. In the midst of fragile relationships, thinning community, and a loss of basic decency, this sort of tale—as unique as it appears—may become less extraordinary.

Even cell phone communication that links parents and children more thoroughly across time and space can also undermine other kinds of substantive interaction. As in civic life, the family is a setting in which we are increasingly more connected to people distant from us and more disconnected to those nearby. A mother interviewed by USA Today comments on the trend of fewer calls on the family phone versus more use of private cell phones and e-mail. "On the one hand it's nice and peaceful at home. On the other hand it's hard to figure out which boys are calling."[84]

Likewise, an uncle of mine tells me that friends of his teenage daughters rarely enter his home or speak to him on the phone. "They call on the cell phone to talk, never on the home phone. And when they drive up to pick up the girls, they don't get out of the car for me to greet them. Instead they just send a text message, "I'm here." He knows less and less about the friends and the connections they are making with his children.

SPATIAL AND SOCIAL FRAGMENTATION

Not surprisingly, when family members do slow down from all the "productive" activity, turn off the computers and cell phones, and turn toward one another, they don't know how to be together.[85] As Peter C. Whybrow notes, "Frequently, in the family's fragmentation, members retreat to their own interests—playing video games, watching television, writing e-mails, working on the computer, talking on the phone—such that the house is no longer a home but a way station to another world."[86] "It is too bad my cousins are coming to visit," my colleague's five-year-old daughter, Hannah, recently lamented, "and I won't get to play with them while they're here because they will be listening to their iPods." Like many kids their age, the cousins, respectively twelve, fourteen, and fifteen years old, each has an MP3 player.

The combination of frenzy and atomization reduces the amount of time and energy devoted to emotional literacy, the art of conversation, and the forging of enduring relationships in general.[87] And such fragmentation yields overwhelming work for caretakers trying to hold the household together, get the work done, instill children with a sense of rootedness, *and* build a coherent, meaningful identity for themselves.

Ironically, this kind of disconnection and the burdens extending from it may be partly derived from parents' efforts to provide more for their children. More in the way of comfort and ease. Sometimes more entertainment (e.g., TVs and videogames), or information (e.g., computers and phones), or just space (e.g., larger bedrooms, play areas, and private bathrooms). "I wanted them to have their own space that inspires them to do more," says Deanna Nowell, a mom of two children in Atlanta. In their home, the children have their own suite with a TV, play room, arts and crafts area, and separate bathrooms. "They get theirs because I didn't get mine. I just had a bed, a dresser and a desk growing up. That was it." The new, expanded space for children is part of a broad trend in growing cities like Atlanta.[88]

The most expansive living arrangements for children appear to be set aside for teenagers. Kevin Clifford has a large bedroom with a queen-sized bed and a thirty-six-inch television, two bathrooms, a den, and a study/game room that includes three computers. This fifteen-year-old's suite is surely not typical of how all teenagers live now, but it does seem to represent a widespread pattern of households' expanding size and extravagance. As a parent of three young children, I am very sympathetic to the desire for more household space, a sensibility I expect will only deepen when they become teenagers. From a sociological perspective, though, I believe there are real costs (in addition to the added expense) associated with more space. There are valuable lessons learned from living in close quarters and interacting on a daily basis, from figuring out how to negotiate, share, and resolve conflict.

This apprehension brings to mind *The Naked Sun*, a science-fiction novel written by Isaac Azimov. On a planet named Solaria, each human lives alone in a large manor with the aid of vast technology, including thousands of robot servants. Solarians happily encounter one another in personal ways via telecommunication (including intimate phone conversations and appearing naked on television screens) without any qualms. However, interacting with another person in physical proximity in the same room is deeply abhorrent, the most distasteful kind of violation of personal space.

One of the points of the story is that over generations, people on Solaria lost any sense of how and why the human collective is important. They lost the society, the tribe, and even the family. In that setting, the consequences were devastating. Most importantly, they lost love.

Somewhere between the overcrowded areas of the world in which a dozen people dwell in one small room and the unencumbered but loveless isolation of Solaria, there is surely a range of living circumstances that enables some reasonable balance. I do not know where the threshold is, but it feels to me like the dimensions of Kevin Clifford's and Deanna Nowell's homes are on the wrong side of it.

Certainly it requires no stretch of the imagination to credibly predict that valuable skills (e.g., sharing, negotiation, conflict resolution, humility, frugality) learned through socialization in the average housing dimensions of our previous era will be diminished in the bigger Mc-Mansions being built now. The impact on family coherence will likely be substantial. This is to say nothing of the consequences for public space, neighborhood interactions, limited natural resources, and other concerns raised by a torrent of letters to the editor that appeared in the pages of the *Atlanta Journal Constitution* in the weeks after these reports.

CONCLUSION

We see in these different challenges facing families multiple manifestations of encroaching market logic. In addition to efficiency and innovation, the market promotes consumerism, competition, and disposability. As I have said, each of these principles can benefit society in numerous ways when situated in the right, balanced context of other moral boundaries. In the absence of such balance, however, they are wreaking havoc in the family. The authority of the family in our lives is weakening, as Tony Soprano discovered.

Even smart, sincere parents are bewildered by the contending claims made on their children, how they should dress, speak, act, and so on. "Mom, you don't get the world anymore!" My colleague whose teenage daughter made this pronouncement had to agree. The images of bare midriffs and pierced noses are so ubiquitous (on TV and on the neighbor's kids), who is she to forbid such choices? But the real issues are much more important than fashion. How will we relate to one another? What moral precedents will guide us? Like different fashion choices, there are now countless divergent answers expressed every day. It appears that a lot of devoted, thoughtful parents concede, who am I to assert decisive answers?

Like other institutions, the family is de-centered. And, as in other institutions, this development is positive in that it represents the expansion of various freedoms, in this case freedom from the kinds of ethnic tribalism and patriarchal authority Tony Soprano struggles to keep intact. Extended negotiation with our children is considered part of healthy and advantageous "cultivation."[89]

The primary family roles we perform as individuals are up for grabs, not just because of the women's movement but also because of a heightened sense of individualism. We are in some sense each more free to make of life what we want. But the pressures to be someone are adding up. The competing claims on our time force us into Taylorized planning at home, and especially on the job, which offers some chance for camaraderie, and daily rewards both monetary and symbolic. A professional opportunity in another city away from our extended family must be taken seriously, even though many of the top firms do not reward loyalty in any way.[90] More generally, the goal of personal ambition, that of adults in their professional aspirations and that of children in pursuit of achievement and fulfillment, increasingly trumps our hopes for the coherence of family relations.

Some of the time and energy that used to be spent cultivating cohesion in the home has been reallocated as a result of the new opportunities and motives women have to enter the labor force. Beyond that historic shift, enabled in part by the heroic accomplishments of the women's movement, there are other factors. Working for economic stability, especially against constraining pressures, is an understandable distraction from full devotion to life at home. But somewhere along the way, many Americans—women and men—cross the line between stability and indulgence, a serious problem that certainly cannot be laid at the feet of the women's movement.

Insofar as sustaining that indulgence requires long hours of work from women and men and the neglect of family life, it is the wrong choice. Unnecessarily adding to the scarcity of time facilitates less contact between family members and puts undue pressure on the time that *is* spent together. Moreover, as Hochschild notes, "Weakened family prepares the soil for a commercialized spirit of domestic life," becoming more materialistic and ephemeral.[91]

It does not help that that spirit coincides with a new sense of time and space; we want more of both and both can be bought. We see an evolving outlook on time evident in the rapidly increasing use of technology in our daily lives. While cell phones and the Internet connect us to all kinds of people, at times they also distance us from the family member in the next room or the next seat. The hunger for space is reflected in larger houses that makes each one of us more comfortable but also more separated.

These trends do not fully explain the problems of marital disruption, unhappiness, and maltreatment noted at the beginning of this chapter, but they do illuminate an essential development central to this nexus of problems. Meaningful relationships take time and contact. In the context of the hurry and fragmentation at home, we are losing the capacity to build relationships. This is one of the most fundamentally problematic symptoms of the current moral crisis, one that will continue to have rippling implications in all parts of society.

We should not deny the contribution to the destabilization of family that the changing roles of women have generated. Nor should we romanticize the stability of repressive constraints imposed on women in the previous era. Indeed, the repression helped bring about the destabilization. It is a worthwhile and ambitious project to figure out how to stabilize the postmodern family in all its complex and varied forms, and to realize normalized ways of meeting both the necessary functions historically served in the family and the new challenges of our time. A fitting way to start would be to interrogate the unnecessary causes of the frenzy and atomization. By unnecessary, I mean that which does not serve the important goals of nurturing relations, healthy socialization, economic security, and freedom of self-realization.

8

RESETTING THE
MORAL COMPASS

MARKET CULTURE

We have seen how the defining American ideals (highlighted at the end of chapter 3) have been warped in ways that undermine our work, civic, and family lives. Problematic norms associated with "progress," "freedom," "prosperity," "productivity," "equality," and "authority" have fundamentally altered American society. They are no longer American values, at least in the original sense, nor simply a matter of market logic, since they have not emerged in the same way in other market economies. But (as noted in chapter 4) they have become entangled with specific goals of the market: efficiency, technological innovation, and especially profit. In addition (as evident in the last three chapters), we have developed certain excessive habits derived from the market that are not rational in the conventional sense. They revolve around quasi-market values such as competition, marketing, consumerism, and disposability.

Together, these transformed American ideals, market principles, and quasi-market values have become the core around which American culture orbits. Most of these themes are not altogether new, but as a whole this kind of market culture has changed in terms of intensity and scale with respect to it how shapes our way of life. The substantive or internal changes of these values and principles are due chiefly to particular historical processes (delineated in chapter 3). The growing influence or external changes are related to how the counterbalancing institutions have faltered (as explained in chapter 4).

It is easy to imagine that the primary agents of the market—economic policymakers, board directors, top executives, stockholders, and advertisers—regard gluttony, narcissism, and frenzy in this culture as regrettable signs of moral decay, which is after all not really economic business. Obviously, though, such issues are related to the internal ideals and practices of the market and how they influence people in its sphere. It turns out, for example, if clever advertisers spend a lot of time and money trying to convince others to eat unhealthy food—and nobody questions the truth of their claims—people will eat a lot of it. Plus, the same is true with high interest loans, long hours at work, gas guzzling cars, bigger appliances, and so on.

The real trouble arises when other institutions are not able to counterbalance the certitudes and expansion of the organizational logic intrinsic in capitalist firms. The resulting problems take on a foreign quality, characteristics inimical to the prescribed values of high-functioning corporations. As a consequence, the organizational parents (capitalistic firms) do not recognize their own cultural children (destructive moral patterns). Again, moral problems are not economic problems and therefore not the business of capitalists.

In the United States, where the economy has until recently so clearly succeeded in its primary intended function, generating resources, it is not altogether obvious that the market has in fact given birth to a brood of dysfunctional offspring. One clear signal, however, which we strain to avoid looking at, is that the organizational logic of the market is both historically and currently more pure and unrestrained here than elsewhere *and* the toxic combination of materialism, selfishness, and community decline is as bad here as anywhere. While the lineage is not obvious at first glance, these two patterns are kin.

We could talk about the influence of market culture on architecture, art, criminal justice, education, medicine, politics, religion, sports, and various other institutions, which has been quite destructive. The broad, ambiguous character of this new culture reflects the complexity of social life in the modern world. As suggested previously, this culture is somehow nebulous and fluid but also potent and unrelenting, and seeps in to every space of our lives. There are very few institutions not tainted by it. The focus in the previous three chapters—economic, civic, and family life—reflects the settings where most Americans spend the bulk of their time and where key relationships are formed.

That our economic lives are profoundly shaped by market logic and that they have a strong rational element is hardly surprising and, in some fundamental way, appropriate. Still, the patterns described here reveal choices that in many cases are not rational, sensible or healthy—choices shaped not just by market principles but also quasi-market values. Hence, economic behavior characterized by excessive consumerism and disposability is considered normal. The contradictory expansion of rational organization and simultaneous spread of nonrational behavior is also not new.[1] Part of the crisis we are encountering is simply deepening paradox as these trends intensify.[2]

That our civic and family lives are infected by this market culture— both the market principles and the quasi-market values—is more startling. Needless to say, neighborhoods and homes cannot maintain their substantive integrity if they are only organized around profit, efficiency, marketing, or other elements of market culture. As a result, we see the widespread deterioration of meaningful relationships, which then ripples through every kind of social group.

To become accustomed to the features of this culture, which is exceedingly difficult to resist at some level, represents a kind of surrender. To actively and purposefully pursue the goals of this culture entails a more thorough kind of capitulation. Either way, we enter the metaphorical Death Zone I mentioned at the outset. All of this is bad news. But this is not the whole story. Not yet, at least. As ugly as our situation is, there is a growing realization that something is not right, a hunger for something better. In such awareness there is hope.

HUMAN RESOURCES

I recently joined 25,000 people to run down the middle of Broad Street in Philadelphia. I love that charged atmosphere among all the jittery runners just before a road-race like the Broad Street Run. The confidence of training combined with the anxiety of a challenge, conspicuous appreciation of our genuine diversity, and a shared commitment to this event always make that moment just before the start exciting.

I had a strangely similar feeling at a recent baptism too. As we watched the little baby get unwrapped and dipped into the holy water, listening to the parents' promises, making our own as a congregation, it felt very safe and portentous. We welcomed our newest member into the community. Hundreds of us made a hopeful commitment that day in a spirit of wonder, generosity, and joy that babies tend to evoke. But I also felt a sense of apprehension I am sure others shared. What a world this baby will face. Like my own children, I thought, he will need God by his side along with his family and community.

In those two different settings people had gathered to do something important to them. They were open to something special happening that day, something that cannot be bought or encountered alone. In both places I think what I felt was a kind of authentic social solidarity, what Émile Durkheim calls "collective effervescence."[3] In lots of different ways, religious ritual, sporting contests, concerts, speeches, family gatherings, and countless other events have the capacity to arouse this volatile feeling.[4]

All the factors described in these pages—that is, the expansion of market culture and the weakening of other kinds of countervailing institutions and relationships—have become aligned for disastrous possibilities in our society. This is a real moral crisis that stands to get worse. In spite of that, however, the appeal of solidarity felt throughout social life, whether it is a road race or a baptism, and the growing awareness that something is wrong, suggest that we are sitting on huge potential for changed circumstances. Things could be different. There is much more that unites us than divides us, not the least of which is a desire for such change.[5]

Let's imagine what a changed society with restored balance could look like. Within two decades from now, there will be an amazing renaissance of American society. A new era of prosperity, justice, and well-being will prevail. Long-dormant forces of hope will rise to the surface and express themselves in new, powerful ways. The United States will no longer be the supreme economic leader of the world, but robust, novel institutions that integrate rich traditions of political inclusiveness, imaginative innovation, and basic fairness will bring such hopes to fruition. Renewed patriotic American ideals will be articulated in humble, universalistic terms understood and admired throughout the world. Churches, museums, and cafés will become vibrant social settings. Schools will be revered. A few antiquated malls and fast food restaurants will limp along against all the odds. Teenagers will consider shopping boring. A profound sense of stewardship will affect how we think about scarce resources, technology, and human health. Questions about whether science and spirituality are mutually exclusive will be passé.

Enormous support will spread across American communities for innovative urban planning and careful organization of social space. A more complicated but stable notion of family will become normative in such communities. Along the way, we will cultivate novel ways of nurturing families and communities, through which neighbors will recognize the common destinies they share and the need to coordinate how social institutions function. Political processes with more integrity will capture, negotiate, and advance the complex, overlapping interests of American citizens.

Such images may appear fuzzy or improbable from our current vantage point, but stranger things have happened. Think of 1776 or 1865, Thomas Edison or the Wright Brothers, Abraham Lincoln or Harry Truman, Selma or Stonewall, the rights of children or of women, the rise of science or of environmentalism, penicillin or the World Wide Web, the costs of secondhand smoke and the benefits of nutrition. Ingenious technology put a man on the moon. Unionists helped make safe working conditions and fair pay unassailable ideals. A powerful social movement with remarkable leadership brought an end to legal segregation. History reveals vast possibilities. If we can imagine a renaissance of sorts, working backwards from the year 2030, the question then is what has to happen for such a scenario to unfold? What events must come to pass, what choices must we make to realize the promise of our society?

More than a decade ago, Robert Putnam pondered how we might restore meaningful relationships. "Creating (or re-creating) social capital is no simple task. It would be eased by a palpable national crisis, like war or depression or natural disaster, but for better *and* for worse, America at the dawn of the new century faces no such galvanizing crisis."[6] And now, the new century well under way—for worse yes, and for better we don't yet know—we have hit the trifecta. The first defining event of the era, 9/11, brought Americans together in a rare moment of national unity. The effects of the war it triggered were more complicated. Hurricane Katrina was the most devastating natural disaster faced by Americans in decades. The thousands of helping hands available to its victims coupled with the failures of government at multiple levels was a mixed bag too. The most plausible prospects now seem to extend from an economic recession. We do not yet know where things will go, but there are clear signs that many think of this moment in terms of a "crisis" that is "galvanizing." Two astounding numbers demonstrate what I mean.

Fifty-three and 1.2 trillion. Hearing these two numbers over and over near the end of 2008 startled Americans. The first figure is the percentage of the popular vote won by Barack Obama. The second is what experts projected the federal budget deficit would be for 2009. We figured we would encounter these numbers at some point. A black man would one day be elected president, surely, and we would triumph over our racist past. And of course deficits and budgets would eventually be measured in the trillions. But to hear these two numbers when we first did was astonishing. It was unimaginably soon. Our economy is in trouble and our political leaders appear unprepared to deal with it. That is what the deficit meant to many people. Various factors motivated people to vote for Barack Obama but certainly one of the most important ones was the desire for broad change in our society, especially in relation to our economy. In short, things are bad and getting worse yet people want to head in a different direction.

The question of what can be done about the moral crisis described here is much more profound than leadership in government, though that is certainly relevant. It must involve a transformation of our culture and institutions. The election of Barack Obama gives some indication of many Americans' desire for something different. But, for now, that is all. And there is great risk in the opportunity of the moment. One scenario (mentioned in chapter 2) is that the focus on revitalizing the economy will distract us from the deeper problems of our society. Restoring market value and lowering the unemployment rate will not be enough. Another possibility is that the messianic hopes projected on to the leadership of President Obama will actually obscure how broad the solutions need to be.

RESPONDING ALONE AND RESPONDING TOGETHER

I believe the most promising answers lie in two kinds of related re-
sponses on the part of Americans in general. We need to *make wise
personal choices* and *restore vital social institutions*. The first answer
pertains to the choices individuals can make for enhancing their lives,
for resisting the destructive impact of market culture. The value of such
choices have been well documented in social research and are probably
understood and recognized somewhere in the back of most people's
minds. Slow down. Don't spend so much time and energy at work.
Turn off the TV and computer. Interact with people. Encounter nature.
Reflect. Attend to things that matter beyond your immediate context.
Spend and consume wisely.

On this front, it is almost as simple as a recent comic in my local
newspaper: "If you'd like to talk to a real person at any time during this
recording, simply hang up the phone and find one."[7] One encouraging
sign is the countless instances of such judicious wisdom modeled across
the country every day. Even amid the power of expanding market logic,
the human resources of anger and hope among ordinary people suggest
such heartening possibilities are viable. We can make different choices
and, against all the pressures, many people do.

For most of us, such choices are simple but not easy. For leaders with significant institutional responsibilities, such choices are
neither simple nor easy. Two problems in particular make such
steps tough. First, the benefits of market culture are much easier to
identify than the drawbacks. That is because what the market values
most—money—is measurable. What it values least—human relationships—is difficult to measure.[8] In the kind of cost-benefit analyses
carried out all the time in our society—formally by economists and
bankers and informally by parents and teachers, for example—what
is easy to measure tends to trump what is difficult to measure.[9] The
cost of economic choices is easier to discern than the value of moral
ones. So, we do not always see clearly the impact on our families and
neighbors of working long hours, relocating frequently, or going in to
debt, but we can grasp the specific gain of extra pay, a job promotion,
or a new car.

The key to clear sight here is appropriately calibrated cultural lenses. That is, to be able to focus on fuzzy but important concepts like relationships, neighborhood, or morality, and emphasize less vehemently material gain, we need the assistance of certain ideals that bring the human value of how we relate to one another into stark relief. In this way, cultural guideposts can trump rational utilitarianism. Consider, for example, how cafés, schools, churches, or soccer fields are revered in some societies. In those settings, people feel devoted to talking, learning, worshipping, and playing, regardless of any utilitarian consideration. They feel collective effervescence. The question then is, how are cultural norms or ethical habits transformed? How do we create cultural guideposts that can inform moral sensibilities?

The second challenge that makes it hard for many people to opt for healthy, sane choices that serve the greater good and their own well-being is that we lack vibrant institutional settings in which such discourse is nurtured. The loss of countervailing institutions (reviewed in chapter 4) is central in this regard. Civic life and its offspring, social capital, have declined precipitously since the 1970s. The most important institutions that have the capacity to resist market culture, that have historically helped provide cultural guideposts, include religion, unions, media, education, and government. As ineffective as these institutions have become in their historical countervailing capacity, some of them could be reinvigorated or other new ones could be created. At any rate, we must try to restore viable moral hardware that will help individuals make such choices.

There is vast power in virtue and character. There are special moments in history when the actions of a single individual become consequential. During periods of broad social change, the individual choices of a small group of people, those with power or even those without it, can become contagious. Sometimes it is ordinary people who behave in extraordinary ways. Sometimes it is important leaders who transcend the troubles of their time. And there is great promise in the daily decisions regular people make to protect the moral viability of their lives.

Parents turn off the TV. Teenagers spend less time with "friends" on Facebook and more with friends in person. Families scale back on the consumerism associated with Christmas, birthdays, weddings, and other milestones. Significant others express what they mean to one another through emotional generosity rather than material generosity. Professionals turn down the promotion because of its impact on their children. Teachers stay after school to assist students who need extra attention. Managers blend goals of productivity and accountability with decency and humanity. Public servants render their best judgment with integrity over and over. Neighbors attend to one another in an hour of need. And so on.

Under current conditions, however, it is difficult for many people to see that such choices are plausible and/or actually make them. The market culture—with all its rational appeal for prosperity and its nonrational commercials for the unattainable "good life"—blinds us. This is why we need moral contexts—that is, decent institutional settings—that can cultivate the propensity to comprehend and embrace such choices. Again, whether we like it or not, our individual lives are intricately tied to the well-being of others. Moreover, our voluntarism, charity, activism, and activity are much more consequential when we coordinate our efforts with others in a sustained way. Behavior that is morally healthy can be contagious just like behavior that is immoral. So, the key is to be around other people morally sensitized to the fact that we all have shared interests that must be protected.

HOW?

The question of how we make wise personal choices and restore vital social institutions brings to mind advice two famous sociologists gave to their students. In a quiet conversation during the final months of his life, Morrie Schwartz declared to Mitch Albom that, "Love is the only rational act."[10] As corny as this might sound, there is a deep tradition of sociology extending from Émile Durkheim behind it. In coherent societies, human lives are comprised of shared meaning that cannot be reduced to rational calculations. In other words, we must nurture relationships. C. Wright Mills exhorted numerous students to "Take it big!"[11] He meant, be ambitious, sophisticated, and visionary. Again, there is sociological wisdom in this familiar kind of guidance, which in this case is rooted in Mills's pragmatic radicalism; we should strive to see the big connections behind any given social problem and really do something about it.

With my main argument in mind—that the market is too influential and we are consequently losing the capacity for meaningful relationships—we should heed the advice of Schwartz and Mills as often as possible: *nurture relationships; think big*. If we stay focused on nurturing relationships and thinking big, the best models will be "communities of discourse," settings where discussions occur that engage at once the personal feelings, experiences, and sensibilities of the individuals involved as well as consideration of large, complex issues of the world.[12] In addition, the most productive collectives in this regard carry on conversations among members of a given group and also between those people and members of other groups. The intra-group conversation is most crucial for nurturing relationships and thereby generates "bonding" social capital. The intergroup conversation is important for thinking big, and helps foster "bridging" social capital.[13]

Generally speaking, the genuine tension between these goals will in the long run be productive on both counts. Substantive relationships, which we learn how to enact at home and then can pursue in other settings, enable difficult conversations required for solving real problems. Coming to terms with the complexity of the world and the significance of our choices helps us resist instant gratification and short-term solutions.

Despite the overall trend of our time, a number of civic institutions have been effective in negotiating these tensions and resisting the pull of market logic. This includes organizations as diverse as Arts Engine, the Association of Waldorf Schools, B'nai B'rith International, Boy and Girl Scouts, Disabled Veterans of America, the Emerging Church, Promise Keepers, the Industrial Areas Foundation, Interfaith Worker Justice, Share Our Strength, Slow Food, or the Union of Concerned Scientists.

In service of nurturing relationships and thinking big several specific qualities tend to characterize these and other effective groups. (1) Most importantly, they are not primarily interested in profit. All of them have bills to pay and must attend to the bottom line. But that work is a means to some other goal, not an end in itself. (2) Their main goal is in some fundamental way cosmopolitan, pertaining to an expansive agenda beyond the people directly involved in this time and place. (3) Organizationally, they include small units situated in larger networks. This allows them to build meaningful local relationships while also participating in broader conversations about big issues. (4) They are open to lots of different kinds of people, but have certain criteria that require and promote "buy-in." This makes each one both accessible to many and, through self-selection, distinctively meaningful to participants who join. (5) Each one is situated in a tradition that allows members to share rooted memory. They have history, of one kind or another, a story to tell. (6) Each one looks forward to the problems and opportunities of the future. This includes the issues of the day, planning for tomorrow, and an understanding of changing culture and/or technology.

Notice that there is no religious, moral, or political litmus test. Such organizations can be religious or secular, left-leaning or right-leaning. They also need not be explicitly moralistic or critical of market logic. This is less about confronting private corporations and more about caring about something else instead.

In general, this set of characteristics and the corresponding examples of organizations give some indication of the kinds of settings conducive to nurturing relationships and thinking big. Needless to say, various groups have different combinations of favorable characteristics and are thereby better equipped for dealing with certain aspects of the moral crisis.

What if the persistent frustration many Americans feel with respect to where our country is headed and the widespread urge to join other people in worthwhile activities were channeled into these kinds of institutions with countervailing potential? If courageous moral actions of individuals were focused into these kinds of organizations, and the organizations themselves became increasingly vibrant, what would it mean?

It would likely invigorate the individuals involved, help them cultivate moral software, and perhaps alleviate numerous specific problems the organizations care about. It could also help stabilize the foundational institutions of the family and community. If real countervailing institutions were restored, they could then imbue generations of Americans with a keen moral sensibility, that is, the conviction that money is a means, not an end, and that society needs all of us to make contributions. If such broad enculturation occurred, then we would see the beginning of a real social movement.

Students, customers, clients, voters, residents, taxpayers, union members, parishioners, viewers, readers, consumers, donors, and other kinds of stakeholders would be motivated to pressure those in positions of authority to rethink the goals of the institutions they run. To the extent that rational market logic dominates most powerful institutions—and clearly such pressure is profound—then the influence of morally engaged stakeholders' leverage ought to be significant. In other words, executives should be influenced by stockholders and customers, college administrators would listen to applicants and benefactors, developers will respond to investors and municipalities, politicians will be persuaded by voters and donors. In addition, powerful individuals may be swayed by the moral authority of civic institutions outside their institutional sphere—parishioners at church, fellow members of clubs, volunteers with shared goals, leaders they respect, their own children, parents of their children's friends, neighbors, and so on.

Perhaps it would be at that point that some of the trickiest, most consequential discourse would take place. Leaders would have to have long, hard conversations with their colleagues about how the cultures and systems of their institutions function. In that context, with lots of support and pressure from other stakeholders, is it possible to imagine that a few powerful players would become real leaders, not just of their firm or their industry, but of a larger vision for society? Could they reconceive the goals of their organizations in genuine ways?

We are talking about the most influential policymakers, executives, developers, college presidents, bishops, rabbis, labor leaders, and other elites. The many problems connected to this crisis—including rudeness, workaholism, marital disruption, overscheduling, anxiety disorders, substance abuse, obesity, declining literacy, healthcare costs, environmental sustainability, suburban sprawl, loss of good-paying jobs, debt, poverty, corruption, and all the rest—each require different kinds of specific solutions. When leaders study such problems, needless to say, we would neither want nor expect an immediate rejection of all market logic. Rather, they might be compelled to have honest discussions about different tradeoffs, which sometimes involve the legal authority of government, the active engagement of civil institutions, and/or basic market logic.

Would all this really alter the trajectory of our society? Maybe. A slight adjustment among important institutions could lead to a big turn over time. In the long run, we would need to restore a kind of balance in social life between the great institutions of the civil society, the polity, and the market. Any of these spheres could hypothetically become too powerful for organizational parity and moral equilibrium. At this moment, though, it is the market that is too dominant. So, rebuilding countervailing institutions with a genuine sense of authority and community that can provide moral hardware is the key to facilitating a fundamental shift toward this kind of balance.

A FINAL WORD

There are numerous other related issues that are important that I have mentioned only in passing or not at all.[14] I do not attempt to explain or inventory all the moral problems of our time. Rather, the focus here is based on the conclusion that the Death Zone of market culture represents the most central, encompassing challenge we face.

The not so hidden agenda here is to promote discourse among thoughtful people who think we can do better. Liberals should accept that we have a serious moral problem, some parts of the solution are beyond government's purview, regular people matter, and individuals can make different choices. Conservatives should recognize that morality is not simply a matter of individual character, the market is not always the solution, and sometimes government can help. All people of good will should endeavor much more strenuously to find and protect the common ground they can identify and never give up the shared discourse.

NOTES

CHAPTER I

1. Allen G. Breed and Binaj Gurubacharya, "Everest Remains Deadly Draw for Climbers," *USA Today*, July 16, 2006, www.usatoday.com/tech/science/2006-07-16-everest-david-sharp_x.htm.

2. See Jon Krakauer, *Into Thin Air: A Personal Account of the Mount Everest Disaster* (New York: Villard, 1997). Special expeditions from Japan and Nepal have removed more than 20,000 pounds of garbage since 2000. "Trash Mountain," *New York Times*, June 3, 2007.

3. Richard A. Posner, *A Failure of Capitalism: The Crisis of '08 and the Descent into Depression* (Cambridge, MA: Harvard University Press, 2009), 89.

4. Émile Durkheim, *Suicide: A Study in Sociology* (New York: Free Press, 1996 [1897]).

5. He also argued that while there is always a chance that society will exert its will on individuals in crushingly repressive ways, the greater risk in modern life is that society will provide insufficient guidance and control for individuals. See also Francis Fukuyama, "Social Capital and Civil Society," International Monetary Fund, October 1, 1999, www.imf.org/external/pubs/ft/seminar/1999/reforms/fukuyama.htm.

6. That is, I am dwelling on those between the bottom quintile who live in or near poverty and the top 5 percent who can live off of their assets. As devastating as the recent recession has been for many in this large category, by

historical and international standards, I believe it still makes sense to think of them as middle class and affluent.

7. A significant parameter of this inquiry is the focus on domestic matters. There are a lot of complex dynamics related to how the United States is situated in global political economy and culture that are not investigated here. I do not mean to suggest that those issues are unimportant. Quite the contrary is true. But there is a particular set of problems distinctive to the American experience that warrants special attention.

8. In keeping with mainstream social science, civil society refers here to all public institutions, voluntary organizations and community groups that are not a part of government or the economy.

9. Numerous citations reference analytical or anecdotal evidence in support of various points made throughout this book. Others merely give credit to sources from which terms or ideas are drawn. Following the convention in ethnographic research, I have changed the names of all individuals mentioned in this text on the basis of personal observation.

10. Albert Borgmann, *Real American Ethics: Taking Responsibility for Our Country* (Chicago: University of Chicago Press, 2006), 150.

CHAPTER 2

1. Alan Wolfe, *Moral Freedom: The Search for Virtue in a World of Choice* (New York: W. W. Norton, 2001), 1.

2. Robert H. Bork, *Slouching Towards Gomorrah: Modern Liberalism and American Decline* (New York: Harper Collins, 1996), 18.

3. See Amitai Etzioni, "Creating Good Communities and Good Societies," *Contemporary Sociology* 29, no. 1 (2000): 188–95.

4. Alan Wolfe, *One Nation, After All: What Middle-Class Americans Really Think About: God, Country, Family, Racism, Welfare, Immigration, Homosexuality, Work, the Right, the Left, and Each Other* (New York: Viking, 1998); Morris P. Fiorina with Samuel J. Abrams and Jeremy C. Pope, *Culture War? The Myth of a Polarized America*, 2nd ed. (New York: Pearson Education, 2006); Wayne Baker, *America's Crisis of Values* (Princeton, NJ: Princeton University Press, 2005).

5. Quoted in Albert Borgmann, *Real American Ethics: Taking Responsibility for Our Country* (Chicago: University of Chicago Press, 2006), 35.

6. Steven M. Cahn, "A Supreme Moral Principle?" in *Exploring Philosophy: An Introductory Anthology*, ed. Steven M. Cahn (New York: Oxford University Press, 2005), 272.

7. See Amitai Etzioni, *The New Golden Rule: Community and Morality in a Democratic Society* (New York: Basic Books, 1996).

8. Etzioni, "Creating Good Communities and Good Societies."

9. Émile Durkheim, *Division of Labor in Modern Society* (New York: Free Press, 1997 [1893]), 329.

10. Peter L. Berger and Thomas Luckmann, *The Social Construction of Reality: A Treatise in the Sociology of Knowledge* (New York: Anchor, 1966).

11. Etzioni, *The New Golden Rule*, 121–23. See also Amitai Etzioni, *The Moral Dimension: Toward a New Economics* (New York: Free Press, 1988); and Borgmann, *Real American Ethics*.

12. See Francis Fukuyama, "Social Capital and Civil Society," International Monetary Fund, October 1, 1999, www.imf.org/external/pubs/ft/seminar/1999/reforms/fukuyama.htm.

13. See Christopher Lasch, *The True and Only Heaven: Progress and Its Critics* (New York: W. W. Norton, 1991). One category of exceptions to this generalization involves dominant parties in power relationships such as men, whites, heterosexuals, capitalists, industrialized nations, and so on. They are implicated in various forms of control, which range from intentional and systematic kinds of cruelty to unintended, indirect means of maltreatment. But in regard to such parties as well as the population in general, we encounter little discourse about virtue or character. See Peter Berger, "Whatever Happened to Sociology," *First Things* 126 (2002): 27–29. A few notable exceptions like Robert Bellah, Amitai Etzioni, and Alan Wolfe notwithstanding, not many sociologists make judgments about the choices individuals make.

14. See Gabriel Abend, "Two Main Problems in the Sociology of Morality," *Theory and Society* 37, no. 2 (2008): 87–125. The American Sociological Association has dozens of sections organized around substantive, methodological, and theoretical themes, such as gender, culture, theory, rationality, global political economy, religion, family, comparative historical sociology, and so on. But, as Abend notes, it has no section on morality.

15. Orlando Patterson, "About Public Sociology," in *Public Sociology: Fifteen Eminent Sociologists Debate Politics and the Profession in the Twenty-first Century*, ed. Dan Clawson, Robert Zussman, Joya Misra, Naomi Gerstel, Randall Stokes, Douglas L. Anderton, et al. (Berkeley: University of California Press, 2007), 176–94; Lasch, *The True and Only Heaven*.

16. See Jonathan Haidt and Jesse Graham, "Planet of the Durkheimians: Where Community, Authority, and Sacredness Are Foundations of Morality," in *Social and Psychological Bases of Ideology and System Justification*, ed. John T. Jost, Aaron C. Kay, and Hulda Thorisdottir (New York: Oxford University Press, 2009), 389.

17. See, for example, Christopher Lasch, *The Culture of Narcissism: American Life in an Age of Diminishing Expectations* (New York: W. W. Norton, 1979); Philip Rieff, *The Triumph of the Therapeutic: Uses of Faith after Freud* (Chicago: University of Chicago Press, 1987).

18. Bork, *Slouching Towards Gomorrah*, 2.

19. Francis Fukuyama, *Trust: The Social Virtues and the Creation of Prosperity* (New York: Free Press, 1996), 34.

20. For a sophisticated explanation of this interconnection, see William Sewell Jr., "A Theory of Structure: Duality, Agency and Transformation," *American Journal of Sociology* 98, no. 1 (1992): 1–29.

21. Fukuyama, *Trust*, 34.

22. See also David Brooks, "The American Way of Equality," *New York Times*, January 14, 2006.

23. See Bork, *Slouching Towards Gomorrah*, 342–43.

24. Fukuyama, *Trust*; Robert E. Lane, *The Loss of Happiness in Market Democracies* (New Haven, CT: Yale University Press, 2000).

25. Chuck Collins and Felice Yeskel, *Economic Apartheid in America: A Primer on Economic Inequality & Insecurity* (New York: New Press, 2005); Thomas M. Shapiro, *The Hidden Cost of Being African American: How Wealth Perpetuates Inequality* (New York: Oxford University Press, 2004).

26. See, for example, Rick Santorum, *It Takes a Family: Conservatism and the Common Good* (Wilmington, DL: ISI Books, 2005); Kate O'Beirne, *Women Who Make the World Worse: And How Their Radical Feminist Assault Is Ruining Our Families, Military, Schools, and Sports* (New York: Sentinel, 2006).

27. Judith Stacey, *In the Name of the Family: Rethinking Family Values in the Postmodern Age* (Boston: Beacon Press, 1996); James T. Patterson, *Grand Expectations: The United States, 1945–1974* (New York: Oxford University Press, 1996).

28. John Micklethwait and Adrian Wooldridge, *The Right Nation: Conservative Power in America* (New York: Penguin Press, 2004); Sean Alfano, "Poll: Women Strive to Find Balance," *CBS News*, May 14, 2006, www.cbsnews.com/stories/2006/05/14/opinion/polls/main1616577.shtml?tag=mncol;lst;1.

29. See Bork, *Slouching Towards Gomorrah*; Dinesh D'Souza, *The Virtue of Prosperity: Finding Values in an Age of Techno-Affluence* (New York: Free Press, 2000).

30. Judith Stacey, "Backward toward the Postmodern Family: Reflections on Gender, Kinship, and Class in the Silicon Valley," in *America at Century's End*, ed. Alan Wolfe (Berkeley: University of California, 1991), 18.

31. Stephanie Coontz, *The Way We Never Were: American Families and the Nostalgia Trap* (New York: Basic Books, 2000); Ruth Rosen, *The World Split*

Open: How the Modern Women's Movement Changed America (New York: Viking, 2000).

32. Stacey, *In the Name of the Family*, 1.

33. Nancy F. Cott, *The Grounding of Modern Feminism* (New Haven, CT: Yale University Press, 1987); Rosen, *The World Split Open*.

34. Judith Stacey, *Brave New Families: Stories of Domestic Upheaval in Late Twentieth Century America* (New York: Basic Books, 1990), 269; Susan Faludi, *Backlash: The Undeclared War against American Women* (New York: Crown, 1991).

35. Alfano, "Poll: Women Strive to Find Balance."

36. Quoted in Chris Hedges, *American Fascists: The Christian Right and the War on America* (New York: Free Press, 2006), 103. See also James Dobson, *Bringing Up Boys* (Wheaton, IL: Tyndale House, 2001).

37. Paul Krugman, "John and Jerry," *New York Times*, April 3, 2006.

38. Tom Regan, "McCain Has His Own 'Pastor Problems,'" The NPR News Blog, February 29, 2008, www.npr.org/blogs/news/2008/02/mccain_has_his_own_pastor_prob.html.

39. Krugman, "John and Jerry"; Micklethwait and Wooldridge, *The Right Nation*.

40. Maggie Gallagher, "The Stakes: Why We Need Marriage," *National Review*, July 14, 2003, http://article.nationalreview.com/269352/the-stakes/maggie gallagher.

41. Santorum, *It Takes a Family*, 28, 30. See also James Davison Hunter, *Culture Wars: The Struggle to Define America* (New York: Basic Books, 2001), 189.

42. Zell Miller, *A Deficit of Decency* (Macon, GA: Stroud and Hall Publishers, 2005).

43. James C. Dobson, *Marriage Under Fire: Why We Must Win This War* (Sisters, OR: Multnomah Publishers, Inc., 2004).

44. Gallagher, "The Stakes: Why We Need Marriage." See also Linda J. Waite and Maggie Gallagher, *The Case for Marriage: Why Married People Are Happier, Healthier and Better Off Financially* (New York: Doubleday, 2000).

45. Wolfe, *One Nation, After All*.

46. The Pew Research Center, "Less Opposition to Gay Marriage, Adoption and Military Service," The Pew Research Center for the People & the Press, March 22, 2006, http://people-press.org/report/273/less-opposition-to-gay-marriage-adoption-and-military-service; Brian Montopoli, "Poll: Support for Same Sex Marriage Grows," *CBS News*, April 27, 2009, www.cbsnews.com/8301-503544_162-4972643-503544.html?tag=mncol;lst;1.

47. Stacey, *In the Name of the Family*, 130.

48. Bill O'Reilly, *Culture Warrior* (New York: Broadway Books, 2006), 179.

49. Gary S. Becker, *The Economic Approach to Human Behavior* (Chicago: University of Chicago Press, 1976).

50. Quoted in Hunter, *Culture Wars*, 111; Kent Garber, "Behind the Prosperity Gospel: Followers Believe God Wants Them to Be Rich—Not Just Spiritually but Materially," *U.S. News and World Report*, February 15, 2008, www .usnews.com/news/national/articles/2008/02/15/behind-the-prosperity-gospel .html.

51. D'Souza, *The Virtue of Prosperity*, 240.

52. Santorum, *It Takes a Family*.

53. Milton Friedman, *Capitalism and Freedom* (Chicago: University of Chicago Press, 1962).

54. Michael Novak, *The Spirit of Democratic Capitalism* (New York: Simon and Schuster, 1982); Ronald M. Glassman, *The Middle Class and Democracy in Socio-Historical Perspective* (New York: E. J. Brill, 1995).

55. Samuel Bowles and Herbert Gintis, *Democracy and Capitalism: Property, Community, and the Contradictions of Modern Social Thought* (New York: Basic Books, 1986); Robert Kuttner, *Everything for Sale: The Virtues and Limits of Markets* (Chicago: University of Chicago Press, 1999).

56. Robert H. Frank and Philip J. Cook, *The Winner-Take-All Society: Why the Few at the Top Get So Much More Than the Rest of Us* (New York: Penguin, 1996); D. Stanley Eitzen, "The Dark Side of Competition in American Society," *Vital Speeches of the Day* 56 (January 1990).

57. Benjamin R. Barber, *Con$umed: How Markets Corrupt Children, Infantilize Adults, and Swallow Citizens Whole* (New York: W. W. Norton and Company, 2007), 149.

58. Fukuyama, *Trust*, 312.

59. Joel Bakan, *The Corporation: The Pathological Pursuit of Profit and Power* (New York: Free Press, 2004).

60. Alan Wolfe, *Whose Keeper? Social Science and Moral Obligation* (Berkeley: University of California Press, 1989), 103–4. See also Robert B. Reich, "Does the Free Market Corrode Moral Character? We'd Rather Not Know," John Templeton Foundation, 2008, www.templeton.org/market/.

61. Quoted in Charles Derber, *Corporation Nation: How Corporations Are Taking Over Our Lives and What We Can Do about It* (New York: St. Martin's Press, 1998), 141.

62. Todd Gitlin, *Media Unlimited: How the Torrent of Images and Sounds Overwhelms Our Lives* (New York: Henry Holt, 2002), 204.

63. M. Douglas Meeks, *God the Economist: The Doctrine of God and Political Economy* (Minneapolis: Fortress Press, 2000); Wolfe, *Whose Keeper?*; Fukuyama, *Trust*.

64. See, for example, Bork, *Slouching Towards Gomorrah*; Novak, *The Spirit of Democratic Capitalism*; D'Souza, *The Virtue of Prosperity*; Dobson, *Marriage Under Fire*; Santorum, *It Takes a Family*.

65. See, for example, Richard J. Herrnstein and Charles Murray, *The Bell Curve: Intelligence and Class Structure in American Life* (New York: Free Press, 1994).

66. Wolfe, *Whose Keeper?*; Amitai Etzioni, *The Spirit of Community: Rights, Responsibilities, and the Communitarian Agenda* (New York: Crown Publishers, 1993).

67. See Haidt and Graham, "Planet of the Durkheimians"; Stephen L. Carter, *Civility: Manners, Morals and the Etiquette of Democracy* (New York: Basic Books, 1998).

68. Tim Rutten, "The Real 'Outrage' Behind AIG's Bonuses," *Los Angeles Times*, March 18, 2009, http://articles.latimes.com/2009/mar/18/opinion/oe-rutten18.

69. See, for example, Peter A. Hall and David Soskice, eds., *Varieties of Capitalism: The Institutional Foundations of Comparative Advantage* (New York: Oxford University Press, 2001). Plenty of scholars like Hall and Soskice systematically compare the political economy of different nations. And many others, mostly anthropologists, study different cultures, though usually without comparative perspective. But there is not a lot of research that systematically pays attention to economics, politics, and culture across societies. And among the few studies that attempt to integrate these topics, the focus is usually on economic outcomes, as opposed to civic life, morality, or social solidarity.

70. Kuttner, *Everything for Sale*, 55. See also Michael Walzer, "Does the Free Market Corrode Moral Character? Of Course It Does," John Templeton Foundation, 2008, www.templeton.org/market/; Carter, *Civility*.

71. John C. Bogle, *The Battle for the Soul of Capitalism* (New Haven, CT: Yale University Press, 2005); John C. Bogle, "Does the Free Market Corrode Moral Character? It All Depends," John Templeton Foundation, 2008, www.templeton.org/market/; Rick Santorum, "Does the Free Market Corrode Moral Character? No," John Templeton Foundation, 2008, www.templeton.org/market/; Fareed Zakaria, "The Capitalist Manifesto: Greed Is Good (to a Point)," *Newsweek*, June 22, 2009.

72. Fukuyama, *Trust*. See also Daniel Bell, *The Cultural Contradictions of Capitalism* (New York: Basic Books, 1996), xv; Orlando Patterson, "Taking Culture Seriously: A Framework and an Afro-American Illustration," *Culture Matters: How Values Shape Human Progress*, ed. Lawrence E. Harrison and Samuel P. Huntington (New York: Basic Books, 2000); Orlando Patterson, "A Poverty of the Mind," *New York Times*, March 26, 2006.

73. Both of these failures, of the Left and the Right, have been described previously with respect to how social action is treated in sociology versus economics. See James S. Coleman, "Social Capital in the Creation of Human Capital," *American Journal of Sociology* 94, Supplement (1988).

74. This was one of the main points behind the formulation of the concept of "social capital." See Coleman, "Social Capital in the Creation of Human Capital." See also Borgmann, *Real American Ethics*; Amitai Etzioni, *The Monochrome Society* (Princeton, NJ: Princeton University Press, 2001); Carter, *Civility*.

75. See Malcolm Gladwell, *Outliers: The Story of Success* (New York: Little, Brown and Company, 2008); Daniel Coyle, *The Talent Code: Greatness Isn't Born. It's Grown. Here's How.* (New York: Bantam Books, 2009); Robert Wuthnow, *Communities of Discourse: Ideology and Social Structure in the Reformation, the Enlightenment, and European Socialism* (Cambridge, MA: Harvard University Press, 1989).

CHAPTER 3

1. Immanuel Wallerstein, *The Modern World-System*, vol. 1 (New York: Academic Press, 1974); Jared M. Diamond, *Guns, Germs, and Steel: The Fates of Human Societies* (New York: W. W. Norton, 1999).

2. Edward Countryman, *The American Revolution* (New York: Hill and Wang, 1985); Elise Marienstras, "Nationality and Citizenship," in *A Companion to the American Revolution*, ed. Jack P. Greene and J. R. Pole (Malden, MA: Blackwell Publishers, 2000), 680–85; David Shields, "The Emergence of Civic Culture in the Colonies to about 1770," in *A Companion to the American Revolution*, ed. Jack P. Greene and J. R. Pole (Malden, MA: Blackwell Publishers, 2000), 82–87; Joseph J. Ellis, *Founding Brothers: The Revolutionary Generation* (New York: Vintage Books, 2000); Stephen G. Kurtz and James H. Hutson, eds., *Essays on the American Revolution* (Chapel Hill: University of North Carolina Press, 1973).

3. Alexis de Tocqueville, *Democracy in America* (New York: Schicken Books, 1970 [1835]); Francis Fukuyama, *Trust: The Social Virtues and the Creation of Prosperity* (New York: Free Press, 1996).

4. See Milton Friedman, *Capitalism and Freedom* (Chicago: University of Chicago Press, 1962); Max Weber, *The Protestant Ethic and the Spirit of Capitalism*, trans. Stephen Kalberg, 3rd ed. (New York: Oxford University Press, 2002); Victor Nee and Richard Swedberg, eds., *The Economic Sociology of Capitalism* (Princeton, NJ: Princeton University Press, 2005).

5. Richard Harvey Brown, *Culture, Capitalism, and Democracy in the New America* (New Haven, CT: Yale University Press, 2005); Paul Starr, *The Creation of the Media: Political Origins of Modern Communications* (New York: Basic Books, 2004); Theda Skocpol, *Diminished Democracy: From Membership to Management in American Civic Life* (Norman: University of Oklahoma Press, 2003).

6. Tocqueville, *Democracy in America*; Skocpol, *Diminished Democracy*; Peter C. Whybrow, *American Mania: When More Is Not Enough* (New York: W. W. Norton and Company, 2005); Alan Wolfe, *Whose Keeper? Social Science and Moral Obligation* (Berkeley: University of California Press, 1989).

7. Countryman, *The American Revolution*; Mary M. Schweitzer, "The Economic and Demographic Consequences of the American Revolution," in *A Companion to the American Revolution*, ed. Jack P. Greene and J. R. Pole (Malden, MA: Blackwell Publishers, 2000), 560–78; Edwin J. Perkins, "Socioeconomic Development of the Colonies," in *A Companion to the American Revolution*, ed. Jack P. Greene and J. R. Pole (Malden, MA: Blackwell Publishers, 2000), 51–59.

8. See Samuel Bowles and Herbert Gintis, *Democracy and Capitalism: Property, Community, and the Contradictions of Modern Social Thought* (New York: Basic Books, 1986); Samuel Bowles and Herbert Gintis, *Schooling in Capitalist America: Educational Reform and the Contradictions of Economic Life* (New York: Basic Books, 1976).

9. Ellis, *Founding Brothers*; Tocqueville, *Democracy in America*.

10. Ellis, *Founding Brothers*; Schweitzer, "The Economic and Demographic Consequences of the American Revolution," 560–78; Sylvia R. Frey, "Slavery and Anti-slavery," in *A Companion to the American Revolution*, ed. Jack P. Greene and J. R. Pole (Malden, MA: Blackwell Publishers, 2000), 402–12; James H. Merrell, "Amerindians and the New Republic," in *A Companion to the American Revolution*, ed. Jack P. Greene and J. R. Pole (Malden, MA: Blackwell Publishers, 2000), 413–18.

11. See Brown, *Culture, Capitalism, and Democracy in the New America*; Bowles and Gintis, *Democracy and Capitalism*.

12. Thomas Bender, *Community and Social Change in America* (New Brunswick, NJ: Rutgers University Press, 1978).

13. Fukuyama, *Trust*.

14. Wolfe, *Whose Keeper?*; Karl Polanyi, *The Livelihood of Man*, ed. Harry W. Pearson (New York: Academic Press, 1977).

15. See James M. McPherson, *Battle Cry of Freedom: The Civil War Era* (New York: Oxford University Press, 1988); James M. McPherson, *For Cause*

and Comrades: Why Men Fought in the Civil War (New York: Oxford University Press, 1997).

16. Bender, *Community and Social Change in America*; McPherson, *Battle Cry of Freedom*.

17. See Fukuyama, *Trust*.

18. Bender, *Community and Social Change in America*.

19. Wolfe, *Whose Keeper?*

20. Ron Chernow, *Titan: The Life of John D. Rockefeller, Sr.* (New York: Vintage, 2004).

21. Skocpol, *Diminished Democracy*.

22. William Julius Wilson, *The Declining Significance of Race: Blacks and Changing American Institutions* (Chicago: University of Chicago Press, 1978).

23. Stanley Lieberson, *A Piece of the Pie: Blacks and White Immigrants since 1880* (Berkeley: University of California Press, 1980).

24. Wilson, *The Declining Significance of Race*; John Brueggemann, "Racial Considerations and Social Policy in the 1930s: Economic Change and Political Opportunities," *Social Science History* 26, no. 1 (2002): 139–77.

25. Whybrow, *American Mania*.

26. See Rubén G. Rumbaut, "Passages to America: Perspectives on the New Immigration," in *America at Century's End*, ed. Alan Wolfe (Berkeley: University of California Press, 1991), 208–44.

27. Lieberson, *A Piece of the Pie*; Alejandro Portes and Robert D. Manning, "The Immigrant Enclave: Theory and Empirical Examples," in *Competitive Ethnic Relations*, ed. Susan Olzak and Joane Nagel (Orlando: Academic Press, 1986), 43–59.

28. Bender, *Community and Social Change in America*.

29. Gunnar Myrdal, *An American Dilemma: The Negro Problem and Modern Democracy* (New York: Harper and Brothers, 1944).

30. Theda Skocpol, "How Americans Became Civic," in *Civic Engagement in American Democracy*, ed. Theda Skocpol and Morris P. Fiorina (Washington, DC: Brookings Institution Press, 1999), 27–80.

31. Skocpol, *Diminished Democracy*.

32. John Brueggemann and Cliff Brown, "Strategic Labor Organization in the Era of Industrial Transformation: A Comparative Historical Analysis of Unionization in Steel and Coal, 1870–1916," *Review of Radical Political Economics* 32, no. 4 (2000): 541–76; John Brueggemann and Cliff Brown, "The Decline of Industrial Unionism in the Meatpacking Industry: Event-Structure Analysis of Labor Unrest, 1946–1987," *Work and Occupations* 30, no. 3 (2003): 327–60.

33. Arthur M. Schlesinger Jr., *The Coming of the New Deal* (Boston: Houghton Mifflin Company, 1959).

34. Arthur M. Schlesinger Jr., *The Politics of Upheaval* (Boston: Houghton Mifflin Company, 1960); Thomas Ferguson, "Industrial Conflict and the Coming of the New Deal: The Triumph of Multinational Liberalism in America," in *The Rise and Fall of the New Deal Order, 1930–1980*, ed. Steve Fraser and Gary Gerstle (Princeton, NJ: Princeton University Press, 1989), 3–31.

35. Richard A. Posner, *A Failure of Capitalism: The Crisis of '08 and the Descent into Depression* (Cambridge, MA: Harvard University Press, 2009).

36. David M. Kennedy, *Freedom from Fear: The American People in Depression and War, 1929–1945* (New York: Oxford University Press, 1999).

37. David Halberstam, *The Fifties* (New York: Villard Books, 1993); James T. Patterson, *Grand Expectations: The United States, 1945–1974* (New York: Oxford University Press, 1996).

38. Harry A. Millis and Emily Clark Brown, *From the Wagner Act to Taft-Hartley: A Study of National Labor Policy and Labor Relations* (Chicago: University of Chicago Press, 1950).

39. Marvin Harris, *America Now: The Anthropology of a Changing Culture* (New York: Simon and Schuster, 1981).

40. See Robert Kuttner, *Everything for Sale: The Virtues and Limits of Markets* (Chicago: University of Chicago Press, 1999).

41. Lizabeth Cohen, *A Consumer's Republic: The Politics of Mass Consumption in Postwar America* (New York: Alfred A. Knopf, 2003).

42. See Stephanie Coontz, *The Way We Never Were: American Families and the Nostalgia Trap* (New York: Basic Books, 2000).

43. William H. Whyte Jr., *The Organization Man* (New York: Simon and Schuster, 1956); Juliet B. Schor, *The Overworked American: The Unexpected Decline of Leisure* (New York: Basic Books, 1992).

44. Halberstam, *The Fifties*; Coontz, *The Way We Never Were*.

45. Gary Alan Fine and Jay Mechling, "Minor Difficulties: Changing Children in the Late Twentieth Century," in *America at Century's End*, ed. Alan Wolfe (Berkeley: University of California Press, 1991), 36–78.

46. Cohen, *A Consumer's Republic*.

47. Cohen, *A Consumer's Republic*.

48. Patterson, *Grand Expectations*.

49. John Kenneth Galbraith, *The Affluent Society* (New York: Penguin Books, 1958); Paul Krugman, *The Conscience of a Liberal* (New York: W. W. Norton, 2007).

50. Cohen, *A Consumer's Republic*.

51. Gaye Tuchman, "Pluralism and Disdain: American Culture Today," in *America at Century's End*, ed. Alan Wolfe (Berkeley: University of California Press, 1991), 340–58.

52. Lynn Spiegel, *Make Room for TV: Television and the Family Ideal in Postwar America* (Chicago: University of Chicago Press, 1992).

53. Alan Ehrenhalt, *The Lost City: The Forgotten Virtues of Community in the America* (New York: Basic Books, 1995).

54. Patterson, *Grand Expectations*.

55. Coontz, *The Way We Never Were*; Ruth Schwartz Cowan, *More Work for Mother: The Ironies of Household Technology from the Open Hearth to the Microwave* (New York: Basic Books, 1983).

56. Coontz, *The Way We Never Were*.

57. Ira Katznelson, *When Affirmative Action Was White: An Untold History of Racial Inequality in Twentieth-Century America* (New York: W. W. Norton, 2006); Ruth Rosen, *The World Split Open: How the Modern Women's Movement Changed America* (New York: Viking, 2000).

58. Harvey A. Levenstein, *Communism, Anti-Communism, and the CIO* (Westport, CT: Greenwood Press, 1981); David Plotke, *Building a Democratic Political Order: Reshaping American Liberalism in the 1930s and 1940s* (New York: Cambridge University Press, 1996).

59. James Carroll, *House of War: The Pentagon and the Disastrous Rise of American Power* (New York: Mariner Books, 2007); Ellen Schrecker, *Many Are the Crimes: McCarthyism in America* (Princeton, NJ: Princeton University Press, 1998); Godfrey Hodgson, *America in Our Time: From World War II to Nixon—What Happened and Why* (Princeton, NJ: Princeton University Press, 2005).

60. Patterson, *Grand Expectations*.

61. Ehrenhalt, *The Lost City*.

62. David Riesman, *The Lonely Crowd: A Study of the Changing American Character* (New Haven, CT: Yale University Press, 1950).

63. John Micklethwait and Adrian Wooldridge, *The Right Nation: Conservative Power in America* (New York: Penguin Press, 2004).

64. Rosen, *The World Split Open*; Harvard Sitkoff, *The New Deal for Blacks: The Emergence of Civil Rights as a National Issue* (New York: Oxford University Press, 1978).

65. Coontz, *The Way We Never Were*.

66. Sitkoff, *The New Deal for Blacks*.

67. Charles Perrow, *The Radical Attack on Business: A Critical Analysis* (New York: Harcourt Brace Jovanovich, 1972); Todd Gitlin, *The Sixties: Years of Hope, Days of Rage* (New York: Bantam Books, 1987); Robert H. Bork, *Slouching Towards Gomorrah: Modern Liberalism and American Decline* (New York: HarperCollins, 1996).

68. Quoted in Jo Freeman, ed., *Social Movements of the Sixties and Seventies* (New York: Longman, 1983).

69. Freeman, *Social Movements of the Sixties and Seventies*.

70. Fukuyama, *Trust*. See also Patterson, *Grand Expectations*; Amitai Etzioni, *The Spirit of Community: Rights, Responsibilities, and the Communitarian Agenda* (New York: Crown Publishers, 1993).

71. Gitlin, *The Sixties*.

72. Perrow, *The Radical Attack on Business*; *Pentagon Papers: The Defense Department History of United States Decisionmaking on Vietnam*, The Senator Gravel Edition, vols. 1–5 (Boston: Beacon Press, 1972).

73. The number of Vietnamese casualties is still disputed but, counting combatants and civilians, appears to have been at least three million. J. William Gibson, "The Return of Rambo: War and Culture in the Post-Vietnam Era," in *America at Century's End*, ed. Alan Wolfe (Berkeley: University of California Press, 1991), 376–95. See also H. R. McMaster, *Dereliction of Duty: Lyndon Johnson, Robert McNamara, the Joint Chiefs, and the Lies That Led to Vietnam* (New York: HarperCollins, 1997).

74. Patterson, *Grand Expectations*; Richard Rorty, *Achieving Our Country: Leftist Thought in Twentieth-Century America* (Cambridge, MA: Harvard University Press, 1998); Jeremy Varon, "Between Revolution 9 and Thesis 11: Or, Will We Learn (Again) to Start Worrying and Change the World?" in *The New Left Revisited*, ed. John McMillian and Paul Buhle (Philadelphia: Temple University Press, 2003), 214–40.

75. Patterson, *Grand Expectations*; Richard Sennett, *The Corrosion of Character: the Personal Consequences of Work in the New Capitalism* (New York: W. W. Norton, 1998); David Brooks, *Bobos in Paradise: The New Upper Class and How They Got There* (New York: Simon and Schuster, 2000).

76. Frank Furstenberg, "Values, Policy and the Family," in *The Future of the Family*, ed. Daniel P. Moynihan, Timothy M. Smeeding, and Lee Rainwater (New York: Russell Sage, 2004), 267–75.

77. Barbara Ehrenreich, *The Hearts of Men: American Dreams and the Flight from Commitment* (New York: Anchor Books, 1984).

78. Eric Alterman, *When Presidents Lie: A History of Official Deception and Its Consequences* (New York: Viking, 2004).

79. Patterson, *Grand Expectations*.

80. Brink Lindsey, *The Age of Abundance: How Prosperity Transformed America's Politics and Culture* (New York: Collins, 2007).

81. Samuel P. Huntington, "The United States," in *The Crisis of Democracy: Report on the Governability of Democracies to the Trilateral Commission,*

Michael Crozier, Samuel P. Huntington, and Joji Watanuki (New York: New York University Press, 1975), 59–118.

82. See Philip Jenkins, *Decade of Nightmares: The End of the Sixties and the Making of Eighties America* (New York: Oxford University Press, 2006); Francis Fukuyama, *The Great Disruption: Human Nature and the Reconstitution of Social Order* (New York: Free Press, 1999).

83. See Alan Wolfe, *Moral Freedom: The Search for Virtue in a World of Choice* (New York: W. W. Norton, 2001).

84. Lynne Truss, *Talk to the Hand: The Utter Bloody Rudeness of the World Today, or, Six Good Reasons to Stay Home and Bolt the Door* (New York: Gotham Books, 2005). See also Stephen L. Carter, *Civility: Manners, Morals and the Etiquette of Democracy* (New York: Basic Books, 1998).

85. Skocpol, *Diminished Democracy*; Morris P. Fiorina, "Extreme Voices: The Dark Side of Civic Engagement," in *Civic Engagement in American Democracy*, ed. Theda Skocpol and Morris P. Fiorina (Washington, DC: Brooking Institution Press, 1999).

86. Lindsey, *The Age of Abundance*; Francis Fukuyama, "The Great Disruption: Human Nature and the Reconstitution of the Social Order," *Atlantic Monthly*, May 1999, 55–80.

87. Rosen, *The World Split Open*.

88. Thomas Frank, *The Conquest of Cool: Business Culture, Counterculture, and the Rise of Hip Consumerism* (Chicago: University of Chicago Press, 1997).

89. Cohen, *A Consumer's Republic*.

90. Quoted in Cohen, *A Consumer's Republic*.

91. Posner, *A Failure of Capitalism*.

92. Frank, *The Conquest of Cool*.

93. See Naomi Klein, *No Logo: Taking Aim at the Brand Bullies* (New York: Picador, 2002).

94. Robert D. Putnam, *Bowling Alone: The Collapse and Revival of American Community* (New York: Simon and Schuster, 2000).

95. Cohen, *A Consumer's Republic*.

96. Freeman, *Social Movements of the Sixties and Seventies*.

97. Bruce J. Schulman, *The Seventies: the Great Shift in American Culture, Society, and Politics* (Cambridge, MA: Da Capo, 2002).

98. Patterson, *Grand Expectations*.

99. Klein, *No Logo*.

100. Fred Block, "Mirrors and Metaphors: The United States and Its Trade Rivals," in *America at Century's End*, ed. Alan Wolfe (Berkeley: University of California Press, 1991), 93–111.

101. Katherine S. Newman, "Uncertain Seas: Cultural Turmoil and the Domestic Economy," in *America at Century's End*, ed. Alan Wolfe (Berkeley: University of California Press, 1991), 112–30.

102. Howard Rosenthal, "Politics, Public Policy, and Inequality: A Look Back at the Twentieth Century," in *Social Inequality*, ed. Katherine M. Neckerman (New York: Russell Sage Foundation, 2004), 861–92.

103. William Julius Wilson, *The Truly Disadvantaged: The Inner City, the Underclass, and Public Policy* (Chicago: University of Chicago Press, 1987); Marc Miringoff and Marque-Luisa Miringoff, *The Social Health of the Nation: How America Is Really Doing* (New York: Oxford University Press, 1999).

104. Schulman, *The Seventies*.

105. Philip Rieff, *The Triumph of the Therapeutic: Uses of Faith after Freud* (Chicago: University of Chicago Press, 1987); Richard Sennett, *The Fall of Public Man* (New York: Vintage, 1977); Christopher Lasch, *The Culture of Narcissism: American Life in an Age of Diminishing Expectations* (New York: W. W. Norton, 1979).

106. Steve Fraser and Gary Gerstle, eds., *The Rise and Fall of the New Deal Order, 1930–1980* (Princeton, NJ: Princeton University Press, 1989).

107. Charles Derber, *The Wilding of America: How Greed and Violence Are Eroding Our Nation's Character* (New York: St. Martin's Press, 1996).

108. Derber, *The Wilding of America*.

109. Putnam, *Bowling Alone*.

110. Wolfe, *Whose Keeper?*; Nicolaus Mills, "The Culture of Triumph and the Spirit of the Times," in *Culture in an Age of Money: The Legacy of the 1980s in America*, ed. Nicolaus Mills (Chicago: Ivan R. Dee, 1990), 11–28; Robert B. Reich, "A Culture of Paper Tigers," in *Culture in an Age of Money*, ed. Nicolaus Mills (Chicago: Ivan R. Dee, 1990), 95–108.

111. Bennett Harrison and Barry Bluestone, *The Great U-Turn: Corporate Restructuring and the Polarizing of America* (New York: Basic Books, 1988).

112. Jeremy Brecher, *Strike!* (Boston: South End Press, 1997); Nelson Lichtenstein, *State of the Union: A Century of American Labor* (Princeton, NJ: Princeton University Press, 2002).

113. William B. Greider, *Who Will Tell the People: The Betrayal of American Democracy* (New York: Simon and Schuster, 1992).

114. Judith Stacey, *Brave New Families: Stories of Domestic Upheaval in Late Twentieth-Century America* (New York: Basic Books, 1990).

115. Jenkins, *Decade of Nightmares*.

116. "Lee Atwater's Last Campaign," *Life*, February 1991.

117. James Davison Hunter, *Culture Wars: The Struggle to Define America* (New York: Basic Books, 1991).

118. Micklethwait and Wooldridge, *The Right Nation*.

119. Whybrow, *American Mania*; Hunter, *Culture Wars*.

120. Krugman, *The Conscience of a Liberal*.

121. See the Gramm-Leach-Bliley Act of 1999.

122. Erving Goffman, *The Presentation of Self in Everyday Life* (Garden City, NY: Doubleday, 1959).

123. Todd Gitlin, *Media Unlimited: How the Torrent of Images and Sounds Overwhelms Our Lives* (New York: Henry Holt, 2002); Lee Rainie and Scott Keeter, "Pew Internet Project Data Memo: Cell Phone Use," Pew Internet and American Life Project, 2006, http://pewinternet.org.

124. Paul DiMaggio, Eszter Hargittai, Coral Celeste, and Steven Shafer, "Digital Inequality: From Unequal Access to Differentiated Use," in *Social Inequality*, ed. Katherine M. Neckerman (New York: Russell Sage Foundation, 2004), 355–400.

125. Mary Madden, "Internet Penetration and Impact," Pew Internet and American Life Project, 2006, http://pewinternet.org.

126. Carmen Sirianni and Andrea Walsh, "Through the Prism of Time: Temporal Structures in Postindustrial America," in *America at Century's End*, ed. Alan Wolfe (Berkeley: University of California Press, 1991), 421–39.

127. Madden, "Internet Penetration and Impact"; James E. Katz and Ronald E. Rice, *Social Consequences of Internet Use: Access, Involvement, and Interaction* (Cambridge, MA: MIT Press, 2002).

128. Norman H. Nie, D. Sunshine Hillygus, and Lutz Erbring, "Internet Use, Interpersonal Relations, and Sociability: A Time Diary Study," in *The Internet in Everyday Life*, ed. Barry Wellman and Caroline A. Haythornthwaite (Malden, MA: Blackwell, 2002) 215–44.

129. DiMaggio, Hargittai, Celeste, and Shafer, "Digital Inequality."

130. Lee Siegel, *Against the Machine: Being Human in the Age of the Electronic Mob* (New York: Spiegel and Grau, 2008).

131. Benjamin R. Barber, *Con$umed: How Markets Corrupt Children, Infantilize Adults, and Swallow Citizens Whole* (New York: W. W. Norton and Company, 2007).

132. Barber, *Con$umed*.

133. See Susan Jacoby, *The Age of American Unreason* (New York: Pantheon Books, 2008).

134. Wolfe, *Moral Freedom*; Gitlin, *Media Unlimited*; Siegel, *Against the Machine*; Julia Angwin, *Stealing MySpace: The Battle to Control the Most Popular Website in America* (New York: Random House, 2009).

135. See Eric Klinenberg, *Fighting for Air: The Battle to Control America's Media* (New York: Henry Holt, 2007).

136. Joel Bakan, *The Corporation: The Pathological Pursuit of Profit and Power* (New York: Free Press, 2004).

137. Cohen, *A Consumer's Republic*.

138. Skocpol, *Diminished Democracy*.

139. Bakan, *The Corporation*; Lawrence Mishel, Jared Bernstein, and Heidi Shierholz, *The State of Working America: 2008–2009* (Ithaca, NY: ILR / Cornell University Press, 2009).

140. Bruce Bartlett, *Impostor: How George W. Bush Bankrupted America and Betrayed the Reagan Legacy* (New York: Doubleday, 2006); Eric Foner, "He's the Worst Ever," *Washington Post*, 2006; Bob Woodward, "Ten Take Aways from the Bush Years," *Washington Post*, January 18, 2009.

141. Posner, *A Failure of Capitalism*; Byron L. Dorgan, *Reckless: How Debt, Deregulation, and Dark Money Nearly Bankrupted America (and How We Can Fix It!)* (New York: Thomas Dunne Books, 2009); Scott Lanman, "Fed Said US Economy's Decline Slowed in Some Areas," Bloomberg, April 15, 2008, http://bloomberg.com; Mark Zandi, *Financial Shock: A 360° Look at the Subprime Mortgage Implosion, and How to Avoid the Next Financial Crisis* (Upper Saddle River, NJ: Financial Times Press, 2009).

142. Michael Lewis, "The End," Portfolio, December 2008, http://portfolio.com; Michael Lewis and David Einhorn, "The End of the Financial World as We Know It," *New York Times*, January 4, 2009, www.nytimes.com; John Irons and Ethan Pollack, "A Rescue Plan for Main Street," Economic Policy Institute, December 17, 2008, http://epi.org.

143. Posner, *A Failure of Capitalism*. Posner suggests that the economic crisis of 2008 is strongly rooted in the "deregulation movement" that can be traced back to the 1970s.

144. Dorgan, *Reckless*; Paul Krugman, *The Return of Depression Economics and the Crisis of 2008* (New York: W. W. Norton, 2009).

145. Cal Thomas, "Where Are Reagan's Successors?" *Saratogian*, June 9, 2009, 8.

146. Krugman, *The Conscience of a Liberal*.

147. Jeffrey Jones, "Obama's Initial Approval Ratings in Historical Context," Gallup, January 26, 2009, www.gallup.com.

148. Richard Sennett, *The Culture of the New Capitalism* (New Haven, CT: Yale University Press, 2006).

149. Juliet B. Schor, *The Overspent American: Why We Want What We Don't Need* (New York: HarperPerennial, 1998).

150. Peter Singer, *The Life You Can Save: Acting Now to End World Poverty* (New York: Random House, 2009).

151. Ehrenhalt, *The Lost City*.

CHAPTER 4

1. Peter A. Hall and David Soskice, eds., *Varieties of Capitalism: The Institutional Foundations of Comparative Advantage* (New York: Oxford University Press, 2001); Francis Fukuyama, *Trust: The Social Virtues and the Creation of Prosperity* (New York: Free Press, 1996).

2. Alan Wolfe, *Whose Keeper? Social Science and Moral Obligation* (Berkeley: University of California Press, 1989).

3. Karl Polanyi, *The Great Transformation* (Boston: Beacon Press, 1957).

4. Of course, buying is not the same thing as fully possessing or completely understanding something. Sometimes an experience does not last or an object gets used up. Indeed, the misunderstood distinction between a purchase and an intrinsic connection probably accounts for a great deal of disappointment. But the legal relationship of ownership does enable significant control for a time, which keeps the allure of shopping strong.

5. Gunnar Myrdal, *An American Dilemma: The Negro Problem and Modern Democracy* (New York: Harper and Brothers, 1944).

6. Stephen L. Carter, *Civility: Manners, Morals and the Etiquette of Democracy* (New York: Basic Books, 1998).

7. The concept of countervailing institutions here extends from the economist John Kenneth Galbraith's notion of countervailing power, which involves the structured capacity to stand up to private economic power. See John Kenneth Galbraith, *American Capitalism: The Concept of Countervailing Power* (Boston: Houghton Mifflin, 1952). Whereas his reasoning focused on the economic sphere, my use of the term involves broader institutional forces that inform, motivate, and empower people to enact ethics and principles that are not market-driven. See also Charles Derber, *Corporation Nation: How Corporations Are Taking Over Our Lives and What We Can Do about It* (New York: St. Martin's Press, 1998).

8. Francis Fukuyama, "Social Capital and Civil Society," International Monetary Fund, October 1, 1999, www.imf.org/external/pubs/ft/seminar/1999/reforms/fukuyama.htm.

9. John Brueggemann, "Negotiating the Meaning of Power and the Power of Meaning," *Theology Today* 63, no. 4 (2007): 485–92.

10. Robert Wuthnow, *The Restructuring of American Religion: Society and Faith since World War II* (Princeton, NJ: Princeton University Press, 1988); Roger Finke, "An Unsecular America," in *Religion and Modernization: Sociologists and Historians Debate the Secularization Thesis*, ed. Steve Bruce (New York: Oxford University Press, 1992), 145–69; Alan Wolfe, *The Transformation of American Religion: How We Actually Live Our Faith* (New York: Free Press, 2003).

11. Robert D. Putnam, *Bowling Alone: The Collapse and Revival of American Community* (New York: Simon and Schuster, 2000).

12. Don S. Browning, "Altruism, Civic Virtue, and Religion," in *Seedbeds of Virtue: Sources of Competence, Character, and Citizenship in American Society*, ed. Mary Ann Glendon and David Blankenhorn (Lanham, MD: Madison Books, 1995), 105–29; Mark D. Regnerus, Christian Smith, and David Sikkink, "Who Gives to the Poor? The Influence of Religious Tradition and Political Location on the Personal Generosity of Americans toward the Poor," *Journal for the Scientific Study of Religion* 37, no. 3 (1998): 481–93; Robert Wuthnow, *Saving America? Faith-Based Services and the Future of Civil Society* (Princeton, NJ: Princeton University Press, 2004).

13. Roger J. Nemeth and Donald A. Luidens, "The Religious Basis of Charitable Giving in America: A Social Capital Perspective," in *Religion as Social Capital: Producing the Common Good*, ed. Corwin Smidt (Waco, TX: Baylor University Press, 2003), 107–20; David E. Campbell and Steven J. Yonish, "Religion and Volunteering in America," in *Religion as Social Capital: Producing the Common Good*, ed. Corwin Smidt (Waco, TX: Baylor University Press, 2003), 87–106.

14. Shalom H. Schwartz and Sipke Huismans, "Value Priorities and Religiosity in Four Western Religions," *Social Psychological Quarterly* 58, no. 2 (1995): 88–107; Janel Curry, "Social Capital and Societal Vision: A Study of Six Farm Communities in Iowa," in *Religion as Social Capital: Producing the Common Good*, ed. Corwin Smidt (Waco, TX: Baylor University Press, 2003), 139–52.

15. Robert Wuthnow, *Sharing the Journey: Support Groups and America's New Quest for Community* (New York: Free Press, 1994); Harvey Cox, "Mammon and the Culture of the Market: A Socio-Theological Critique," in *Meaning and Modernity: Religion, Polity, and Self*, ed. Richard Madsen, William M. Sullivan, Ann Swidler, and Steven M. Tipton (Berkeley: University of California Press, 2002), 124–34.

16. Mark D. Regnerus and Christian Smith, "Selective Deprivatization among American Religious Traditions: The Reversal of the Great Reversal," *Social Forces* 76, no. 4 (1998): 1347–72; Mark Chaves, *Congregations in America* (Cambridge, MA: Harvard University Press, 2004).

17. See Michael Novak, *The Spirit of Democratic Capitalism* (New York: Simon and Schuster, 1982); James Davison Hunter, *Culture Wars: The Struggle to Define America* (New York: Basic Books, 1991); Kent Garber, "Behind the Prosperity Gospel: Followers Believe God Wants Them to Be Rich—Not Just Spiritually but Materially," *U.S. News and World Report*, February 15, 2008, www.usnews.com/articles/news/national/2008/02/15/behind-the-prosperity gospel.html; Rick Santorum, *It Takes a Family: Conservatism and the Common Good* (Wilmington, DL: ISI Books, 2005).

18. Jeremy Brecher, *Strike!* (Boston: South End Press, 1997); Michael Goldfield, *The Decline of Organized Labor in the United States* (Chicago: University of Chicago Press, 1987).

19. Peter Dreier, "The United States in Comparative Perspective," *Contexts* 6, no. 3 (2007): 39–47; Nelson Lichtenstein, *State of the Union: A Century of American Labor* (Princeton, NJ: Princeton University Press, 2002).

20. See John Brueggemann and Cliff Brown, "The Decline of Industrial Unionism in the Meatpacking Industry: Event-Structure Analysis of Labor Unrest, 1946–1987," *Work and Occupations* 30, no. 3 (2003): 327–60.

21. Brueggemann and Brown, "The Decline of Industrial Unionism"; Dan Clawson and Mary Ann Clawson, "What Happened to the US Labor Movement? Union Decline and Renewal," *Annual Review of Sociology* 25 (1999): 95–121; Thomas C. Kohler, "Civic Virtue at Work: Unions as Seedbeds of the Civic Virtues," in *Seedbeds of Virtue: Sources of Competence, Character, and Citizenship in American Society*, ed. Mary Ann Glendon and David Blankenhorn (Lanham, MD: Madison Books, 1995), 131–59.

22. Gretchen Morgenson, "Are Enrons Bustin' Out All Over?" *New York Times*, May 28, 2006; Erik Lie, "On the Timing of CEO Stock Option Awards," *Management Science* 51, no. 5 (2005): 802–12; John C. Bogle, *The Battle for the Soul of Capitalism* (New Haven, CT: Yale University Press, 2005); James Lardner, "The Specter Haunting Your Office," *New York Review of Books*, June 14, 2007, 62–65.

23. Ten of the top twenty campaign contributors in 2000 were labor unions. See Thomas R. Dye, *Who's Running America? The Bush Restoration*, 7th ed. (Upper Saddle River, NJ: Prentice Hall, 2002). But business has been outspending labor by more than 15 to 1. See Dan Clawson "Money and Politics," in *Inequality and Society: Social Science Perspectives on Social Stratification*, ed. Jeff Manza and Michael Sauder (New York: W. W. Norton, 2009), 819–31.

24. Todd Gitlin, *Media Unlimited: How the Torrent of Images and Sounds Overwhelms Our Lives* (New York: Henry Holt, 2002).

25. Theodor W. Adorno, *The Culture Industry: Selected Essays on Mass Culture* (New York: Routledge, 1991); Neil Postman, *Amusing Ourselves to Death: Public Discourse in the Age of Show Business* (New York: Viking, 1985); David J. Jackson, *Entertainment and Politics: The Influence of Pop Culture on Young Adult Political Socialization* (New York: Peter Lang, 2002).

26. Milan Kundera, *Immortality*, trans. Peter Kussi (New York: Grove Weidenfeld, 1991).

27. Stacy Schiff, "Know It All: Can Wikipedia Conquer Expertise?" *New Yorker*, July 31, 2006. Wikipedia had nearly 3 million entries in 2009.

28. Lee Rainie, Jeffrey Boase, John Horrigan, and Barry Wellman, "The Strength of Internet Ties," Pew Internet and American Life Project, January 25, 2006, www.pewinternet.org/Reports/2006/The-Strength-of-Internet-Ties.aspx.

29. Benjamin Barber, Con$umed: How Markets Corrupt Children, Infantilize Adults, and Swallow Citizens Whole (New York: W. W. Norton and Company, 2007).

30. Jackson, Entertainment and Politics; Susan Jacoby, The Age of American Unreason (New York: Pantheon Books, 2008).

31. Ben H. Bagdikian, The New Media Monopoly (Boston: Beacon Press, 2004).

32. Katie Hafner, "Lifting Corporate Fingerprints from the Editing of Wikipedia," New York Times, 2007; Lee Siegel, Against the Machine: Being Human in the Age of the Electronic Mob (New York: Spiegel and Grau, 2008).

33. Alan Wolfe, Does American Democracy Still Work? (New Haven, CT: Yale University Press, 2006); Michael Bugeja, Interpersonal Divide: The Search for Community in a Technological Age (New York: Oxford University Press, 2005).

34. Thomas Frank, "Coming to an Airport Checkpoint Near You: Ads in the Security Bins," USA Today, January 10, 2007; Julie Bosman, "Place Your Ad Here, and Here," New York Times, July 23, 2006.

35. Gitlin, Media Unlimited. See also Eric Klinenberg, Fighting for Air: The Battle to Control America's Media (New York: Henry Holt, 2007).

36. Putnam, Bowling Alone.

37. William G. Bowen and Derek Bok, The Shape of the River: Long-Term Consequences of Considering Race in College and University Admissions (Princeton, NJ: Princeton University Press, 1998); Kenneth Arrow, Samuel Bowles, and Steven Durlauf, eds., Meritocracy and Economic Inequality (Princeton, NJ: Princeton University Press, 2000); Peter W. Cookson Jr. and Caroline Hodges Persell, Preparing for Power: America's Elite Boarding Schools (New York: Basic Books, 1985).

38. Richard Rubinson, "Class Formation, Politics, and Institutions: Schooling in the United States," American Journal of Sociology 92, no. 3 (1986): 519–38.

39. Daniel Golden, The Price of Admission: How America's Ruling Class Buys Its Way into Elite Colleges—and Who Gets Left Outside the Gates (New York: Crown, 2006); William G. Bowen, Martin A. Kurzweil, and Eugene M. Tobin, Equity and Excellence in American Higher Education (Charlottesville: University of Virginia Press, 2006).

40. The decline of such proficiency is particularly disconcerting in light of the preeminent goal of achievement. See Jacoby, The Age of American Unreason.

41. Charles J. Sykes, *Dumbing Down Our Kids: Why America's Children Feel Good about Themselves but Can't Read, Write, or Add* (New York: St. Martin's Press, 1995).

42. Maureen Stout, *The Feel-Good Curriculum: The Dumbing-Down of America's Kids in the Name of Self-Esteem* (Cambridge, MA: Perseus Books, 2000).

43. Barber, *Con$umed*; Michael Bugeja, *Interpersonal Divide: The Search for Community in a Technological Age* (New York: Oxford University Press, 2005).

44. Robert N. Bellah, "Freedom, Coercion and Authority," *Academe*, January–February 1999, 16–21.

45. Academics do tend to vote Democratic, but such liberal leanings do not translate into widespread engagement and efficacy in public discourse. See Michael Bérubé, *What's Liberal About the Liberal Arts? Classroom Politics and "Bias" in Higher Education* (New York: W. W. Norton, 2006).

46. See Amitai Etzioni, *The Spirit of Community: Rights, Responsibilities, and the Communitarian Agenda* (New York: Crown Publishers, 1993).

47. Alan Wolfe, *Marginalized in the Middle* (Chicago: University of Chicago Press, 1996). See also Mark C. Taylor, "End the University as We Know It," *New York Times*, April 27, 2009.

48. See John Brueggemann, "Racial Considerations and Social Policy in the 1930s: Economic Change and Political Opportunities," *Social Science History* 26, no. 1 (2002): 139–79.

49. Dye, *Who's Running America?*; G. William Domhoff, *Who Rules America? Power and Politics in the Year 2000* (Mountain View, CA: Mayfield, 1998).

50. Jeanne Cummings, "2008 Campaign Costliest in U.S. History," Politico, January 15, 2008, http://politico.com.

51. Robert Kuttner, *Everything for Sale: The Virtues and Limits of Markets* (Chicago: University of Chicago Press, 1999).

52. See Barber, *Con$umed*; Alan Wolfe, *Does American Democracy Still Work?* (New Haven, CT: Yale University Press, 2006); Etzioni, *The Spirit of Community*; Michael Parenti, *Democracy for the Few*, 6th ed. (New York: St. Martin's Press, 1995); Charles Derber, *Corporation Nation: How Corporations Are Taking Over Our Lives and What We Can Do about It* (New York: St. Martin's Press, 1998).

53. The Supreme Court's 2010 ruling expanding the First Amendment rights of Corporations allows for unlimited corporate spending in political campaigns.

54. See Kuttner, *Everything for Sale*; Derber, *Corporation Nation*; Joel Bakan, *The Corporation: The Pathological Pursuit of Profit and Power* (New York: Free Press, 2004); Byron L. Dorgan, *Reckless: How Debt, Deregulation, and Dark Money Nearly Bankrupted America (and How We Can Fix It!)* (New York: Thomas Dunne Books, 2009).

55. Fukuyama, "Social Capital and Civil Society."

56. Eric Alterman, *When Presidents Lie: A History of Official Deception and Its Consequences* (New York: Viking, 2004); Marc J. Hetherington, *Why Trust Matters: Declining Political Trust and the Demise of American Liberalism* (Princeton, NJ: Princeton University Press, 2005); Douglas Brinkley, *The Great Deluge: Hurricane Katrina, New Orleans, and the Mississippi Gulf Coast* (New York: Harper, 2007); Thomas E. Ricks, *Fiasco: The American Military Adventure in Iraq* (New York: Penguin, 2007).

57. Carter, *Civility*; Amitai Etzioni, *The New Golden Rule: Community and Morality in a Democratic Society* (New York: Basic Books, 1996).

CHAPTER 5

1. Lauren Greenfield, "Money Talks," *New York Times*, June 10, 2007.

2. C. Wright Mills, *The Sociological Imagination* (New York: Oxford University Press, 1959).

3. See Richard A. Posner, *A Failure of Capitalism: The Crisis of '08 and the Descent into Depression* (Cambridge, MA: Harvard University Press, 2009).

4. See chapter 3.

5. John P. Robinson and Geoffrey Godbey, *Time for Life: The Surprising Ways Americans Use Their Time* (University Park: Pennsylvania State University Press, 1997).

6. Nelson Lichtenstein, *Labor's War at Home: The CIO in World War II* (New York: Cambridge University Press, 1982).

7. Juliet B. Schor, *The Overworked American: The Unexpected Decline of Leisure* (New York: Basic Books, 1992).

8. Peter Dreier, "The United States in Comparative Perspective," *Contexts* 6, no. 3 (2007): 39–47.

9. Fred Block, "Mirrors and Metaphors: The United States and Its Trade Rivals," in *America at Century's End*, ed. Alan Wolfe (Berkeley: University of California Press, 1991), 93–111; Katherine S. Newman, *Falling From Grace: The Experience of Downward Mobility in the American Middle Class* (New York: Free Press, 1988).

10. "The World Factbook," Central Intelligence Agency, 2008, www.cia.gov/library/publications/the-world-factbook/index.html.

11. Paul Taylor, Cary Funk, and April Clark, "Luxury or Necessity? Things We Can't Live Without: The List Has Grown in the Past Decades," Pew Research Center, December 14, 2006, http://pewsocialtrends.org/assets/pdf/Luxury.pdf.

12. Marion Nestle, *Food Politics: How the Food Industry Influences Nutrition and Health* (Berkeley: University of California Press, 2002).

13. Juliet B. Schor, *Born to Buy: The Commercialized Child and the New Consumer Culture* (New York: Scribner, 2004).

14. Schor, *The Overworked American*; Newman, *Falling From Grace*; Arlie Russell Hochschild, *The Time Bind: When Work Becomes Home and Home Becomes Work* (New York: Metropolitan Books, 1997).

15. Donald E. Super and Branimir Sverko, eds., *Life Roles, Values, and Careers: International Findings of the Work Importance Study* (San Francisco: Jossey-Bass, 1995).

16. MOW International Research Team, *The Meaning of Work* (London: Academic Press, 1987); Stefan Svallfors, *The Moral Economy of Class: Class and Attitudes in Comparative Perspective* (Stanford, CA: Stanford University Press, 2006).

17. Robinson and Godbey, *Time for Life*; Jerry A. Jacobs and Kathleen Gerson, *The Time Divide: Work, Family, and Gender Inequality* (Cambridge, MA: Harvard University Press, 2004).

18. Robert E. Lane, *The Loss of Happiness in Market Democracies* (New Haven, CT: Yale University Press, 2000); Richard Sennett, *The Corrosion of Character: The Personal Consequences of Work in the New Capitalism* (New York: W. W. Norton, 1998).

19. Christine M. Pearson, Lynne M. Andersson, and Christine L. Porath, "Assessing and Attacking Workplace Incivility," *Organizational Dynamics* 29, no. 2 (2000): 123–48; Christine M. Pearson and Christine L. Porath, "On the Nature, Consequences and Remedies of Workplace Incivility: No Time for 'Nice'? Think Again," *Academy of Management Executive* 19, no.1 (2005): 1–12; Dawn Sagario, "Rudeness Can Hurt More Than Work Force's Feelings," *Times Union*, November 27, 2005.

20. Alan Wolfe, *Whose Keeper? Social Science and Moral Obligation* (Berkeley: University of California Press, 1989); Tim Kasser, *The High Price of Materialism* (Cambridge, MA: MIT Press, 2002).

21. Hochschild, *The Time Bind*; MOW International Research Team, *The Meaning of Work*.

22. Sennett, *The Corrosion of Character*.

23. D. Stanley Eitzen, "The Dark Side of Competition in American Society," *Vital Speeches of the Day* 56 (January 1990): 185–86; Robert H. Frank and Philip J. Cook, *The Winner-Take-All Society: Why the Few at the Top Get So Much More Than the Rest of Us* (New York: Penguin, 1996).

24. Barry Schwartz, *Queuing and Waiting: Studies in the Social Organization of Access and Delay* (Chicago: University of Chicago Press, 1975); Carmen Sirianni and Andrea Walsh, "Through the Prism of Time: Temporal Structures in Postindustrial America," in *America at Century's End*, ed. Alan Wolfe (Berkeley: University of California Press, 1991), 421–39.

25. Alvin A. Rosenfeld and Nicole Wise, *The Over-Scheduled Child: Avoiding the Hyper-Parenting Trap* (New York: St. Martin's Griffin, 2000); Arlie Russell Hochschild, *The Commercialization of Intimate Life: Notes from Home and Work* (Berkeley: University of California Press, 2003).

26. Jacobs and Gerson, *The Time Divide*; Peter C. Whybrow, *American Mania: When More Is Not Enough* (New York: W. W. Norton and Company, 2005); Ellen Galinsky, *Ask the Children: What America's Children Really Think about Working Parents* (New York: William Morrow, 1991).

27. Janet W. Salaff, "Where Home Is the Office: The New Form of Flexible Work," in *The Internet in Everyday Life*, ed. Barry Wellman and Caroline A. Haythornthwaite (Malden, MA: Blackwell, 2002), 464–495.

28. Galinsky, *Ask the Children*.

29. This mobility is of course dampened during a recession but in global, historical terms, the pattern continues to hold in the United States. See William Julius Wilson, *When Work Disappears: The World of the New Urban Poor* (New York: Vintage Books, 1996); Kenneth Arrow, Samuel Bowles, and Steven Durlauf, eds., *Meritocracy and Economic Inequality* (Princeton, NJ: Princeton University Press, 2000); Chuck Collins and Felice Yeskel, *Economic Apartheid in America: A Primer on Economic Inequality & Insecurity* (New York: New Press, 2005).

30. Robert L. Frank, *Richistan: A Journey through the American Wealth Boom and the Lives of the New Rich* (New York: Crown Publishers, 2007).

31. Barbara Ehrenreich, *Bait and Switch: The (Futile) Pursuit of the American Dream* (New York: Henry Holt and Company, 2006); Louis Uchitelle, *The Disposable American: Layoffs and Their Consequences* (New York: Alfred A. Knopf, 2006).

32. See Erik Olin Wright, *Classes* (London: Verso, 1985).

33. Garance Franke-Ruta, "Remapping the Culture Debate," *The American Prospect*, January 16, 2006, http://prospect.org/cs/articles?article=remapping_the_culture_debate_011606.

34. Melvin L. Oliver and Thomas M. Shapiro, *Black Wealth/White Wealth: A New Perspective on Racial Inequality* (New York: Routledge, 1995); Thomas M. Shapiro, *The Hidden Cost of Being African American: How Wealth Perpetuates Inequality* (New York: Oxford University Press, 2004).

35. Collins and Yeskel, *Economic Apartheid in America*.

36. "The 400 Richest Americans," *Forbes*, 2006, www.forbes.com. The proportion of wealth that is inherited has declined in recent years, but it is still substantial. See Frank, *Richistan*.

37. Posner, *A Failure of Capitalism*.

38. Collins and Yeskel, *Economic Apartheid in America*.

39. John Kenneth Galbraith, *Annals of an Abiding Liberal*, ed. Andrea D. Williams (New York: New American Library, 1980).

40. Erik Lie, "On the Timing of CEO Stock Option Awards," *Management Science* 51, no. 5 (2005): 802–12.

41. James Lardner, "The Specter Haunting Your Office," *New York Review of Books*, June 14, 2007, 62–65.

42. John C. Bogle, *The Battle for the Soul of Capitalism* (New Haven, CT: Yale University Press, 2005).

43. Posner, *A Failure of Capitalism*.

44. Robert Kuttner, *Everything for Sale: The Virtues and Limits of Markets* (Chicago: University of Chicago Press, 1999); Byron L. Dorgan, *Take This Job and Ship It: How Corporate Greed and Brain-Dead Politics Are Selling Out America* (New York: St. Martin's Press, 2006).

45. Frank, *Richistan*.

46. Collins and Yeskel, *Economic Apartheid in America*.

47. Simon Head, "They're Micromanaging Your Every Move," *New York Review of Books*, August 16, 2007, 42–44.

48. The poverty rate is the proportion of American citizens whose household income is below the poverty line designated by the federal government. Dreier, "The United States in Comparative Perspective"; "Current Population Survey, 2006 Annual Social and Economic (ASEC) Supplement," U.S. Census Bureau, 2006, www.census.gov/apsd/techdoc/cps/cpsmar06.pdf.

49. Kimberley A. Bobo, *Wage Theft in America: Why Millions of Working Americans Are Not Getting Paid—and What We Can Do about It* (New York: New Press, 2009).

50. William J. Dixon and Terry Boswell, "Dependency, Disarticulation, and Denominator Effects: Another Look at Foreign Capital Penetration," *American Journal of Sociology* 102, no. 2 (1996): 543–63; George Ritzer, *The Globalization of Nothing* (Thousand Oaks, CA: Pine Forge Press, 2004).

51. David Brooks, "Friedman's Glow Was the Smile of Reason," *New York Times*, November 19, 2006. See also Posner, *A Failure of Capitalism*.

52. Dreier, "The United States in Comparative Perspective"; Wilson, *When Work Disappears*; Shapiro, *The Hidden Cost of Being African American*; Douglas S. Massey and Nancy A. Denton, *American Apartheid: Segregation and the Making of the Underclass* (Cambridge, MA: Harvard University Press, 1993); William Julius Wilson, *The Truly Disadvantaged: The Inner City, the Underclass, and Public Policy* (Chicago: University of Chicago Press, 1987).

53. Barry Schwartz, *The Costs of Living: How Market Freedom Erodes the Best Things in Life* (New York: Xlibris, 2000).

54. Dreier, "The United States in Comparative Perspective."

55. Schor, *Born to Buy*; Lane, *The Loss of Happiness in Market Democracies*; Hochschild, *The Commercialization of Intimate Life*; Juliet B. Schor, *The*

Overspent American: Why We Want What We Don't Need (New York: Harper Perennial, 1998).

56. Taylor, Funk, and Clark, "Luxury or Necessity?"; Pamela N. Danziger, *Why People Buy Things They Don't Need* (Ithaca, NY: Paramount Market Publishing, 2002).

57. Schor, *The Overworked American*; Paul Nunes and Brian Johnson, *Mass Affluence: Seven New Rules of Marketing to Today's Consumer* (Boston: Harvard Business School Press, 2004).

58. Mark Zandi, *Financial Shock: A 360° Look at the Subprime Mortgage Implosion, and How to Avoid the Next Financial Crisis* (Upper Saddle River, NJ: Financial Times Press, 2009).

59. Quoted in Gary Rivlin, "The Millionaires Who Don't Feel Rich," *New York Times*, August 5, 2007. See also Frank, *Richistan*.

60. Allen Salkin, "Pimp My Grill," *New York Times*, May 28, 2006.

61. Robert H. Frank, *Falling Behind: How Rising Inequality Harms the Middle Class* (Berkeley: University of California Press, 2007).

62. Nunes and Johnson, *Mass Affluence*.

63. Schor, *The Overspent American*.

64. "Fortune 500," *Fortune*, April 17, 2006, 329–36.

65. Theodor W. Adorno, *The Culture Industry: Selected Essays on Mass Culture* (New York: Routledge, 1991); Ben H. Bagdikian, *The New Media Monopoly* (Boston: Beacon Press, 2004); Todd Gitlin, *Media Unlimited: How the Torrent of Images and Sounds Overwhelms Our Lives* (New York: Henry Holt, 2002).

66. Robinson and Godbey, *Time for Life*.

67. On a 10-point scale of satisfaction, one study reports a decline from 6.0 in 1975 to 4.8 in 1995. Robinson and Godbey, *Time for Life*. See also Schor, *The Overworked American*.

68. Benjamin R. Barber, *Con$umed: How Markets Corrupt Children, Infantilize Adults, and Swallow Citizens Whole* (New York: W. W. Norton and Company, 2007); Neil Postman, *Amusing Ourselves to Death: Public Discourse in the Age of Show Business* (New York: Viking, 1985); David J. Jackson, *Entertainment and Politics: The Influences of Pop Culture on Young Adult Political Socialization* (New York: Peter Lang, 2002).

69. Lane, *The Loss of Happiness in Market Democracies*.

70. Schor, *Born to Buy*. See also Nestle, *Food Politics*.

71. Lane, *The Loss of Happiness in Market Democracies*.

72. Quoted in Greenfield, "Money Talks."

73. Nestle, *Food Politics*.

74. Kasser, *The High Price of Materialism*.

75. Hochschild, *The Commercialization of Intimate Life*.

76. Advertisements for children alone in 2004 cost $15 billion. Schor, *Born to Buy*; Regis McKenna, *Total Access: Giving Customers What They Want in an Anytime, Anywhere World* (Boston: Harvard Business School Press, 2002).

77. McKenna, *Total Access*.

78. Jackson Lears, "The American Way of Debt," *New York Times*, June 11, 2006, 13-16.

79. One estimate calculated more than $15 billion of revenue for the year 2006 in global online gambling. Half of the customers generating that amount were in the United States. Nancy Zuckerbrod, "House of Representatives Passes Bill to Limit Online Gambling," *Saratogian*, July 12, 2006.

80. Lendol Calder, *Financing the American Dream: A Cultural History of Consumer Credit* (Princeton, NJ: Princeton University Press, 1999); Edward N. Wolff, *Recent Trends in Household Wealth in the United States: Rising Debt and the Middle-Class Squeeze* (New York: The Levy Economics Institute of Bard College, 2007). Total consumer credit reached $2 trillion in 2006, about 18 percent of the gross domestic product; and the national savings rate dropped below zero, which has proven to be extremely destructive for both the government and individual households. See also Byron L. Dorgan, *Reckless: How Debt, Deregulation, and Dark Money Nearly Bankrupted America (and How We Can Fix It!)* (New York: Thomas Dunne Books, 2009); Niall Ferguson, "Reason to Worry," *New York Times*, June 11, 2006; "Consumer Credit," U.S. Federal Reserve, 2006, http://federalreserve.gov.

81. Nestle, *Food Politics*.

82. Naomi Wolf, *The Beauty Myth: How Images of Beauty Are Used against Women* (New York: Perennial, 2002); Sharlene Hesse-Biber, Patricia Leavy, Courtney E. Quinn, and Julia Zoino, "The Mass Marketing of Disordered Eating and Eating Disorders: The Social Psychology of Women, Thinness and Culture," *Women's Studies International Forum* 29, no. 2 (2006): 208-24; Bianca N. Loya, Gloria Cowan, and Christine Walters, "The Role of Social Comparison and Body Consciousness in Women's Hostility towards Women," *Sex Roles* 54, nos. 7-8 (2006): 575-83; Marika Tiggemann and Belinda McGill, "The Role of Social Comparison in the Effect of Magazine Advertisements on Women's Mood and Body Dissatisfaction," *Journal of Social and Clinical Psychology* 23, no. 1 (2004): 23-44.

83. In 2005 Americans spent some $12.4 billion on cosmetic medical treatments in the United States and about $49 billion on cosmetics and toiletries. Natasha Singer, "Is Looking Your Age Taboo?" *New York Times*, March 1, 2007.

84. See Peter Singer, *The Life You Can Save: Acting Now to End World Poverty* (New York: Random House, 2009).

85. Dreier, "The United States in Comparative Perspective."

86. "Overweight and Obesity: Obesity Trends: U.S. Obesity Trends, 1985–2004," Centers for Disease Control and Prevention, 2006, www.cdc.gov/nccdphp/dnpa/obesity.

87. Michael Gard and Jan Wright, *The Obesity Epidemic: Science, Morality, and Ideology* (New York: Routledge, 2005).

88. Nestle, *Food Politics*.

89. Nestle, *Food Politics*.

90. Barber, *Consumed*.

91. See Singer, *The Life You Can Save*.

92. Approximately 7.4 percent of U.S. adults were dependent on or abusive of alcohol in 1991–1992 compared to 8.4 percent in 2001–2002. "2001–2002 National Epidemiological Survey on Alcohol and Related Conditions," National Institute on Alcohol Abuse and Alcoholism, 2004, www.beersoaksamerica.org.

93. "Beer Consumption," Alcohol Policies Project, 2006, beersoaksamerica.org/ consumption.

94. "Beer Consumption"; "2006 American Community Survey," U.S. Census Bureau, 2007, www.census.gov/acs.

95. Dorgan, *Take This Job and Ship It*; "CIA World Factbook," Central Intelligence Agency, 2006, www.cia.gov/library/publications/the-world-factbook.

96. "Fortune 500," *Fortune*, April 17, 2006, 329–36.

97. Dreier, "The United States in Comparative Perspective."

98. Frank Sesno, "Poll: Most Americans Fear Vulnerability of Oil Supply," *CNN*, March 16, 2006, www.cnn.com/2006/US/03/16/oil.poll/index.html.

99. James Howard Kunstler, *The Long Emergency: Surviving the Converging Catastrophes of the Twenty-first Century* (New York: Atlantic Monthly Press, 2005).

100. Danziger, *Why People Buy Things They Don't Need*.

101. Claudia Wallis, "The Multitasking Generation," *Time*, March 27, 2006, 48–55.

102. "School Daze: Kids, Computers and Sleep," National Sleep Foundation, 2003, www.sleepfoundation.org.

103. Dawn Fallik, "Just Too Wired: Why Teens Don't Get Enough Sleep," *Philadelphia Inquirer*, March 28, 2006.

104. Wallis, "The Multitasking Generation."

105. Lori Aratani, "Teens Can Multitask, But What Are the Costs?" *Washington Post*, February 26, 2007; Martin Wainwright, "Emails 'Pose Threat to IQ,'" *Guardian*, April 22, 2005; Karin Foerde, Barbara J. Knowlton, and Russell A. Poldrack, "Modulation of Competing Memory Systems by Distraction," *Proceedings of the National Academy of Science* 103, no. 31 (2006): 11778–83.

106. Matt Richtel, "Dismissing the Risks of a Deadly Habit," *New York Times*, July 19, 2009.

107. Schwartz, *Queuing and Waiting*.

108. Barry Schwartz, *The Paradox of Choice: Why More Is Less* (New York: HarperCollins, 2004).

109. Lane, *The Loss of Happiness in Market Democracies*; Kasser, *The High Price of Materialism*; Whybrow, *American Mania*; Schwartz, *The Paradox of Choice*; Tim Kasser and Richard M. Ryan, "A Dark Side of the American Dream: Correlates of Financial Success as a Central Life Aspiration," *Journal of Personality and Social Psychology* 65, no. 2 (1993): 410–22.

110. Schor, *Born to Buy*; Tim Kasser and Kennon M. Sheldon, "Of Wealth and Death: Materialism, Mortality Salience, and Consumption Behavior," *Psychological Science* 11, no. 4 (2000): 348–51; Suniya S. Luthar and Karen D'Avanzo, "Contextual Factors in Substance Use: A Study of Suburban and Inner-City Adolescents," *Development of Psychopathology* 11, no. 4 (1999): 845–67; Suniya S. Luthar and Bronwyn E. Becker, "Privileged but Pressured? A Study of Affluent Youth," *Child Development* 73, no. 5 (2002): 1593–610.

CHAPTER 6

1. One of the most ambitious longitudinal studies ever carried out, the Grant Study, has tracked the lives of 268 men since the late 1930s. Its primary researcher for several decades has been George Vaillant. See Joshua Wolf Shenk, "What Makes Us Happy?" *Atlantic Monthly*, June 2009.

2. Anthony P. Cohen, *The Symbolic Construction of Community* (New York: Tavistock Publications, 1985); Émile Durkheim, *Division of Labor in Society* (New York: Free Press, 1997 [1893]); Amitai Etzioni, "The Responsive Community: A Communitarian Perspective," *American Sociological Review* 61, no. 1 (1996): 1–11.

3. Jeffrey C. Alexander, *The Civil Sphere* (New York: Oxford University Press, 2006); Alan Wolfe, *Whose Keeper? Social Science and Moral Obligation* (Berkeley: University of California Press, 1989).

4. Robert N. Bellah, Richard Madsen, William M. Sullivan, Ann Swidler, and Steven M. Tipton, *Habits of the Heart: Individualism and Commitment in American Life* (Berkeley: University of California Press, 1985); Stephen L. Carter, *Civility: Manners, Morals and the Etiquette of Democracy* (New York: Basic Books, 1998); Theda Skocpol, *Diminished Democracy: From Membership to Management in American Civic Life* (Norman: University of Oklahoma Press, 2003).

5. Thomas Bender, *Community and Social Change in America* (New Brunswick, NJ: Rutgers University Press, 1978).

6. Albert Borgmann, *Real American Ethics: Taking Responsibility for Our Country* (Chicago: University of Chicago Press, 2006), 191.

7. "Weak ties" serve an important function for those seeking jobs or allies for social movements or politics. But they are less valuable for fostering self-esteem and meaningful relationships, functions usually served by substantive community. See Mark Granovetter, "The Strength of Weak Ties," *American Journal of Sociology* 78, no. 6 (1973): 1360–80.

8. James S. Coleman, "Social Capital and the Creation of Human Capital," *American Journal of Sociology* 94, Supplement (1988): S95–S120.

9. Jerry A. Jacobs and Kathleen Gerson, *The Time Divide: Work, Family, and Gender Inequality* (Cambridge, MA: Harvard University Press, 2004).

10. Richard Harvey Brown, *Culture, Capitalism, in the New America* (New Haven, CT: Yale University Press, 2005); Carmen Sirianni and Andrea Walsh, "Through the Prism of Time: Temporal Structures in Postindustrial America," in *America at Century's End*, ed. Alan Wolfe (Berkeley: University of California Press, 1991), 421–39.

11. David Brooks, "The Organization Kid," *Atlantic Monthly* 287, no. 4 (2001): 40–55; Juliet B. Schor, *Born to Buy: The Commercialized Child and the New Consumer Culture* (New York: Scribner, 2004); Judith Warner, "Kids Gone Wild," *New York Times*, November 27, 2005; Alex Williams, "The Lost Summer: For the College-Bound, the Grind Is Endless," *New York Times*, June 4, 2006.

12. Robert Andersen, James Curtis, and Edward Grabb, "Trends in Civic Association Activity in Four Democracies: The Special Case of Women in the United States," *American Sociological Review* 71, no. 3 (2006): 376–400.

13. Mary Madden, "Internet Penetration and Impact," Pew Internet and American Life Project, 2006, http://pewinternet.org; Lee Rainie and Scott Keeter, "Pew Internet Project Data Memo: Cell Phone Use," Pew Internet and American Life Project, 2006. http://pewinternet.org; "Internet: The Mainstreaming of Online Life," Pew Internet and American Life Project, 2006, http://pewinternet.org.

14. Miller McPherson, Lynn Smith-Lovin, and Matthew E. Brashears, "Social Isolation in America: Changes in Core Discussion Networks over Two Decades," *American Sociological Review* 71, no. 3 (2006): 353–75. Some methodological questions have been raised about this important research but without any decisive evidence. And the basic thrust of the argument appears on target. See Claude S. Fischer, "Comment: The 2004 GSS Finding of Shrunken Social Networks: An Artifact?" *American Sociological Review* 74, no. 4 (2009): 657–56;

David Glenn, "Is 2.08 Really the Loneliest Number? Sociologist Casts Doubt on a Study," *Chronicle of Higher Education*, September 30, 2008, http://chronicle .com/article/Is-208-Really-the-Lonelies/1205/; Miller McPherson, Lynn Smith-Lovin, and Matthew E. Brashears, "Reply: Models and Marginals: Using Survey Evidence to Study Social Networks," *American Sociological Review* 74, no. 4 (2009): 670–81; Miller McPherson, Lynn Smith-Lovin, and Matthew E. Brashears, "The Ties That Bind Are Fraying," *Contexts* 7, no. 3 (2008): 32–36.

15. Norman H. Nie, "Sociability, Interpersonal Relations, and the Internet: Reconciling Conflicting Findings," *American Behavioral Scientist* 45, no. 3 (2001): 420–35; Norman H. Nie, D. Sunshine Hillygus, and Lutz Erbring, "Internet Use, Interpersonal Relations, and Sociability: A Time Diary Study," in *The Internet in Everyday Life*, ed. Barry Wellman and Caroline A. Haythorn-thwaite (Malden, MA: Blackwell, 2002), 215–44.

16. Andrea L. Kavanaugh and Scott J. Patterson, "The Impact of Community Computer Networks on Social Capital and Community Involvement," *American Behavioral Scientist* 45, no. 3 (2001): 496–509; Barry Wellman, Anabel Quan Haase, James Witte, and Keith Hampton, "Does the Internet Increase, Decrease or Supplement Social Capital? Social Networks, Participation, and Community Commitment," *American Behavioral Scientist* 45, no. 3 (2001): 436–55.

17. Lee Rainie, John Horrigan, Barry Wellman, and Jeffrey Boase, "The Strength of Internet Ties," Pew Internet and American Life Project, January 25, 2006, www.pewinternet.org/Reports/2006/The-Strength-of-Internet-Ties .aspx; James E. Katz and Ronald E. Rice, *Social Consequences of Internet Use: Access, Involvement, and Interaction* (Cambridge, MA: MIT Press, 2002).

18. John Horrigan, "Cities Online: Urban Development and the Internet," Pew Internet and American Life Project, November 20, 2001, www.pew internet.org/Reports/2001/Cities-Online-Urban-Development-and-the-Internet.aspx; Katz and Rice, *Social Consequences of Internet Use*; Andrea L. Kavanaugh and Scott J. Patterson, "The Impact of Community Computer Networks on Social Capital and Community Involvement," *American Behavioral Science* 45, no. 3 (2001): 496–509.

19. Lee Siegel, *Against the Machine: Being Human in the Age of the Electronic Mob* (New York: Spiegel and Grau, 2008).

20. Lynne Truss, *Talk to the Hand: The Utter Bloody Rudeness of the World Today, or, Six Good Reasons to Stay Home and Bolt the Door* (New York: Gotham Books, 2005).

21. Thomas M. Jones, "Ethical Decision Making by Individuals in Organizations: An Issue-Contingent Model," *Academy of Management Review* 16, no. 2 (1991): 366–95. See also Melissa F. Pirkey, "The Social Genesis of Moral Con-

sumption: How Social Groups Support Moral Consumers and Fight Off Care Fatigue" (Paper presented at the annual meeting of the American Sociological Association, San Francisco, California, August 8, 2009).

22. Lori Aratani, "Teens Can Multitask, But What Are the Costs?" *Washington Post*, February 26, 2007; Karin Foerde, Barbara J. Knowlton, and Russell A. Poldrack, "Modulation of Competing Memory Systems by Distraction," *Proceedings of the National Academy of Science* 103, no. 31 (2006): 11778–83; Martin Wainwright, "Emails 'Pose Threat to IQ,'" *Guardian*, April 22, 2005.

23. Recent data indicates that among teenagers who use e-mail and cell phones, 53 percent communicate with their friends mostly by way of written messages. Virgin Mobile reports that a quarter of its teen customers use their phones for texting more than talking. See Olivia Barker, "Technology Leaves Teens Speechless," *USA Today*, May 30, 2006; Pew Internet and American Life Project, "Internet: The Mainstreaming of Online Life."

24. McPherson, Smith-Lovin, and Brashears, "Social Isolation in America"; Barry Wellman and Scot Wortley, "Different Strokes from Different Folks: Community Ties and Social Support," *American Journal of Sociology* 96, no. 3 (1990): 558–88.

25. Julia Angwin, *Stealing MySpace: The Battle to Control the Most Popular Website in America* (New York: Random House, 2009); Siegel, *Against the Machine*.

26. Robert D. Putnam, *Bowling Alone: The Collapse and Revival of American Community* (New York: Simon and Schuster, 2000), 113.

27. Charles Derber, *The Pursuit of Attention: Power and Ego in Everyday Life* (New York: Oxford University Press, 2000).

28. Putnam, *Bowling Alone*, 114.

29. Theda Skocpol, "Advocates without Members: The Recent Transformation of American Civic Life," in *Civic Engagement in American Democracy*, ed. Theda Skocpol and Morris P. Fiorina (Washington, DC: Brookings Institution Press, 1999); Robert Wuthnow, *Sharing the Journey: Support Groups and America's New Quest for Community* (New York: Free Press, 1994).

30. See Putnam, *Bowling Alone*; Wolfe, *Whose Keeper?*

31. In one study, the proportion of respondents who said they "discussed local problems with people they knew" dropped from 66 percent in 1992 to 39 percent in 2004. See Garance Franke-Ruta, "Remapping the Culture Debate," *The American Prospect*, February 5, 2006, www.prospect.org/cs/articles?article =remapping_the_culture_debate_011606.

32. Wuthnow, *Sharing the Journey*.

33. See Putnam, *Bowling Alone*.

34. Whereas the modal number of confidants went from three to zero, the average number went from three to two. McPherson, Smith-Lovin, and Brashears, "Social Isolation in America." In this study, such a network was defined as two or more confidants. See also McPherson, Smith-Lovin, and Brashears, "The Ties That Bind Are Fraying."

35. Amitai Etzioni, *The Spirit of Community: Rights, Responsibilities, and the Communitarian Agenda* (New York: Crown Publishers, 1993); Pamela Paxton, "Is Social Capital Declining in the United States? A Multiple Indicator Assessment," *American Journal of Sociology* 105, no. 1 (1999): 88–127; Robert Wuthnow, *Saving America? Faith-Based Services and the Future of Civil Society* (Princeton, NJ: Princeton University Press, 2004).

36. Robert J. Sampson, Doug McAdam, Heather MacIndoe, and Simon Weffer-Elizondo, "Civil Society Reconsidered: The Durable Nature and Community Structure of Collective Civic Action," *American Journal of Sociology* 111, no. 3 (2005): 673–714.

37. Skocpol, "Advocates without Members," 471–80.

38. C. Wright Mills, *The Sociological Imagination* (New York: Oxford University Press, 1959), 3.

39. Pamela Paxton, "Social Capital and Democracy: An Interdependent Relationship," *American Sociological Review* 67, no. 2 (2002): 254–77; Pamela Paxton, "Trust in Decline?" *Contexts* 4, no. 1 (2005): 40–46.

40. James Howard Kunstler, *The Geography of Nowhere: The Rise and Decline of America's Man-Made Landscape* (New York: Simon and Schuster, 1993).

41. Christine M. Pearson, Lynne M. Andersson, and Christine L. Porath, "Assessing and Attacking Workplace Incivility," *Organizational Dynamics* 29, no. 2 (2000): 123–48.

42. Paxton, "Social Capital and Democracy."

43. Truss, *Talk to the Hand*, 35.

44. The National Highway Safety Administration, *National Survey of Speeding and Unsafe Driving Attitude and Behaviors: 2002* (Washington, DC: U.S. Department of Transportation 2002); John Trinkaus, "Stop Sign Compliance: A Final Look," *Perpetual and Motor Skills* 85, no. 1 (1997): 217–18.

45. Matthew L. Wald, "Temper Cited as Cause of 28,000 Road Deaths a Year," *New York Times*, July 18, 1997.

46. Matt Richtel, "Dismissing the Risks of a Deadly Habit," *New York Times*, July 19, 2009.

47. The National Highway Safety Administration, *National Survey of Speeding and Unsafe Driving Attitude and Behaviors*; Tara E. Galovski, Loretta S. Malta, and Edward B. Blanchard, "Road Rage: A Domain for Psychological

Intervention?" *Aggression and Violent Behavior* 9, no. 2 (2004): 105–27; Public Agenda, "Land of the Rude: Americans in New Survey Say Lack of Respect Is Getting Worse," Public Agenda Press Release, April 3, 2002, www.public agenda.org/press-releases/land-rude-americans-new-survey-say-lack-respect-getting-worse.

48. Public Agenda, "Land of the Rude"; Mark Roth, "Dissatisfaction Guaranteed—Consumers Seem to Be Getting Shortchanged on Customer Service," *Pittsburgh Post-Gazette*, October 16, 2005.

49. Charles Walsh, "Civilization Grumpily Faces a Ride Awakening," *Connecticut Post*, December 15, 2005.

50. Public Agenda, "Land of the Rude"; Rainie and Keeter, "Pew Internet Project Data Memo: Cell Phone Use."

51. Pearson, Andersson, and Porath, "Assessing and Attacking Workplace Incivility"; Eileen Roche, "Do Something—He's About to Snap," *Harvard Business Review* 81, no. 7 (2003): 23–31; Dawn Sagario, "Rudeness Can Hurt More Than Work Force's Feelings," *Times Union*, November 27, 2005.

52. Christine Pearson and Christine L. Porath, "On the Nature, Consequences and Remedies of Workplace Incivility: No Time for 'Nice'? Think Again," *Academy of Management Executive* 19, no. 1 (2005): 1–12.

53. Carter, *Civility*.

54. Bill O'Reilly, *Culture Warrior* (New York: Broadway Books, 2006), 166. Nicholas Lemann, "Fear Factor: Bill O'Reilly's Baroque Period," *New Yorker*, March 27, 2006.

55. Robert H. Bork, *Slouching Towards Gomorrah: Modern Liberalism and American Decline* (New York: HarperCollins, 1996); Alan Ehrenhalt, *The Lost City: The Forgotten Virtues of Community in America* (New York: Basic Books, 1995); Truss, *Talk to the Hand*.

56. Carter, *Civility*, 32–36.

57. Truss, *Talk to the Hand*, 45.

58. Paxton, "Is Social Capital Declining in the United States?"

59. Paxton, "Trust in Decline?" In 2007 some 57 percent of adults expressed high or moderate degrees of social trust in general. Paul Taylor, Cary Funk, and April Clark, "Americans and Social Trust: Who, Where and Why," Pew Research Center, February 22, 2007, http://pewresearch.org/pubs/414/americans-and-social-trust-who-where-and-why.

60. Neil Howe and William Strauss, *Millennials Rising: The Next Great Generation* (New York: Vintage Books, 2000).

61. Marc J. Hetherington, *Why Trust Matters: Declining Political Trust and the Demise of American Liberalism* (Princeton, NJ: Princeton University Press, 2005); Robert E. Lane, *The Loss of Happiness in Market Democracies* (New

Haven, CT: Yale University Press, 2000); James Q. Wilson, *The Moral Sense* (New York: Free Press, 1993).

62. Paxton, "Is Social Capital Declining in the United States?"; Paxton, "Trust in Decline?"

63. Ehrenhalt, *The Lost City*; Paxton, "Trust in Decline?" Carter, *Civility*; Francis Fukuyama, *Trust: The Social Virtues and the Creation of Prosperity* (New York: Free Press, 1996).

64. Susan Weich, "Football Dad, Brother Face Charges in Taser Incident," *St. Louis Post-Dispatch*, October 11, 2006.

65. Fox Butterfield, "A Fatality, Parental Violence and Youth Sports," *New York Times*, July 11, 2000. See also John Manasso, "Foul Language, Dirty Play Stain Soccer," *Atlantic Journal Constitution*, April 25, 2007; Paxton, "Trust in Decline?"

66. Richard Rosenfeld, "Crime Decline in Context," *Contexts* 1, no. 1 (2002): 25–34; U.S. Bureau of Justice Statistics, "Key Crimes and Justice Facts at a Glance," U.S. Department of Justice, 2007, www.justice.gov.

67. See Michael Bugeja, *Interpersonal Divide: The Search for Community in a Technological Age* (New York: Oxford University Press, 2005).

68. Francis Fukuyama, "Social Capital and Civil Society," International Monetary Fund, October 1, 1999, www.imf.org/external/pubs/ft/seminar/1999/reforms/fukuyama.htm; Fukuyama, *Trust*; Wolfe, *Whose Keeper?*

69. Steven Pinker, *The Blank Slate: The Modern Denial of Human Nature* (New York: Viking, 2002), 48.

70. Geoffrey Colvin, *Talent Is Overrated: What Really Separates World-Class Performers from Everybody Else* (New York: Portfolio, 2008); Barry Schwartz, *The Battle for Human Nature: Science, Morality, and Modern Life* (New York: W. W. Norton and Company, 1986); Wilson, *The Moral Sense*.

71. Amitai Etzioni, *The New Golden Rule: Community and Morality in a Democratic Society* (New York: Basic Books, 1996s).

72. George H. Mead, *Mind, Self, and Society: From the Standpoint of a Social Behaviorist*, ed. Charles W. Morris (Chicago: University of Chicago Press, 1934), 162.

73. Derber, *The Pursuit of Attention*; Charles Derber, *The Wilding of America: How Greed and Violence Are Eroding Our Nation's Character* (New York: St. Martin's Press, 1996).

74. Sheldon Solomon, Jeff Greenberg, and Tom Pyszczynski, "Fear of Death and Social Behavior: The Anatomy of Human Destructiveness," in *Evolutionary Psychology and Violence: A Primer for Policymakers and Public Policy Advocates*, ed. N. Dess and R. Bloom (Westport, CT: Greenwood / Praeger, 2003), 129–56.

75. Sheldon Solomon, Jeff Greenberg, and Tom Pyszczynski, "Tales from the Crypt: On the Role of Death in Life," *Zygon* 33, no. 1 (1998): 9–43.

76. Peter C. Whybrow, *American Mania: When More Is Not Enough* (New York: W. W. Norton and Company, 2005); Peter C. Whybrow, *A Mood Apart: Depression, Mania, and Other Afflictions of the Self* (New York: Basic Books, 1997).

77. Whybrow, *American Mania*, 3.

78. Ronald C. Kessler, Patricia Berglund, Olga Demler, Robert Jin, Doreen Koretz, Kathleen R. Merikangas, et al., "The Epidemiology of Major Depressive Disorder: Results from the National Comorbidity Survey Replication (NCS-R)," *Journal of the American Medical Association* 289, no. 23 (2003): 3095–105; Lane, *The Loss of Happiness in Market Democracies*.

79. U.S. Department of Health and Human Services, *Mental Health: A Report of the Surgeon General—Executive Summary* (Rockville, MD: U.S. Department of Health and Human Services, Substance Abuse and Mental Health Services Administration, Center for Mental Health Services, National Institutes of Health, 1999); The National Institute of Mental Health, "Youth in a Difficult World," National Institutes of Health, 2006, http://nimh.nih.gov.

80. Common patterns have occurred among the dozens of school shootings in recent decades, including the following: Mitchell Johnson and Andrew Golden killed four students and a teacher in 1998 at the Jonesboro school in Arkansas; Todd Cameron Smith killed another student at W. R. Myers High School in Alberta, Canada in 1999; Jeffrey Weise of Red Lake High School in Minnesota killed ten people in 2005; Seung-Hui Cho established a new level of violence when he killed thirty-three people at Virginia Tech in 2007. More recently, Steven Kazmierczak killed six people at Northern Illinois University in 2008.

81. Steven F. Messner and Richard Rosenfeld, *Crime and the American Dream*, 3rd ed. (Belmont, CA: Wadsworth, 2001).

82. Gregory Gibson, *Gone Boy: A Walkabout, a Father's Search for the Truth in His Son's Murder* (New York: Anchor Books, 2000); James W. Messerschmidt, *Nine Lives: Adolescent Masculinities, the Body, and Violence* (Boulder, CO: Westview Press, 2000); Solomon, Greenberg, and Pyszczynski, "Fear of Death and Social Behavior."

83. Steven F. Messner, Eric P. Baumer, and Richard Rosenfeld, "Dimensions of Social Capital and Rates of Criminal Homicide," *American Sociological Review* 69, no. 6 (2004): 882–903.

84. Lane, *The Loss of Happiness in Market Democracies*; Solomon, Greenberg, and Pyszczynski, "Fear of Death and Social Behavior"; Whybrow, *American Mania*.

85. Derber, *The Pursuit of Attention*.

86. U.S. Bureau of Justice Statistics, "Key Crimes and Justice Facts at a Glance."

87. Whybrow, *American Mania*, 228–29.

CHAPTER 7

1. Naomi Gerstel and Natalia Sarkisian, "Marriage: The Good, the Bad, and the Greedy," *Contexts* 5, no. 4 (2006): 16–21.

2. Between 1970 and 2004, the proportion of families with five or more people dropped from 21 to 10 percent. The average number of individuals per household decreased from 3.14 to 2.57. See Peter Grier and Sara B. Miller, "Incredible Shrinking Family," *Christian Science Monitor*, December 2, 2004.

3. Kristin Luker, *Abortion and the Politics of Motherhood* (Berkeley: University of California Press, 1984); James Davison Hunter, *Culture Wars: The Struggle to Define America* (New York: Basic Books, 1991); Susan Walzer, *Thinking about the Baby: Gender and Transitions into Parenthood* (Philadelphia: Temple University Press, 1998); Judith Warner, *Perfect Madness: Motherhood in the Age of Anxiety* (New York: Riverhead Books, 2005).

4. Andrew J. Cherlin, *Marriage, Divorce, Remarriage*, rev. ed. (Cambridge, MA: Harvard University Press, 1992); David Popenoe, *Disturbing the Nest: Family Change and Decline in Modern Societies* (New York: Aldine de Gruyter, 1988); David Popenoe, "Modern Marriage: Revisiting the Cultural Script," in *The Gendered Society Reader*, ed. Michael S. Kimmel and Amy Aronson, 2nd ed. (New York: Oxford University Press, 2004).

5. The proportion of married couples who report being "very happy" declined from 53.5 percent in 1973–1976 to 37.8 percent in 1996. See Stephanie Coontz, *The Way We Never Were: American Families and the Nostalgia Trap* (New York: Basic Books, 2000), xiv. In 2000 the proportion was found to be 40 percent. Despite this decline, married people do tend to be happier. A quarter of singles describe themselves as "very happy," compared to 15 percent of those separated and 18 percent of those divorced. See Linda J. Waite and Maggie Gallagher, *The Case for Marriage: Why Married People Are Happier, Healthier and Better Off Financially* (New York: Doubleday, 2000), 67.

6. Between 1960 and 1999, the percentage of people living alone between the ages of twenty-five and forty-five went from under 3 percent to over 12 percent. Among those between forty-five and sixty-four, the shift was from 7.5 percent to over 13 percent. See Douglas A. Wolfe, "Demography, Public Policy, and 'Problem' Families," in *The Future of the Family*, ed. Daniel P.

Moynihan, Timothy M. Smeeding, and Lee Rainwater (New York: Russell Sage, 2004), 176.

7. Paul Taylor, Cary Funk, and April Clark, "Luxury or Necessity? Things We Can't Live Without: The List Has Grown in the Past Decades," Pew Research Center, December 14, 2006, http://pewsocialtrends.org/assets/pdf/Luxury.pdf.

8. Timothy M. Smeeding, Daniel P. Moynihan, and Lee Rainwater, "The Challenge of Family System Changes for Research and Policy," in *The Future of the Family*, ed. Daniel P. Moynihan, Timothy M. Smeeding, and Lee Rainwater (New York: Russell Sage, 2004), 6.

9. Paul Taylor, Cary Funk, and April Clark, "Generation Gap in Values and Behaviors as Marriage and Parenthood Drift Apart, Public Is Concerned about Social Impact," Pew Research Center, July 1, 2007, pp. 15, 20, http://pew research.org/assets/social/pdf/Marriage.pdf.

10. David Popenoe, "American Family Decline, 1960–1990: A Review and Appraisal," *Journal of Marriage and the Family* 55, no. 3 (1993): 526–55; David Popenoe, *Life without Father* (New York: Free Press, 1996); Maxine Seaborn Thompson, Karl L. Alexander, and Doris R. Entwisle, "Household Composition, Parental Expectations, and School Achievement," *Social Forces* 67, no. 2 (1988): 424–45, Maxine Seaborn Thompson, Doris R. Entwisle, Karl L. Alexander, and M. Jane Sundius, "The Influence of Family Composition on Children's Conformity to the Student Role," *American Educational Research Journal* 29, no. 2 (1992): 405–24.

11. Amitai Etzioni, *The Spirit of Community: Rights, Responsibilities, and the Communitarian Agenda* (New York: Crown Publishers, 1993); Waite and Gallagher, *The Case for Marriage*; Wade F. Horn, "Marriage, Family, and the Welfare of Children: A Call for Action," in *The Future of the Family*, ed. Daniel P. Moynihan, Timothy M. Smeeding, and Lee Rainwater (New York: Russell Sage, 2004); Wendy Sigle-Rushton and Sara McLanahan, "Father Absence and Child Well-Being: A Critical Review," in *The Future of the Family*, ed. Daniel P. Moynihan, Timothy M. Smeeding, and Lee Rainwater (New York: Russell Sage, 2004), 116–58.

12. Karen Struening, *New Family Values: Liberty, Equality, and Diversity* (Lanham, MD: Rowman and Littlefield, 2002); Judith Stacey, *In the Name of the Family: Rethinking Family Values in the Postmodern Age* (Boston: Beacon Press, 1996); David H. Demo and Martha J. Cox, "Families with Young Children: A Review of Research in the 1990s," *Journal of Marriage and the Family* 62, no. 4 (2000): 876–95.

13. Child Health USA, *Children in Poverty* (Washington, DC: U.S. Department of Health and Human Services, Health Resources and Services Administration, Maternal and Child Health Bureau, 2004); Hsien-Hen Lu and Heather

Koball, "Living at the Edge Research Brief No. 2: The Changing Demographics of Low-Income Families and Their Children," National Center for Children in Poverty, August 2003.

14. Marc Miringoff and Marque-Luisa Miringoff, *The Social Health of the Nation: How America Is Really Doing* (New York: Oxford University Press, 1999), 75, 87.

15. Coontz, *The Way We Never Were*, 17.

16. The National Institute of Mental Health, "Youth in a Difficult World," National Institutes of Health, 2006, http://nimh.nih.gov.

17. Arlie Hochschild with Anne Machung, *The Second Shift* (New York: Avon Books, 1989).

18. David T. Ellwood and Christopher Jencks, "The Spread of Single-Parent Families in the United States since 1960," in *The Future of the Family*, ed. Daniel P. Moynihan, Timothy M. Smeeding, and Lee Rainwater (New York: Russell Sage, 2004).

19. Robert E. Lane, *The Loss of Happiness in Market Democracies* (New Haven, CT: Yale University Press, 2000), 54.

20. Juliet B. Schor, *The Overworked American: The Unexpected Decline of Leisure* (New York: Basic Books, 1992); Jerry A. Jacobs and Kathleen Gerson, *The Time Divide: Work, Family, and Gender Inequality* (Cambridge, MA: Harvard University Press, 2004); Miller McPherson, Lynn Smith-Lovin, and Matthew E. Brashears, "Social Isolation in America: Changes in Core Discussion Networks over Two Decades," *American Sociological Review* 71, no. 3 (2006): 353–75; Suzanne M. Bianchi, John P. Robinson, and Melissa A. Milkie, *Changing Rhythms of American Family Life* (New York: Russell Sage Foundation, 2006).

21. One recent study suggests that for some families, leisure time has actually increased in recent years. See John P. Robinson and Geoffrey Godbey, *Time for Life: The Surprising Ways Americans Use Their Time* (University Park: Pennsylvania State University Press, 1997). But the overwhelming trend for most families appears to be significant constraints due to more time spent at work. This pattern is most intense among professionals and managers. See Jacobs and Gerson, *The Time Divide*; Warner, *Perfect Madness*.

22. Bianchi, Robinson, and Milkie, *Changing Rhythms of American Family Life*.

23. Robinson and Godbey, *Time for Life*; Ellen Galinsky, *Ask the Children* (New York: Harper, 2000).

24. Steven Ruggles, "The Transformation of American Family Structure," *The American Historical Review* 99, no. 1 (1994): 103–28; Demo and Cox, "Families with Young Children."

25. Daniel P. Moynihan, "A Dahrendorf Inversion and the Twilight of the Family: The Challenge to the Conference," in *The Future of the Family*, ed. Daniel P. Moynihan, Timothy M. Smeeding, and Lee Rainwater (New York: Russell Sage, 2004).

26. Robert H. Bork, *Slouching Towards Gomorrah: Modern Liberalism and American Decline* (New York: HarperCollins, 1996); Waite and Gallagher, *The Case for Marriage*; Rick Santorum, *It Takes a Family: Conservatism and the Common Good* (Wilmington, DL: ISI Books, 2005); Kate O'Beirne, *Women Who Make the World Worse: And How Their Radical Feminist Assault Is Ruining Our Families, Military, Schools, and Sports* (New York: Sentinel, 2006).

27. Jo Freeman, *The Politics of Women's Liberation: A Case Study of an Emerging Social Movement and Its Return to the Policy Process* (New York: McKay, 1975); Nancy F. Cott, *The Grounding of Modern Feminism* (New Haven, CT: Yale University Press, 1987); Susan Faludi, *Backlash: The Undeclared War against American Women* (New York: Crown, 1991); Demie Kurz, *For Richer for Poorer: Mothers Confront Divorce* (New York: Routledge, 1995); Ruth Rosen, *The World Split Open: How the Modern Women's Movement Changed America* (New York: Viking, 2000).

28. Judith Stacey, *Brave New Families: Stories of Domestic Upheaval in Late Twentieth-Century America* (New York: Basic Books, 1990), 269.

29. "Progress and Perils: New Agenda for Women," Center for the Advancement of Women, 2003, www.advancewomen.org.

30. Stacey, *Brave New Families*, 269.

31. Demo and Cox, "Families with Young Children"; Stacey, *In the Name of the Family*; Stephanie Coontz, *The Way We Really Are: Coming to Terms with America's Changing Families* (New York: Basic Books, 1997).

32. Stacey, *Brave New Families*, 270.

33. Taylor, Funk, and Clark, "Generation Gap in Values and Behaviors as Marriage and Parenthood Drift Apart"; Stephanie Coontz, Maya Parson, and Gabrielle Raley, eds., *American Families: A Multicultural Reader* (New York: Routledge, 1999); Frank Furstenberg, "Values, Policy and the Family," in *The Future of the Family*, ed. Daniel P. Moynihan, Timothy M. Smeeding, and Lee Rainwater (New York: Russell Sage, 2004): 267–75.

34. Hochschild, *The Second Shift*.

35. Quoted in Walzer, *Thinking about the Baby*, 53.

36. Arlie Russell Hochschild, *The Commercialization of Intimate Life: Notes from Home and Work* (Berkeley: University of California Press, 2003), 28.

37. Barbara Ehrenreich, *The Hearts of Men: American Dreams and the Flight from Commitment* (New York: Anchor Books, 1984).

38. Walzer, *Thinking about the Baby*.

39. Arlie Russell Hochschild, *The Time Bind: When Work Becomes Home and Home Becomes Work* (New York: Metropolitan Books, 1997).

40. Hochschild, *The Second Shift*.

41. Hochschild, *The Second Shift*, 211.

42. Between 1969 and 1987 Juliet B. Schor estimates Americans in the labor force increased their average time at work annually by about 163 hours. The biggest shift is women's additional time doing work for pay (305 hours) and a related decrease in their work at home (145 hours). By the 1990s, men had increased their time working at home (68 hours per year), while also spending more time (98 hours) at their jobs. See Schor, *The Overworked American*, 35. Between 1989 and 1996, Hochschild reports, married middle-class couples together increased their work hours outside the home by 235 hours, or more than three 40-hour weeks. See Hochschild, *The Time Bind*, xxi. Twenty-one percent of men in general worked fifty hours or more per week in 1970. In 2000, more than 26 percent did so. The percentage of male managers, professionals, and technical workers who worked that hard in 2000 was 37. See Jacobs and Gerson, *The Time Divide*, 34.

43. Etzioni, *The Spirit of Community*.

44. Schor, *The Overworked American*.

45. Lane, *The Loss of Happiness in Market Democracies*.

46. Schor, *The Overworked American*; Coontz, *The Way We Never Were*.

47. Katherine S. Newman, *Falling from Grace: The Experience of Downward Mobility in the American Middle Class* (New York: Free Press, 1988); Alan Wolfe, *Whose Keeper? Social Science and Moral Obligation* (Berkeley: University of California Press, 1989).

48. Hochschild, *The Commercialization of Intimate Life*, 144.

49. Hochschild, *The Time Bind*.

50. Hochschild, *The Second Shift*, 263.

51. Robert H. Frank, *Falling Behind: How Rising Inequality Harms the Middle Class* (Berkeley: University of California Press, 2007).

52. Juliet B. Schor, *The Overspent American: Why We Want What We Don't Need* (New York: HarperPerennial, 1998), 107.

53. Barry Wellman and Scot Wortley, "Different Strokes from Different Folks: Community Ties and Social Support," *American Journal of Sociology* 96, no. 3 (1990): 558–88.

54. Hochschild, *The Commercialization of Intimate Life*; Peter C. Whybrow, *American Mania: When More Is Not Enough* (New York: W. W. Norton and Company, 2005).

55. Robert Andersen, James Curtis, and Edward Grabb, "Trends in Civic Association in Four Democracies: The Special Case of Women in the United States," *American Sociological Review* 71, no. 3 (2006): 376–400.

56. McPherson, Smith-Lovin, and Brashears, "Social Isolation in America"; Amy Caiazza and Robert D. Putnam, "Women's Status and Social Capital across the States: A Briefing Paper," Briefing paper, Institute for Women's Policy Research, July 2002.

57. George Ritzer, ed., *McDonaldization: The Reader* (Thousand Oaks, CA: Pine Forge Press, 2002).

58. Benjamin Barber, *Con$umed: How Markets Corrupt Children, Infantilize Adults, and Swallow Citizens Whole* (New York: W. W. Norton and Company, 2007), 83.

59. Hochschild, *The Time Bind*; Arlie Russell Hochschild, "'Rent a Mom' and Other Services: Markets, Meanings and Emotions," *International Journal of Work, Organisation and Emotions* 1, no. 1 (2005): 74–86.

60. Galinsky, *Ask the Children*; PBS, "Interview with Ellen Galinsky," *Frontline*, 2009, www.pbs.org/wgbh/pages/frontline/shows/teenbrain/interviews/galinsky.html.

61. Hochschild, "'Rent a Mom' and Other Services," 77.

62. See Galinsky, *Ask the Children*, 33.

63. Alvin A. Rosenfeld and Nicole Wise, *The Over-Scheduled Child: Avoiding the Hyper-Parenting Trap* (New York: St. Martin's Griffin, 2000).

64. One Touch, "Maddy," One Touch: Our Commitment, 2008, www.one touchdiabetes.com/our_commitment.

65. David Brooks, "The Organization Kid," *Atlantic Monthly* 287, no. 4 (2001): 42.

66. Juliet B. Schor, *Born to Buy: The Commercialized Child and the New Consumer Culture* (New York: Scribner, 2004); Alex Williams, "The Lost Summer: For the College-Bound, the Grind Is Endless," *New York Times*, June 4, 2006; Neil Howe and William Strauss, *Millennials Rising: The Next Great Generation* (New York: Vintage Books, 2000).

67. Warren St. John, "Hey Coach, Do You Need a Time Out?" *New York Times*, October 15, 2006.

68. Gina Kolata, "A Big-Time Injury Striking Little Players' Knees," *New York Times*, February 18, 2008.

69. See Suniya S. Luthar and Bronwyn E. Becker, "Privileged but Pressured? A Study of Affluent Youth," *Child Development* 73, no. 5 (2002): 1593–610.

70. Luthar and Becker, "Privileged but Pressured?"; Claudia Wallis, "The Multitasking Generation," *Time*, March 27, 2006.

71. Lori Aratani, "Teens Can Multitask, But What Are the Costs?" *Washington Post*, February 26, 2007; Walter Kirn, "The Autumn of the Multitaskers," *The Atlantic*, November 2007, 66–80.

72. Olivia Barker, "Technology Leaves Teens Speechless," *USA Today*, May 30, 2006.

73. Barry Schwartz, *Queuing and Waiting: Studies in the Social Organization of Access and Delay* (Chicago: University of Chicago Press, 1975); Barry Schwartz, *The Paradox of Choice: Why More Is Less* (New York: Harper Collins, 2004).

74. George Ritzer, *The McDonaldization of Society: An Investigation into the Changing Character of Contemporary Social Life* (Thousand Oaks, CA: Pine Forge Press, 1993).

75. Hochschild, *The Commercialization of Intimate Life*; Hochschild, "'Rent a Mom' and Other Services."

76. "Internet: The Mainstreaming of Online Life," Pew Internet and American Life Project, 2006, http://pewinternet.org.

77. Lee Rainie and Scott Keeter, "Pew Internet Project Data Memo: Cell Phone Use," Pew Internet and American Life Project, 2006, http://pewinternet .org; Mary Madden, "Internet Penetration and Impact," Pew Internet and American Life Project, 2006, http://pewinternet.org.

78. Howe and Strauss, *Millennials Rising*.

79. Neil Postman, *Amusing Ourselves to Death: Public Discourse in the Age of Show Business* (New York: Viking, 1985); David J. Jackson, *Entertainment and Politics: The Influences of Pop Culture on Young Adult Political Socialization* (New York: Peter Lang, 2002).

80. Michael Bugeja, *Interpersonal Divide: The Search for Community in a Technological Age* (New York: Oxford University Press, 2005).

81. Judith Warner, "Loosen the Apron Strings," *New York Times*, July 20, 2006.

82. Erin Wade, "Eight Ways to Avoid 'Helicopter Parenting,'" kvue.com, August 15, 2005; Sue Shellenbarger, "Colleges Ward Off Overinvolved Parents," wjs.com, July 19, 2005.

83. Leonard Pitts Jr., "When the Laughing Stopped," *Philadelphia Inquirer*, November 22, 2007; Bonnie Goldstein, "The Stock Puppet Who Loved Me," *Slate*, November 29, 2007; Kim Zetter, "Lori Drew Not Guilty of Felonies in Landmark Cyberbullying Trial," Wired.com, 2008.

84. Barker, "Technology Leaves Teens Speechless."

85. Jeffrey P. Dennis, "The Disneyization of Society," in *McDonaldization: The Reader*, ed. George Ritzer (London: Pine Forge Press, 2002).

86. Whybrow, *American Mania*, 242. See also James Q. Wilson, *The Moral Sense* (New York: Free Press, 1993).

87. Michael Bugeja argues that this separateness among family members is the result of targeted marketing, which is why different individuals each want

to have their own television, DVD player, iPod, and so on. See Bugeja, *Interpersonal Divide*.

88. On average, the square footage of American homes has increased from 1,695 in 1974 to 2,400 in 2007, while during the same period families shrank from an average of 3.1 members to 2.6. Alma E. Hill, "Kids Living the Suite Life," *The Atlanta Journal Constitution*, March 11, 2007.

89. Annette Lareau, *Unequal Childhoods: Class, Race, and Family Life* (Berkeley: University of California Press, 2003), 31.

90. Richard Sennett, *The Culture of the New Capitalism* (New Haven, CT: Yale University Press, 2006); Henry Farber, "Is the Company Man an Anachronism? Trends in Long-Term Employment in the United States, 1973–2006," in *The Price of Independence: The Economics of Early Adulthood*, ed. Sheldon Danziger and Cecilia Elena Rouse (New York: Russell Sage Foundation, 2007); Alan Wolfe, *Moral Freedom: The Search for Virtue in a World of Choice* (New York: W. W. Norton, 2001).

91. Hochschild, *The Commercialization of Intimate Life*, 31. See also Jackson, *Entertainment and Politics*.

CHAPTER 8

1. See Daniel Bell, *The Cultural Contradictions of Capitalism*, 20th anniversary ed. (New York: Basic Books, 1996); George Ritzer, *The McDonaldization of Society: An Investigation into the Changing Character of Contemporary Life* (Thousand Oaks, CA: Pine Forge, 1993).

2. Richard Sennett, *The Corrosion of Character: The Personal Consequences of Work in the New Capitalism* (New York: W. W. Norton, 1998).

3. Émile Durkheim, *The Elementary Forms of Religious Life*, trans. Karen E. Fields (New York: Free Press, 1995 [1912]), 217.

4. Rebecca Solnit suggests that such social solidarity routinely abounds in the context of crises, a regular pattern often neglected in mainstream accounts. See Rebecca Solnit, *A Paradise Built in Hell: The Extraordinary Communities that Arise in Disaster* (New York: Viking, 2009).

5. Morris P. Fiorina with Samuel J. Abrams and Jeremy C. Pope, *Culture War? The Myth of a Polarized America* (New York: Pearson, 2005); Alan Wolfe, *One Nation, After All: What Middle-Class Americans Really Think About: God, Country, Family, Racism, Welfare, Immigration, Homosexuality, Work, the Right, the Left, and Each Other* (New York: Viking, 1998).

6. Robert D. Putnam, *Bowling Alone: The Collapse and Revival of American Community* (New York: Simon and Schuster, 2000), 402.

7. Bliss, HarryBliss.com, September 6, 2006.

8. John Kenneth Galbraith, *The Affluent Society* (New York: Penguin Books, 1958), 309.

9. See Steven Levitt and Stephen J. Dubner, *Freakonomics: A Rogue Economist Explores the Hidden Side of Everything* (New York: HarperCollins, 2005).

10. Mitch Albom, *Tuesdays with Morrie: An Old Man, a Young Man, and Life's Greatest Lesson* (New York: Doubleday, 1997).

11. Kathryn Mills, ed., *C. Wright Mills: Letters and Autobiographical Writings* (Berkeley: University of California Press, 2000), 8.

12. See Robert Wuthnow, *Communities of Discourse: Ideology and Social Structure in the Reformation, the Enlightenment, and European Socialism* (Cambridge, MA: Harvard University Press, 1989).

13. Putnam, *Bowling Alone*, 22; Corwin Smidt, ed., *Religion as Social Capital: Producing the Common Good* (Waco, TX: Baylor University Press, 2003).

14. The interconnectedness of the global community and all the problems that concern nations of the world, as well as specific matters of American security, are foremost among them. The experience of particular groups marginalized by discrimination is another example. A particular threat in this regard is when civic groups become too cohesive, insular, or belligerent, which has occurred countless times throughout history. There are also complicated moral questions less directly related to the main argument of this book, including abortion, for instance.

BIBLIOGRAPHY

Abend, Gabriel. "Two Main Problems in the Sociology of Morality." *Theory and Society* 37, no. 2 (2008): 87–125.

Adorno, Theodor W. *The Culture Industry: Selected Essays on Mass Culture.* New York: Routledge, 1991.

Albom, Mitch. *Tuesdays with Morrie: An Old Man, a Young Man, and Life's Greatest Lesson.* New York: Doubleday, 1997.

Alexander, Jeffrey C. *The Civil Sphere.* New York: Oxford University Press, 2006.

Alfano, Sean. "Poll: Women Strive to Find Balance." *CBS News*, May 14, 2006. www.cbsnews.com/stories/2006/05/14/opinion/polls/main1616577.shtml ?tag=mncol;lst;1.

Alterman, Eric. *When Presidents Lie: A History of Official Deception and Its Consequences.* New York: Viking, 2004.

Andersen, Robert, James Curtis, and Edward Grabb. "Trends in Civic Association Activity in Four Democracies: The Special Case of Women in the United States." *American Sociological Review* 71, no. 3 (2006): 376–400.

Angwin, Julia. *Stealing MySpace: The Battle to Control the Most Popular Website in America.* New York: Random House, 2009.

Aratani, Lori. "Teens Can Multitask, But What Are the Costs?" *Washington Post*, February 26, 2007.

Arrow, Kenneth, Samuel Bowles, and Steven Durlauf, eds. *Meritocracy and Economic Inequality.* Princeton, NJ: Princeton University Press, 2000.

Bagdikian, Ben H. *The New Media Monopoly*. Boston: Beacon Press, 2004.

Bakan, Joel. *The Corporation: The Pathological Pursuit of Profit and Power*. New York: Free Press, 2004.

Baker, Wayne E. *America's Crisis of Values: Reality and Perception*. Princeton, NJ: Princeton University Press, 2005.

Barber, Benjamin R. *Con$umed: How Markets Corrupt Children, Infantilize Adults, and Swallow Citizens Whole*. New York: W. W. Norton and Company, 2007.

Barker, Olivia. "Technology Leaves Teens Speechless." *USA Today*, May 30, 2006.

Bartlett, Bruce. *Impostor: How George W. Bush Bankrupted America and Betrayed the Reagan Legacy*. New York: Doubleday, 2006.

Becker, Gary S. *The Economic Approach to Human Behavior*. Chicago: University of Chicago Press, 1976.

"Beer Consumption." Alcohol Policies Project, 2006. Accessed from www.beer soaksamerica.org/consumption.

Bell, Daniel. *The Cultural Contradictions of Capitalism*. 20th anniversary ed. New York: Basic Books, 1996.

Bellah, Robert N. "Freedom, Coercion and Authority." *Academe*, January–February 1999, 16–21.

Bellah, Robert N., Richard Madsen, William M. Sullivan, Ann Swidler, and Steven M. Tipton. *Habits of the Heart: Individualism and Commitment in American Life*. Berkeley: University of California Press, 1985.

Bender, Thomas. *Community and Social Change in America*. New Brunswick, NJ: Rutgers University Press, 1978.

Berger, Peter. "What Happened to Sociology." *First Things*, no. 126 (2002): 27–29.

Berger, Peter, and Thomas Luckmann. *The Social Construction of Reality: A Treatise in the Sociology of Knowledge*. New York: Anchor, 1966.

Bérubé, Michael. *What's Liberal about the Liberal Arts? Classroom Politics and "Bias" in Higher Education*. New York: W. W. Norton, 2006.

Bianchi, Suzanne M., John P. Robinson, and Melissa A. Milkie. *Changing Rhythms of American Family Life*. New York: Russell Sage Foundation, 2006.

Bliss. HarryBliss.com, September 6, 2006.

Block, Fred. "Mirrors and Metaphors: The United States and Its Trade Rivals." In *America at Century's End*, edited by Alan Wolfe, 93–111. Berkeley: University of California Press, 1991.

Bobo, Kimberley A. *Wage Theft in America: Why Millions of Working Americans Are Not Getting Paid—and What We Can Do about It*. New York: New Press, 2009.

Bogle, John C. *The Battle for the Soul of Capitalism*. New Haven, CT: Yale University Press, 2005.

———. "Does the Free Market Corrode Moral Character? It All Depends." John Templeton Foundation, 2008. www.templeton.org/market/.

Borgmann, Albert. *Real American Ethics: Taking Responsibility for Our Country*. Chicago: University of Chicago Press, 2006.

Bork, Robert H. *Slouching Towards Gomorrah: Modern Liberalism and American Decline*. New York: HarperCollins, 1996.

Bosman, Julie. "Place Your Ad Here, and Here." *New York Times*, July 23, 2006.

Bowen, William G., and Derek Bok. *The Shape of the River: Long-Term Consequences of Considering Race in College and University Admissions*. Princeton, NJ: Princeton University Press, 1998.

Bowen, William G., Martin A. Kurzweil, and Eugene M. Tobin. *Equity and Excellence in American Higher Education*. Charlottesville: University of Virginia Press, 2006.

Bowles, Samuel, and Herbert Gintis. *Democracy and Capitalism: Property, Community, and the Contradictions of Modern Social Thought*. New York: Basic Books, 1986.

———. *Schooling in Capitalist America: Educational Reform and the Contradictions of Economic Life*. New York: Basic Books, 1976.

Brecher, Jeremy. *Strike!* Boston: South End Press, 1997.

Breed, Allen G., and Binaj Gurubacharya. "Everest Remains Deadly Draw for Climbers." *USA Today*, July 16, 2006. www.usatoday.com/tech/science/2006 -07-16-everest-david-sharp_x.htm.

Brinkley, Douglas. *The Great Deluge: Hurricane Katrina, New Orleans, and the Mississippi Gulf Coast*. New York: Harper, 2007.

Brooks, David. "The American Way of Equality." *New York Times*, January 14, 2006.

———. *Bobos in Paradise: The New Upper Class and How They Got There*. New York: Simon and Schuster, 2000.

———. "Friedman's Glow Was the Smile of Reason." *New York Times*, November 19, 2006.

———. "The Organization Kid." *Atlantic Monthly* 287, no. 4 (2001): 40–55.

Brown, Richard Harvey. *Culture, Capitalism, and Democracy in the New America*. New Haven, CT: Yale University Press, 2005.

Browning, Don S. "Altruism, Civic Virtue, and Religion." In *Seedbeds of Virtue: Sources of Competence, Character, and Citizenship in American Society*, edited by Mary Ann Glendon and David Blankenhorn, 105–29. Lanham, MD: Madison Books, 1995.

Brueggemann, John. "Negotiating the Meaning of Power and the Power of Meaning." *Theology Today* 63, no. 4 (2007): 485–92.

———. "Racial Considerations and Social Policy in the 1930s: Economic Change and Political Opportunities." *Social Science History* 26, no. 1 (2002): 139–77.

Brueggemann, John, and Cliff Brown. "The Decline of Industrial Unionism in the Meatpacking Industry: Event-Structure Analysis of Labor Unrest, 1946–1987." *Work and Occupations* 30, no. 3 (2003): 327–60.

———. "Strategic Labor Organization in the Era of Industrial Transformation: A Comparative Historical Analysis of Unionization in Steel and Coal, 1870–1916." *Review of Radical Political Economics* 32, no. 4 (2000): 541–76.

Bugeja, Michael. *Interpersonal Divide: The Search for Community in a Technological Age*. New York: Oxford University Press, 2005.

Butterfield, Fox. "A Fatality, Parental Violence and Youth Sports." *New York Times*, July 11, 2000.

Cahn, Steven M. "A Supreme Moral Principle?" In *Exploring Philosophy*, edited by Steven M. Cahn, 271–75. New York: Oxford University Press, 2005.

Calder, Lendol. *Financing the American Dream: A Cultural History of Consumer Credit*. Princeton, NJ: Princeton University Press, 1999.

Campbell, David E., and Steven J. Yonish. "Religion and Volunteering in America." In *Religion as Social Capital: Producing the Common Good*, edited by Corwin Smidt, 87–106. Waco, TX: Baylor University Press, 2003.

Carroll, James. *House of War: The Pentagon and the Disastrous Rise of American Power*. New York: Mariner Books, 2007.

Carter, Stephen L. *Civility: Manners, Morals and the Etiquette of Democracy*. New York: Basic Books, 1998.

Chaves, Mark. *Congregations in America*. Cambridge, MA: Harvard University Press, 2004.

Cherlin, Andrew J. *Marriage, Divorce, Remarriage*. Rev. ed. Cambridge, MA: Harvard University Press, 1992.

Chernow, Ron. *Titan: The Life of John D. Rockefeller, Sr.* New York: Vintage, 2004.

Child Health USA. *Children in Poverty*. Washington, DC: U.S. Department of Health and Human Services, Health Resources and Services Administration, Maternal and Child Health Bureau, 2004.

Clawson, Dan. "Money and Politics." In *Inequality and Society: Social Science Perspectives on Social Stratification*, edited by Jeff Manza and Michael Sauder, 819–31. New York: W. W. Norton, 2009.

Clawson, Dan, and Mary Ann Clawson. "What Happened to the US Labor Movement? Union Decline and Renewal." *Annual Review of Sociology* 25 (1999): 95–121.

Cohen, Anthony P. *The Symbolic Construction of Community*. New York: Tavistock Publications, 1985.

Cohen, Lizabeth. *A Consumer's Republic: The Politics of Mass Consumption in Postwar America*. New York: Alfred A. Knopf, 2003.

Coleman, James S. "Social Capital and the Creation of Human Capital." *American Journal of Sociology* 94, Supplement (1988): S95–S120.

Collins, Chuck, and Felice Yeskel. *Economic Apartheid in America: A Primer on Economic Inequality & Insecurity*. New York: New Press, 2005.

Colvin, Geoffrey. *Talent Is Overrated: What Really Separates World-Class Performers from Everybody Else*. New York: Portfolio, 2008.

"Consumer Credit." U.S. Federal Reserve, 2006. http://federalreserve.gov.

Cookson, Peter W., Jr., and Caroline Hodges Persell. *Preparing for Power: America's Elite Boarding Schools*. New York: Basic Books, 1985.

Coontz, Stephanie. *The Way We Never Were: American Families and the Nostalgia Trap*. New York: Basic Books, 2000.

———. *The Way We Really Are: Coming to Terms with America's Changing Families*. New York: Basic Books, 1997.

Coontz, Stephanie, Maya Parson, and Gabrielle Raley, eds. *American Families: A Multicultural Reader*. New York: Routledge, 1999.

Cott, Nancy F. *The Grounding of Modern Feminism*. New Haven, CT: Yale University Press, 1987.

Countryman, Edward. *The American Revolution*. New York: Hill and Wang, 1985.

Cowan, Ruth Schwartz. *More Work for Mother: The Ironies of Household Technology from the Open Hearth to the Microwave*. New York: Basic Books, 1983.

Cox, Harvey. "Mammon and the Culture of the Market: A Socio-Theological Critique." In *Meaning and Modernity: Religion, Polity, and Self*, edited by Richard Madsen, William M. Sullivan, Ann Swidler, and Steven M. Tipton, 124–34. Berkeley: University of California Press, 2002.

Coyle, Daniel. *The Talent Code: Greatness Isn't Born. It's Grown. Here's How.* New York: Bantam Books, 2009.

Cummings, Jeanne. "2008 Campaign Costliest in U.S. History." Politico, January 15, 2008. http://politico.com.

"Current Population Survey, 2006 Annual Social and Economic (ASEC) Supplement." U.S. Census Bureau, 2006. www.census.gov/apsd/techdoc/cps/cpsmar06.pdf.

Curry, Janel. "Social Capital and Societal Vision: A Study of Six Farm Communities in Iowa." In *Religion as Social Capital: Producing the Common Good*, edited by Corwin Smidt, 139–52. Waco, TX: Baylor University Press, 2003.

Danziger, Pamela N. *Why People Buy Things They Don't Need*. Ithaca, NY: Paramount Market Publishing, 2002.

Demo, David H., and Martha J. Cox. "Families with Young Children: A Review of Research in the 1990s." *Journal of Marriage and the Family* 62, no. 4 (2000): 876–95.

Dennis, Jeffrey P. "The Disneyization of Society." In *McDonaldization: The Reader*, edited by George Ritzer, 107–15. London: Pine Forge Press, 2002.

Derber, Charles. *Corporation Nation: How Corporations Are Taking Over Our Lives and What We Can Do about It*. New York: St. Martin's Press, 1998.

———. *The Pursuit of Attention: Power and Ego in Everyday Life*. New York: Oxford University Press, 2000.

———. *The Wilding of America: How Greed and Violence Are Eroding Our Nation's Character*. New York: St. Martin's Press, 1996.

Diamond, Jared M. *Guns, Germs, and Steel: The Fates of Human Societies*. New York: W. W. Norton, 1999.

DiMaggio, Paul, Eszter Hargittai, Coral Celeste, and Steven Shafer. "Digital Inequality: From Unequal Access to Differentiated Use." In *Social Inequality*, edited by Kathryn M. Neckerman, 355–400. New York: Russell Sage Foundation, 2004.

Dixon, William J., and Terry Boswell. "Dependency, Disarticulation, and Denominator Effects: Another Look at Foreign Capital Penetration." *American Journal of Sociology* 102, no. 2 (1996): 543–63.

Dobson, James. *Bringing Up Boys*. Wheaton, IL: Tyndale House, 2001.

———. *Marriage Under Fire: Why We Must Win This War*. Sisters, OR: Multnomah Publishers, Inc., 2004.

Domhoff, G. William. *Who Rules America? Power and Politics in the Year 2000*. Mountain View, CA: Mayfield, 1998.

Dorgan, Byron L. *Reckless: How Debt, Deregulation, and Dark Money Nearly Bankrupted America (and How We Can Fix It!)*. New York: Thomas Dunne Books, 2009.

———. *Take This Job and Ship It: How Corporate Greed and Brain-Dead Politics Are Selling Out America*. New York: St. Martin's Press, 2006.

Dreier, Peter. "The United States in Comparative Perspective." *Contexts* 6, no. 3 (2007): 39–47.

D'Souza, Dinesh. *The Virtue of Prosperity: Finding Values in an Age of Techno-Affluence*. New York: Free Press, 2000.

Durkheim, Émile. *Division of Labor in Society*. New York: Free Press, 1997 [1893].

———. *The Elementary Forms of Religious Life*. Translated by Karen E. Fields. New York: Free Press, 1995 [1912].

———. *Suicide: A Study in Sociology*. New York: Free Press, 1996 [1897].

Dye, Thomas R. *Who's Running America? The Bush Restoration*. 7th ed. Upper Saddle River, NJ: Prentice Hall, 2002.

Ehrenhalt, Alan. *The Lost City: The Forgotten Virtues of Community in America*. New York: Basic Books, 1995.

Ehrenreich, Barbara. *Bait and Switch: The (Futile) Pursuit of the American Dream*. New York: Henry Holt and Company, 2006.

———. *The Hearts of Men: American Dreams and the Flight from Commitment*. New York: Anchor Books, 1984.

Eitzen, D. Stanley. "The Dark Side of Competition in American Society." *Vital Speeches of the Day* 56 (January 1990): 185–86.

Ellis, Joseph J. *Founding Brothers: The Revolutionary Generation*. New York: Vintage Books, 2000.

Ellwood, David T., and Christopher Jencks. "The Spread of Single-Parent Families in the United States since 1960." In *The Future of the Family*, edited by Daniel P. Moynihan, Timothy M. Smeeding, and Lee Rainwater, 25–65. New York: Russell Sage, 2004.

Etzioni, Amitai. "Creating Good Communities and Good Societies." *Contemporary Sociology* 29, no. 1 (2000): 188–95.

———. *The Monochrome Society*. Princeton, NJ: Princeton University Press, 2001.

———. *The Moral Dimension: Toward a New Economics*. New York: Free Press, 1988.

———. *The New Golden Rule: Community and Morality in a Democratic Society*. New York: Basic Books, 1996.

———. "The Responsive Community: A Communitarian Perspective." *American Sociological Review* 61, no. 1 (1996): 1–11.

———. *The Spirit of Community: Rights, Responsibilities, and the Communitarian Agenda*. New York: Crown Publishers, 1993.

Fallik, Dawn. "Just Too Wired: Why Teens Don't Get Enough Sleep." *Philadelphia Inquirer*, March 28, 2006.

Faludi, Susan. *Backlash: The Undeclared War against American Women*. New York: Crown, 1991.

Farber, Henry. "Is the Company Man an Anachronism? Trends in Long-Term Employment in the United States, 1973–2006." In *The Price of Independence: The Economics of Early Adulthood*, edited by Sheldon Danziger and Cecilia Elena Rouse, 56–83. New York: Russell Sage Foundation, 2007.

Ferguson, Niall. "Reason to Worry." *New York Times*, June 11, 2006, 46–50.

Ferguson, Thomas. "Industrial Conflict and the Coming of the New Deal: The Triumph of Multinational Liberalism in America." In *The Rise and Fall of the New Deal Order, 1930–1980,* edited by Steve Fraser and Gary Gerstle, 3–31. Princeton, NJ: Princeton University Press, 1989.

Fine, Gary Alan, and Jay Mechling. "Minor Difficulties: Changing Children in the Late Twentieth Century." In *America at Century's End,* edited by Alan Wolfe, 36–78. Berkeley: University of California Press, 1991.

Finke, Roger. "An Unsecular America." In *Religion and Modernization: Sociologists and Historians Debate the Secularization Thesis,* edited by Steve Bruce, 145–69. New York: Oxford University Press, 1992.

Fiorina, Morris P., with Samuel J. Abrams and Jeremy C. Pope. *Culture War? The Myth of a Polarized America.* New York: Pearson, 2005.

———. "Extreme Voices: The Dark Side of Civic Engagement." In *Civic Engagement in American Democracy,* edited by Theda Skocpol and Morris P. Fiorina, 395–426. Washington, DC: Brooking Institution Press, 1999.

Fischer, Claude S. "Comment: The 2004 GSS Finding of Shrunken Social Networks: An Artifact?" *American Sociological Review* 74, no. 4 (2009): 657–56.

Foerde, Karin, Barbara J. Knowlton, and Russell A. Poldrack. "Modulation of Competing Memory Systems by Distraction." *Proceedings of the National Academy of Science* 103, no. 31 (2006): 11778–83.

Foner, Eric. "He's the Worst Ever." *Washington Post,* December 3, 2006.

"Fortune 500." *Fortune,* April 17, 2006, 329–36.

"The 400 Richest Americans." *Forbes,* 2006. www.forbes.com.

Frank, Robert H. *Falling Behind: How Rising Inequality Harms the Middle Class.* Berkeley: University of California Press, 2007.

Frank, Robert H., and Philip J. Cook. *The Winner-Take-All Society: Why the Few at the Top Get So Much More Than the Rest of Us.* New York: Penguin, 1996.

Frank, Robert L. *Richistan: A Journey through the American Wealth Boom and the Lives of the New Rich.* New York: Crown Publishers, 2007.

Frank, Thomas. "Coming to an Airport Checkpoint Near You: Ads in the Security Bins." *USA Today,* January 10, 2007.

———. *The Conquest of Cool: Business Culture, Counterculture, and the Rise of Hip Consumerism.* Chicago: University of Chicago Press, 1997.

Franke-Ruta, Garance. "Remapping the Culture Debate." *The American Prospect,* February 5, 2006. www.prospect.org/cs/articles?article=remapping_the_culture_debate_011606.

Fraser, Steve, and Gary Gerstle. *The Rise and Fall of the New Deal Order, 1930–1980.* Princeton, NJ: Princeton University Press, 1989.

Freeman, Jo. *The Politics of Women's Liberation: A Case Study of an Emerging Social Movement and Its Return to the Policy Process.* New York: McKay, 1975.

———, ed. *Social Movements of the Sixties and Seventies*. New York: Longman, 1983.

Frey, Sylvia R. "Slavery and Anti-slavery." In *A Companion to the American Revolution*, edited by Jack P. Greene and J. R. Pole, 402–12. Malden, MA: Blackwell Publishers, 2000.

Friedman, Milton. *Capitalism and Freedom*. Chicago: University of Chicago Press, 1962.

Fukuyama, Francis. *The Great Disruption: Human Nature and the Reconstitution of Social Order*. New York: Free Press, 1999.

———. "The Great Disruption: Human Nature and the Reconstitution of the Social Order." *The Atlantic Monthly*, May (1999): 55–80.

———. "Social Capital and Civil Society." International Monetary Fund, October 1, 1999. www.imf.org/external/pubs/ft/seminar/1999/reforms/fukuyama.htm.

———. *Trust: The Social Virtues and the Creation of Prosperity*. New York: Free Press, 1996.

Furstenberg, Frank. "Values, Policy and the Family." In *The Future of the Family*, edited by Daniel P. Moynihan, Timothy M. Smeeding, and Lee Rainwater, 267–75. New York: Russell Sage, 2004.

Galbraith, John Kenneth. *The Affluent Society*. New York: Penguin Books, 1958.

———. *American Capitalism: The Concept of Countervailing Power*. Boston: Houghton Mifflin, 1952

———. *Annals of an Abiding Liberal*. Edited by Andrea D. Williams. New York: New American Library, 1980.

Galinsky, Ellen. *Ask the Children: What America's Children Really Think about Working Parents*. New York: Harper, 2000.

Gallagher, Maggie. "The Stakes: Why We Need Marriage." *National Review*, July 14, 2003. http://article.nationalreview.com/269352/the-stakes/maggie gallagher.

Galovski, Tara E., Loretta S. Malta, and Edward B. Blanchard. "Road Rage: A Domain for Psychological Intervention?" *Aggression and Violent Behavior* 9, no. 1 (2004): 105–27.

Garber, Kent. "Behind the Prosperity Gospel: Followers Believe God Wants Them to Be Rich—Not Just Spiritually but Materially." *U.S. News and World Report*, February 15, 2008. www.usnews.com/articles/news/national/2008/02/15/behind-the-prosperity-gospel.html.

Gard, Michael, and Jan Wright. *The Obesity Epidemic: Science, Morality, and Ideology*. New York: Routledge, 2005.

Gerstel, Naomi, and Natalia Sarkisian. "Marriage: The Good, the Bad, and the Greedy." *Contexts* 5, no. 4 (2006): 16–21.

Gibson, Gregory. *Gone Boy: A Walkabout, a Father's Search for the Truth in His Son's Murder*. New York: Anchor Books, 2000.

Gibson, J. William. "The Return of Rambo: War and Culture in the Post-Vietnam Era." In *America at Century's End*, edited by Alan Wolfe, 376–95. Berkeley: University of California Press, 1991.

Gitlin, Todd. *Media Unlimited: How the Torrent of Images and Sounds Overwhelms Our Lives*. New York: Henry Holt, 2002.

———. *The Sixties: Years of Hope, Days of Rage*. New York: Bantam Books, 1987.

Gladwell, Malcolm. *Outliers: The Story of Success*. New York: Little, Brown and Company, 2008.

Glassman, Ronald M. *The Middle Class and Democracy in Socio-Historical Perspective*. New York: E. J. Brill, 1995.

Glenn, David. "Is 2.08 Really the Loneliest Number? Sociologist Casts Doubt on a Study." *Chronicle of Higher Education*, September 30, 2008. http://chronicle.com/article/Is-208-Really-the-Lonelies/1205/.

Goffman, Erving. *The Presentation of Self in Everyday Life*. Garden City, NY: Doubleday, 1959.

Golden, Daniel. *The Price of Admission: How America's Ruling Class Buys Its Way into Elite Colleges—and Who Gets Left Outside the Gates*. New York: Crown, 2006.

Goldfield, Michael. *The Decline of Organized Labor in the United States*. Chicago: University of Chicago Press, 1987.

Goldstein, Bonnie. "The Stock Puppet Who Loved Me." *Slate*, November 29, 2007.

Granovetter, Mark. "The Strength of Weak Ties." *American Journal of Sociology* 78, no. 6 (1973): 1360–80.

Greenfield, Lauren. "Money Talks." *New York Times*, June 10, 2007.

Greider, William B. *Who Will Tell the People: The Betrayal of American Democracy*. New York: Simon and Schuster, 1992.

Grier, Peter, and Sara B. Miller. "Incredible Shrinking Family." *Christian Science Monitor*, December 2, 2004.

Hafner, Katie. "Lifting Corporate Fingerprints from the Editing of Wikipedia." *New York Times*, August 19, 2007.

Haidt, Jonathan, and Jesse Graham. "Planet of the Durkheimians: Where Community, Authority, and Sacredness Are Foundations of Morality." In *Social and Psychological Bases of Ideology and System Justification*, edited by John T. Jost, Aaron C. Kay, and Hulda Thorisdottir, 371–401. New York: Oxford University Press, 2009.

Halberstam, David. *The Fifties*. New York: Villard Books, 1993.

Hall, Peter A., and David Soskice, eds. *Varieties of Capitalism: The Institutional Foundations of Comparative Advantage*. New York: Oxford University Press, 2001.

Harris, Marvin. *America Now: The Anthropology of a Changing Culture*. New York: Simon and Schuster, 1981.

Harrison, Bennett, and Barry Bluestone. *The Great U-Turn: Corporate Restructuring and the Polarizing of America*. New York: Basic Books, 1988.

Head, Simon. "They're Micromanaging Your Every Move." *New York Review of Books*, August 16, 2007, 42–44.

Hedges, Chris. *American Fascists: The Christian Right and the War on America*. New York: Free Press, 2006.

Herrnstein, Richard J., and Charles Murray. *The Bell Curve: Intelligence and Class Structure in American Life*. New York: Free Press, 1994.

Hesse-Biber, Sharlene, Patricia Leavy, Courtney E. Quinn, and Julia Zoino. "The Mass Marketing of Disordered Eating and Eating Disorders: The Social Psychology of Women, Thinness and Culture." *Women's Studies International Forum* 29, no. 2 (2006): 208–24.

Hetherington, Marc J. *Why Trust Matters: Declining Political Trust and the Demise of American Liberalism*. Princeton, NJ: Princeton University Press, 2005.

Hill, Alma E. "Kids Living the Suite Life." *The Atlanta Journal Constitution*, March 11, 2007.

Hochschild, Arlie Russell. *The Commercialization of Intimate Life: Notes from Home and Work*. Berkeley: University of California Press, 2003.

———. "'Rent a Mom' and Other Services: Markets, Meanings and Emotions." *International Journal of Work, Organisation and Emotions* 1, no. 1 (2005): 74–86.

———. *The Time Bind: When Work Becomes Home and Home Becomes Work*. New York: Metropolitan Books, 1997.

Hochschild, Arlie Russell, with Anne Machung. *The Second Shift*. New York: Avon Books, 1989.

Hodgson, Godfrey. *America in Our Time: From World War II to Nixon—What Happened and Why*. Princeton, NJ: Princeton University Press, 2005.

Horn, Wade F. "Marriage, Family, and the Welfare of Children: A Call for Action." In *The Future of the Family*, edited by Daniel P. Moynihan, Timothy M. Smeeding, and Lee Rainwater, 181–97. New York: Russell Sage, 2004.

Horrigan, John. "Cities Online: Urban Development and the Internet." Pew Internet and American Life Project, November 20, 2001. www.pewinternet.org/Reports/2001/Cities-Online-Urban-Development-and-the-Internet.aspx.

Howe, Neil, and William Strauss. *Millennials Rising: The Next Great Generation*. New York: Vintage Books, 2000.

Hunter, James Davison. *Culture Wars: The Struggle to Define America*. New York: Basic Books, 1991.

Huntington, Samuel P. "The United States." In *The Crisis of Democracy: Report on the Governability of Democracies to the Trilateral Commission*, Michael Crozier, Samuel P. Huntington, and Joji Watanuki, 59–118. New York: New York University Press, 1975.

"Internet: The Mainstreaming of Online Life." Pew Internet and American Life Project, 2006. http://pewinternet.org.

Irons, John, and Ethan Pollack. "A Rescue Plan for Main Street." Economic Policy Institute, December 17, 2008. http://epi.org.

Jackson, David J. *Entertainment and Politics: The Influence of Pop Culture on Young Adult Political Socialization*. New York: Peter Lang, 2002.

Jacobs, Jerry A., and Kathleen Gerson. *The Time Divide: Work, Family, and Gender Inequality*. Cambridge, MA: Harvard University Press, 2004.

Jacoby, Susan. *The Age of American Unreason*. New York: Pantheon Books, 2008.

Jenkins, Philip. *Decade of Nightmares: The End of the Sixties and the Making of Eighties America*. New York: Oxford University Press, 2006.

Jones, Jeffrey. "Obama's Initial Approval Ratings in Historical Context." Gallup, January 26, 2009. www.gallup.com.

Jones, Thomas M. "Ethical Decision-Making by Individuals in Organizations: An Issue-Contingent Model." *Academy of Management Review* 16, no. 2 (1991): 366–95.

Kasser, Tim. *The High Price of Materialism*. Cambridge, MA: MIT Press, 2002.

Kasser, Tim, and Richard M. Ryan. "A Dark Side of the American Dream: Correlates of Financial Success as a Central Life Aspiration." *Journal of Personality and Social Psychology* 65, no. 2 (1993): 410–22.

Kasser, Tim, and Kennon M. Sheldon. "Of Wealth and Death: Materialism, Mortality Salience, and Consumption Behavior." *Psychological Science* 11, no. 4 (2000): 348–51

Katz, James E., and Ronald E. Rice. *Social Consequences of Internet Use: Access, Involvement, and Interaction*. Cambridge, MA: MIT Press, 2002.

Katznelson, Ira. *When Affirmative Action Was White: An Untold History of Racial Inequality in Twentieth-Century America*. New York: W. W. Norton, 2006.

Kavanaugh, Andrea L., and Scott J. Patterson. "The Impact of Community Computer Networks on Social Capital and Community Involvement." *American Behavioral Scientist* 45, no. 3 (2001): 496–509.

Kennedy, David M. *Freedom from Fear: The American People in Depression and War, 1929–1945*. New York: Oxford University Press, 1999.

Kessler, Ronald C., Patricia Berglund, Olga Demler, Robert Jin, Doreen Koretz, Kathleen R. Merikangas, et al., "The Epidemiology of Major Depressive Disorder: Results from the National Comorbidity Survey Replication (NCS-R)." *Journal of the American Medical Association* 289, no. 23 (2003): 3095–105.

Kirn, Walter. "The Autumn of the Multitaskers." *The Atlantic*, November 2007, 66–80.

Klein, Naomi. *No Logo: Taking Aim at the Brand Bullies*. New York: Picador, 2002.

Klinenberg, Eric. *Fighting for Air: The Battle to Control America's Media*. New York: Henry Holt, 2007.

Kohler, Thomas C. "Civic Virtue at Work: Unions as Seedbeds of the Civic Virtues." In *Seedbeds of Virtue: Sources of Competence, Character, and Citizenship in American Society*, edited by Mary Ann Glendon and David Blankenhorn, 131–59. Lanham, MD: Madison Books, 1995.

Kolata, Gina. "A Big-Time Injury Striking Little Players' Knees." *New York Times*, February 18 2008.

Krakauer, Jon. *Into Thin Air: A Personal Account of the Mount Everest Disaster*. New York: Villard, 1997.

Krugman, Paul. *The Conscience of a Liberal*. New York: W. W. Norton, 2007.

———. "John and Jerry." *New York Times*, April 4, 2006.

———. *The Return of Depression Economics and the Crisis of 2008*. New York: W. W. Norton, 2009.

Kundera, Milan. *Immortality*. Translated by Peter Kussi. New York: Grove Weidenfeld, 1991.

Kunstler, James Howard. *The Geography of Nowhere: The Rise and Decline of America's Man-Made Landscape*. New York: Simon and Schuster, 1993.

———. *The Long Emergency: Surviving the Converging Catastrophes of the Twenty-first Century*. New York: Atlantic Monthly Press, 2005.

Kurtz, Stephen G., and James H. Hutson, eds. *Essays on the American Revolution*. Chapel Hill, NC: University of North Carolina Press, 1973.

Kurz, Demie. *For Richer for Poorer: Mothers Confront Divorce*. New York: Routledge, 1995.

Kuttner, Robert. *Everything for Sale: The Virtues and Limits of Markets*. Chicago: University of Chicago Press, 1999.

Lane, Robert E. *The Loss of Happiness in Market Democracies*. New Haven, CT: Yale University Press, 2000.

Lanman, Scott. "Fed Said US Economy's Decline Slowed in Some Areas." *Bloomberg*, April 15, 2008. http://bloomberg.com.

Lardner, James. "The Specter Haunting Your Office." *New York Review of Books*, June 14, 2007, 62–65.

Lareau, Annette. *Unequal Childhoods: Class, Race, and Family Life*. Berkeley: University of California Press, 2003.

Lasch, Christopher. *The Culture of Narcissism: American Life in an Age of Diminishing Expectations*. New York: W. W. Norton, 1979.

———. *The True and Only Heaven: Progress and Its Critics*. New York: W. W. Norton, 1991.

Lears, Jackson. "The American Way of Debt." *New York Times*, June 11, 2006, 13–16.

"Lee Atwater's Last Campaign." *Life*, February 1991.

Lemann, Nicholas. "Fear Factor: Bill O'Reilly's Baroque Period." *New Yorker*, March 27, 2006.

Levenstein, Harvey A. *Communism, Anti-Communism, and the CIO*. Westport, CT: Greenwood Press, 1981.

Levitt, Steven, and Stephen J. Dubner. *Freakonomics: A Rogue Economist Explores the Hidden Side of Everything*. New York: HarperCollins, 2005.

Lewis, Michael. "The End." Portfolio, December 2008. http://portfolio.com.

Lewis, Michael, and David Einhorn. "The End of the Financial World as We Know It." *New York Times*, January 4, 2009.

Lichtenstein, Nelson. *Labor's War at Home: The CIO in World War II*. New York: Cambridge University Press, 1982.

———. *State of the Union: A Century of American Labor*. Princeton, NJ: Princeton University Press, 2002.

Lie, Erik. "On the Timing of CEO Stock Option Awards." *Management Science* 51, no. 5 (2005): 802–12.

Lieberson, Stanley. *A Piece of the Pie: Blacks and White Immigrants since 1880*. Berkeley: University of California Press, 1980.

Lindsey, Brink. *The Age of Abundance: How Prosperity Transformed America's Politics and Culture*. New York: Collins, 2007.

Loya, Bianca N., Gloria Cowan, and Christine Walters. "The Role of Social Comparison and Body Consciousness in Women's Hostility towards Women." *Sex Roles* 54, nos. 7–8 (2006): 575–83.

Lu, Hsien-Hen, and Heather Koball. "Living at the Edge Research Brief No. 2: The Changing Demographics of Low-Income Families and Their Children." National Center for Children in Poverty, August 2003.

Luker, Kristin. *Abortion and the Politics of Motherhood*. Berkeley: University of California Press, 1984.

Luthar, Suniya S., and Bronwyn E. Becker. "Privileged but Pressured? A Study of Affluent Youth." *Child Development* 73, no. 5 (2002): 1593–610.

Luthar, Suniya S., and Karen D'Avanzo. "Contextual Factors in Substance Use: A Study of Suburban and Inner-City Adolescents." *Development of Psychopathology* 11, no. 4 (1999): 845–67.

Madden, Mary. "Internet Penetration and Impact." Pew Internet and American Life Project, 2006. http://pewinternet.org.

Manasso, John. "Foul Language, Dirty Play Stain Soccer." *Atlantic Journal Constitution*, April 25, 2007.

Marienstras, Elise. "Nationality and Citizenship." In *A Companion to the American Revolution*, edited by Jack P. Greene and J. R. Pole, 680–85. Malden, MA: Blackwell Publishers, 2000.

Massey, Douglas S., and Nancy A. Denton. *American Apartheid: Segregation and the Making of the Underclass*. Cambridge, MA: Harvard University Press, 1993.

McKenna, Regis. *Total Access: Giving Customers What They Want in an Anytime, Anywhere World*. Boston: Harvard Business School Press, 2002.

McMaster, H. R. *Dereliction of Duty: Lyndon Johnson, Robert McNamara, the Joint Chiefs, and the Lies That Led to Vietnam*. New York: HarperCollins, 1997.

McPherson, James M. *Battle Cry of Freedom: The Civil War Era*. New York: Oxford University Press, 1988.

———. *For Cause and Comrades: Why Men Fought in the Civil War*. New York: Oxford University Press, 1997.

McPherson, Miller, Lynn Smith-Lovin, and Matthew E. Brashears. "Reply: Models and Marginals: Using Survey Evidence to Study Social Networks." *American Sociological Review* 74, no. 4 (2009): 670–81.

———. "Social Isolation in America: Changes in Core Discussion Networks over Two Decades." *American Sociological Review* 71, no. 3 (2006): 353–75.

———. "The Ties That Bind Are Fraying." *Contexts* 7, no. 3 (2008): 32–36.

Mead, George H. *Mind, Self, and Society: From the Standpoint of a Social Behaviorist*. Edited by Charles W. Morris. Chicago: University of Chicago Press, 1934.

Meeks, M. Douglas. *God the Economist: The Doctrine of God and Political Economy*. Minneapolis: Fortress Press, 2000.

Merrell, James H. "Amerindians and the New Republic." In *A Companion to the American Revolution*, edited by Jack P. Greene and J. R. Pole, 413–18. Malden, MA: Blackwell Publishers, 2000.

Messerschmidt, James W. *Nine Lives: Adolescent Masculinities, the Body, and Violence*. Boulder, CO: Westview Press, 2000.

Messner, Steven F., Eric P. Baumer, and Richard Rosenfeld. "Dimensions of Social Capital and Rates of Criminal Homicide." *American Sociological Review* 69, no. 6 (2004): 882–903.

Messner, Steven F., and Richard Rosenfeld. *Crime and the American Dream*. 3rd ed. Belmont, CA: Wadsworth, 2001.

Micklethwait, John, and Adrian Wooldridge. *The Right Nation: Conservative Power in America*. New York: Penguin Press, 2004.

Miller, Zell. *A Deficit of Decency*. Macon, GA: Stroud and Hall Publishers, 2005.

Millis, Harry A., and Emily Clark Brown. *From the Wagner Act to Taft-Hartley: A Study of National Labor Policy and Labor Relations*. Chicago: University of Chicago Press, 1950.

Mills, C. Wright. *The Sociological Imagination*. New York: Oxford University Press, 1959.

Mills, Kathryn, ed. *C. Wright Mills: Letters and Autobiographical Writings*. Berkeley: University of California Press, 2000.

Mills, Nicolaus. "The Culture of Triumph and the Spirit of the Times." In *Culture in an Age of Money: The Legacy of the 1980s in America*, edited by Nicolaus Mills, 11–28. Chicago: Ivan R. Dee, 1990.

Miringoff, Marc, and Marque-Luisa Miringoff. *The Social Health of the Nation: How America Is Really Doing*. New York: Oxford University Press, 1999.

Mishel, Lawrence, Jared Bernstein, and Heidi Shierholz. *The State of Working America: 2008–2009*. Ithaca, NY: ILR / Cornell University Press, 2009.

Montopoli, Brian. "Poll: Support for Same Sex Marriage Grows." *CBS News*, April 27, 2009. www.cbsnews.com/8301-503544_162-4972643-503544 .html?tag=mncol;lst;1.

Morgenson, Gretchen. "Are Enrons Bustin' Out All Over?" *New York Times*, May 28, 2006.

MOW International Research Team. *The Meaning of Work*. London: Academic Press, 1987.

Moynihan, Daniel P. "A Dahrendorf Inversion and the Twilight of the Family: The Challenge to the Conference." In *The Future of the Family*, edited by Daniel P. Moynihan, Timothy M. Smeeding, and Lee Rainwater, xiii–xxviii. New York: Russell Sage, 2004.

Myrdal, Gunnar. *An American Dilemma: The Negro Problem and Modern Democracy*. New York: Harper and Brothers, 1944.

The National Highway Safety Administration. *National Survey of Speeding and Unsafe Driving Attitude and Behaviors: 2002*. Washington, DC: U.S. Department of Transportation, 2002.

The National Institute of Mental Health. "Youth in a Difficult World." National Institutes of Health, 2006. http://nimh.nih.gov.

Nee, Victor, and Richard Swedberg, eds. *The Economic Sociology of Capitalism*. Princeton, NJ: Princeton University Press, 2005.

Nemeth, Roger J., and Donald A. Luidens. "The Religious Basis of Charitable Giving in America: A Social Capital Perspective." In *Religion as Social Capital Producing the Common Good*, edited by Corwin Smidt, 107–20. Waco, TX: Baylor University Press, 2003.

Nestle, Marion. *Food Politics: How the Food Industry Influences Nutrition and Health*. Berkeley: University of California Press, 2002.

Newman, Katherine S. *Falling from Grace: The Experience of Downward Mobility in the American Middle Class*. New York: Free Press, 1988.

———. "Uncertain Seas: Cultural Turmoil and the Domestic Economy." In *America at Century's End*, edited by Alan Wolfe, 112–30. Berkeley: University of California Press, 1991.

Nie, Norman H. "Sociability, Interpersonal Relations, and the Internet: Reconciling Conflicting Findings." *American Behavioral Scientist* 45, no. 3 (2001): 420–35.

Nie, Norman H., D. Sunshine Hillygus, and Lutz Erbring. "Internet Use, Interpersonal Relations, and Sociability: A Time Diary Study." In *The Internet in Everyday Life*, edited by Barry Wellman and Caroline A. Haythornthwaite, 215–44. Malden, MA: Blackwell, 2002.

Novak, Michael. *The Spirit of Democratic Capitalism*. New York: Simon and Schuster, 1982.

Nunes, Paul, and Brian Johnson. *Mass Affluence: Seven New Rules of Marketing to Today's Consumer*. Boston: Harvard Business School Press, 2004.

O'Beirne, Kate. *Women Who Make the World Worse: And How Their Radical Feminist Assault Is Ruining Our Families, Military, Schools, and Sports*. New York: Sentinel, 2006.

Oliver, Melvin L., and Thomas M. Shapiro. *Black Wealth/White Wealth: A New Perspective on Racial Inequality*. New York: Routledge, 1995.

One Touch. "Maddy." One Touch: Our Commitment, 2008. www.onetouch diabetes.com/our_commitment.

O'Reilly, Bill. *Culture Warrior*. New York: Broadway Publishers, 2006.

"Overweight and Obesity: Obesity Trends: U.S. Obesity Trends, 1985–2004." Centers for Disease Control and Prevention, 2006. www.cdc.gov/nccdphp/ dnpa/obesity.

Parenti, Michael. *Democracy for the Few*. 6th ed. New York: St. Martin's Press, 1995.

Patterson, James. *Grand Expectations: The United States, 1945–1974*. New York: Oxford University Press, 1996.

Patterson, Orlando. "About Public Sociology." In *Public Sociology: Fifteen Eminent Sociologists Debate Politics and the Profession in the Twenty-first Century*, edited by Dan Clawson, Robert Zussman, Joya Misra, Naomi Gerstel, Randall Stokes, Douglas L. Anderton, et al., 176–94. Berkeley: University of California Press, 2007.

———. "A Poverty of the Mind." *New York Times*, March 26, 2006.

———. "Taking Culture Seriously: A Framework and an Afro-American Illustration." In *Culture Matters*, edited by Lawrence E. Harrison and Samuel P. Huntington, 202–18. New York: Basic Books, 2000.

Paxton, Pamela. "Is Social Capital Declining in the United States? A Multiple Indicator Assessment." *American Journal of Sociology* 105, no. 1 (1999): 88–127.

———. "Social Capital and Democracy: An Interdependent Relationship." *American Sociological Review* 67, no. 2 (2002): 254–77.

———. "Trust in Decline?" *Contexts* 4, no. 1 (2005): 40–46.

PBS. "Interview with Ellen Galinsky." *Frontline*, 2009, www.pbs.org/wgbh/pages/frontline/shows/teenbrain/interviews/galinsky.html.

Pearson, Christine M., Lynne M. Andersson, and Christine L. Porath. "Assessing and Attacking Workplace Incivility." *Organizational Dynamics* 29, no. 2 (2000): 123–48.

Pearson, Christine M., and Christine L. Porath. "On the Nature, Consequences and Remedies of Workplace Incivility: No Time for 'Nice'? Think Again." *Academy of Management Executive* 19, no. 1 (2005): 1–12.

Pentagon Papers: The Defense Department History of United States Decision-making on Vietnam. The Senator Gravel Edition. Vols. 1–5. Boston: Beacon Press, 1972.

Perkins, Edwin J. "Socio-Economic Development of the Colonies." In *A Companion to the American Revolution*, edited by Jack P. Greene and J. R. Pole, 51–59. Malden, MA: Blackwell Publishers, 2000.

Perrow, Charles. *The Radical Attack on Business: A Critical Analysis*. New York: Harcourt Brace Jovanovich, 1972.

The Pew Research Center. "Less Opposition to Gay Marriage, Adoption and Military Service." The Pew Research Center for the People and the Press, March 22, 2006. http://people-press.org/report/273/less-opposition-to-gay-marriage-adoption-and-military-service.

Pinker, Steven. *The Blank Slate: The Modern Denial of Human Nature*. New York: Viking, 2002.

Pirkey, Melissa F. "The Social Genesis of Moral Consumption: How Social Groups Support Moral Consumers and Fight Off Care Fatigue." Paper presented at the annual meeting of the American Sociological Association, San Francisco, California, August 8, 2009.

Pitts, Leonard, Jr. "When the Laughing Stopped." *Philadelphia Inquirer*, November 22, 2007.

Plotke, David. *Building a Democratic Political Order: Reshaping American Liberalism in the 1930s and 1940s*. New York: Cambridge University Press, 1996.

Polanyi, Karl. *The Great Transformation*. Boston: Beacon Press, 1957.

———. *The Livelihood of Man*. Edited by Harry W. Pearson. New York: Academic Press, 1977.

Popenoe, David. "American Family Decline, 1960–1990: A Review and Appraisal." *Journal of Marriage and the Family* 55, no. 3 (1993): 526–55.

———. *Disturbing the Nest: Family Change and Decline in Modern Societies*. New York: Aldine de Gruyter, 1988.

———. *Life Without Father*. New York: Free Press, 1996.

———. "Modern Marriage: Revisiting the Cultural Script." In *The Gendered Society Reader*, edited by Michael S. Kimmel and Amy Aronson, 2nd ed., 170–86. New York: Oxford University Press, 2004.

Portes, Alejandro, and Robert D. Manning. "The Immigrant Enclave: Theory and Empirical Examples." In *Competitive Ethnic Relations*, edited by Susan Olzak and Joane Nagel, 43–59. Orlando: Academic Press, 1986.

Posner, Richard A. *A Failure of Capitalism: The Crisis of '08 and the Descent into Depression*. Cambridge, MA: Harvard University Press, 2009.

Postman, Neil. *Amusing Ourselves to Death: Public Discourse in the Age of Show Business*. New York: Viking, 1985.

"Progress and Perils: New Agenda for Women." Center for the Advancement of Women, 2003, www.advancewomen.org.

Public Agenda. "Land of the Rude: Americans in New Survey Say Lack of Respect Is Getting Worse." Public Agenda Press Release, April 3, 2002. www.publicagenda.org/press-releases/land-rude-americans-new-survey-say-lack-respect-getting-worse.

Putnam, Robert D. *Bowling Alone: The Collapse and Revival of American Community*. New York: Simon and Schuster, 2000.

Rainie, Lee, Jeffrey Boase, John Horrigan, Barry Wellman. "The Strength of Internet Ties." Pew Internet and American Life Project, January 25, 2006. www.pewinternet.org/Reports/2006/The-Strength-of-Internet-Ties.aspx.

Rainie, Lee, and Scott Keeter. "Pew Internet Project Data Memo: Cell Phone Use." Pew Internet and American Life Project, 2006. http://pewinternet.org.

Regan, Tom. "McCain Has His Own 'Pastor Problems.'" The NPR News Blog, February 29, 2008. www.npr.org/blogs/news/2008/02/mccain_has_his_own_pastor_prob.html.

Regnerus, Mark D., and Christian Smith. "Selective Deprivatization among American Religious Traditions: The Reversal of the Great Reversal." *Social Forces* 76, no. 4 (1998): 1347–72.

Regnerus, Mark D., Christian Smith, and David Sikkink. "Who Gives to the Poor? The Influence of Religious Tradition and Political Location on the Personal Generosity of Americans toward the Poor." *Journal for the Scientific Study of Religion* 37, no. 3 (1998): 481–93.

Reich, Robert B. "A Culture of Paper Tigers." In *Culture in an Age of Money: The Legacy of the 1980s in America*, edited by Nicolaus Mills, 95–108. Chicago: Ivan R. Dee, 1990.

———. "Does the Free Market Corrode Moral Character? We'd Rather Not Know." John Templeton Foundation, 2008. www.templeton.org/market/.

Richtel, Matt. "Dismissing the Risks of a Deadly Habit." *New York Times*, July 19, 2009.

Ricks, Thomas E. *Fiasco: The American Military Adventure in Iraq*. New York: Penguin, 2007.

Rieff, Philip. *The Triumph of the Therapeutic: Uses of Faith after Freud*. Chicago: University of Chicago Press, 1987.

Riesman, David. *The Lonely Crowd: A Study of the Changing American Character*. New Haven, CT: Yale University Press, 1950.

Ritzer, George. *The Globalization of Nothing*. Thousand Oaks, CA: Pine Forge Press, 2004.

———. *The McDonaldization of Society: An Investigation into the Changing Character of Contemporary Social Life*. Thousand Oaks, CA: Pine Forge, 1993.

———, ed. *McDonaldization: The Reader*. Thousand Oaks, CA: Pine Forge, 2002.

Rivlin, Gary. "The Millionaires Who Don't Feel Rich." *New York Times*, August 5, 2007.

Robinson, John P., and Geoffrey Godbey. *Time for Life: The Surprising Ways Americans Use Their Time*. University Park: Pennsylvania State University Press, 1997.

Roche, Eileen. "Do Something—He's About to Snap." *Harvard Business Review* 81, no. 7 (2003): 23–31.

Rorty, Richard. *Achieving Our Country: Leftist Thought in Twentieth-Century America*. Cambridge: Harvard University Press, 1998.

Rosen, Ruth. *The World Split Open: How the Modern Women's Movement Changed America*. New York: Viking, 2000.

Rosenfeld, Alvin A., and Nicole Wise. *The Over-Scheduled Child: Avoiding the Hyper-Parenting Trap*. New York: St. Martin's Griffin, 2000.

Rosenfeld, Richard. "Crime Decline in Context." *Contexts* 1, no. 1 (2002): 25–34.

Rosenthal, Howard. "Politics, Public Policy, and Inequality: A Look Back at the Twentieth Century." In *Social Inequality*, edited by Kathryn M. Neckerman, 861–92. New York: Russell Sage Foundation, 2004.

Roth, Mark. "Dissatisfaction Guaranteed—Consumers Seem to Be Getting Short-changed on Customer Service." *Pittsburgh Post-Gazette*, October 16, 2005.

Rubinson, Richard. "Class Formation, Politics, and Institutions: Schooling in the United States." *American Journal of Sociology* 92, no. 3 (1986): 519–38.

Ruggles, Steven. "The Transformation of American Family Structure." *The American Historical Review* 99, no. 1 (1994): 103–28.

Rumbaut, Rubén G. "Passages to America: Perspectives on the New Immigration." In *America at Century's End*, edited by Alan Wolfe, 208–44. Berkeley: University of California Press, 1991.

Rutten, Tim. "The Real 'Outrage' Behind AIG's Bonuses." *Los Angeles Times*, March 18, 2009. http://articles.latimes.com/2009/mar/18/opinion/oe-rutten18.

Sagario, Dawn. "Rudeness Can Hurt More Than Work Force's Feelings." *Times Union*, November 27, 2005.

Salaff, Janet W. "Where Home Is the Office: The New Form of Flexible Work." In *The Internet in Everyday Life*, edited by Barry Wellman and Caroline A. Haythornthwaite, 464–95. Malden, MA: Blackwell, 2002.

Salkin, Allen. "Pimp My Grill." *New York Times*, May 28, 2006.

Sampson, Robert J., Doug McAdam, Heather MacIndoe, and Simon Weffer-Elizondo. "Civil Society Reconsidered: The Durable Nature and Community Structure of Collective Civic Action." *American Journal of Sociology* 111, no. 3 (2005): 673–714.

Santorum, Rick. "Does the Free Market Corrode Moral Character? No." John Templeton Foundation, 2008. www.templeton.org/market/.

———. *It Takes a Family: Conservatism and the Common Good*. Wilmington, DL: ISI Books, 2005.

Schiff, Stacy. "Know It All: Can Wikipedia Conquer Expertise?" *New Yorker*, July 31, 2006.

Schlesinger, Arthur M., Jr. *The Coming of the New Deal*. Boston: Houghton Mifflin Company, 1959.

———. *The Politics of Upheaval*. Boston: Houghton Mifflin Company, 1960.

"School Daze: Kids, Computers and Sleep." National Sleep Foundation, 2003. www.sleepfoundation.org.

Schor, Juliet B. *Born to Buy: The Commercialized Child and the New Consumer Culture*. New York: Scribner, 2004.

———. *The Overspent American: Why We Want What We Don't Need*. New York: HarperPerennial, 1998.

———. *The Overworked American: The Unexpected Decline of Leisure*. New York: Basic Books, 1992.

Schrecker, Ellen. *Many Are the Crimes: McCarthyism in America*. Princeton, NJ: Princeton University Press, 1998.

Schulman, Bruce J. *The Seventies: The Great Shift in American Culture, Society and Politics*. Cambridge, MA: Da Capo, 2002.

Schwartz, Barry. *The Battle for Human Nature: Science, Morality, and Modern Life*. New York: W. W. Norton and Company, 1986.

———. *The Costs of Living: How Market Freedom Erodes the Best Things in Life*. New York: Xlibris, 2000.

———. *The Paradox of Choice: Why More Is Less*. New York: HarperCollins, 2004.

———. *Queuing and Waiting: Studies in the Social Organization of Access and Delay*. Chicago: University of Chicago Press, 1975.

Schwartz, Shalom H., and Sipke Huismans. "Value Priorities and Religiosity in Four Western Religions." *Social Psychological Quarterly* 58, no. 2 (1995): 88–107.

Schweitzer, Mary M. "The Economic and Demographic Consequences of the American Revolution." In *A Companion to the American Revolution*, edited by Jack P. Greene and J. R. Pole, 560–78. Malden, MA: Blackwell Publishers, 2000.

Sennett, Richard. *The Corrosion of Character: The Personal Consequences of Work in the New Capitalism*. New York: W. W. Norton, 1998.

———. *The Culture of the New Capitalism*. New Haven, CT: Yale University Press, 2006.

———. *The Fall of Public Man*. New York: Vintage, 1977.

Sesno, Frank. "Poll: Most Americans Fear Vulnerability of Oil Supply." *CNN*, March 16, 2006. www.cnn.com/2006/US/03/16/oil.poll/index.html.

Sewell, William, Jr. "A Theory of Structure: Duality, Agency and Transformation." *American Journal of Sociology* 98, no. 1 (1992): 1–29.

Shapiro, Thomas M. *The Hidden Cost of Being African American: How Wealth Perpetuates Inequality*. New York: Oxford University Press, 2004.

Shellenbarger, Sue. "Colleges Ward Off Overinvolved Parents." wjs.com, July 19, 2005.

Shenk, Joshua Wolf. "What Makes Us Happy?" *Atlantic Monthly*, June 2009.

Shields, David. "The Emergence of Civic Culture in the Colonies to about 1770." In *A Companion to the American Revolution*, edited by Jack P. Greene and J. R. Pole, 82–87. Malden, MA: Blackwell Publishers, 2000.

Siegel, Lee. *Against the Machine: Being Human in the Age of the Electronic Mob*. New York: Spiegel and Grau, 2008.

Sigle-Rushton, Wendy, and Sara McLanahan. "Father Absence and Child Well-Being: A Critical Review." In *The Future of the Family*, edited by Daniel P. Moynihan, Timothy M. Smeeding, and Lee Rainwater, 116–58. New York: Russell Sage, 2004.

Singer, Natasha. "Is Looking Your Age Taboo?" *New York Times*, March 1, 2007.

Singer, Peter. *The Life You Can Save: Acting Now to End World Poverty*. New York: Random House, 2009.

Sirianni, Carmen, and Andrea Walsh. "Through the Prism of Time: Temporal Structures in Postindustrial America." In *America at Century's End*, edited by Alan Wolfe, 421–39. Berkeley: University of California Press, 1991.

Sitkoff, Harvard. *The New Deal for Blacks: The Emergence of Civil Rights as a National Issue*. New York: Oxford University Press, 1978.

Skocpol, Theda. "Advocates without Members: The Recent Transformation of American Civic Life." In *Civic Engagement in American Democracy*, edited by Theda Skocpol and Morris P. Fiorina, 461–510. Washington, DC: Brookings Institution Press, 1999.

———. *Diminished Democracy: From Membership to Management in American Civic Life*. Norman: University of Oklahoma Press, 2003.

———. "How Americans Became Civic." In *Civic Engagement in American Democracy*, edited by Theda Skocpol and Morris P. Fiorina, 27–80. Washington, DC: Brookings Institution Press, 1999.

Smeeding, Timothy M., Daniel P. Moynihan, and Lee Rainwater. "The Challenge of Family System Changes for Research and Policy." In *The Future of the Family*, edited by Daniel P. Moynihan, Timothy M. Smeeding, and Lee Rainwater, 1–24. New York: Russell Sage, 2004.

Smidt, Corwin, ed. *Religion as Social Capital: Producing the Common Good*. Waco, TX: Baylor University Press, 2003.

Solnit, Rebecca. *A Paradise Built in Hell: The Extraordinary Communities That Arise in Disaster*. New York: Viking, 2009.

Solomon, Sheldon, Jeff Greenberg, and Tom Pyszczynski. "Fear of Death and Social Behavior: The Anatomy of Human Destructiveness." In *Evolutionary Psychology and Violence: A Primer for Policymakers and Public Policy Advocates*, edited by N. Dess and R. Bloom, 129–56. Westport, CT: Greenwood / Praeger, 2003.

———. "Tales from the Crypt: On the Role of Death in Life." *Zygon* 33, no. 1 (1998): 9–43.

Spiegel, Lynn. *Make Room for TV: Television and the Family Ideal in Postwar America*. Chicago: University of Chicago Press, 1992.

Stacey, Judith. "Backward toward the Postmodern Family: Reflections on Gender, Kinship, and Class in the Silicon Valley." In *America at Century's End*, edited by Alan Wolfe, 17–35. Berkeley: University of California, 1991.

———. *Brave New Families: Stories of Domestic Upheaval in Late Twentieth-Century America*. New York: Basic Books, 1990.

———. *In the Name of the Family: Rethinking Family Values in the Postmodern Age*. Boston: Beacon Press, 1996.

Starr, Paul. *The Creation of the Media: Political Origins of Modern Communications*. New York: Basic Books, 2004.

St. John, Warren. "Hey Coach, Do You Need a Time Out?" *New York Times*, October 15, 2006.

Stout, Maureen. *The Feel-Good Curriculum: The Dumbing-Down of America's Kids in the Name of Self-Esteem*. Cambridge, MA: Perseus Books, 2000.

Struening, Karen. *New Family Values: Liberty, Equality, and Diversity*. New York: Rowman and Littlefield, 2002.

Super, Donald E. and Branimir Sverko, eds. *Life Roles, Values and Careers: International Findings of the Work Importance Study*. San Francisco: Jossey-Bass, 1995.

Svallfors, Stefan. *The Moral Economy of Class: Class and Attitudes in Comparative Perspective*. Stanford, CA: Stanford University Press, 2006.

Sykes, Charles J. *Dumbing Down Our Kids: Why America's Children Feel Good about Themselves but Can't Read, Write, or Add*. New York: St. Martin's Press, 1995.

Taylor, Mark C. "End the University as We Know It." *New York Times*, April 27, 2009.

Taylor, Paul, Cary Funk, and April Clark. "Americans and Social Trust: Who, Where and Why." Pew Research Center, February 22, 2007. http://pew research.org/pubs/414/americans-and-social-trust-who-where-and-why.

———. "Generation Gap in Values and Behaviors as Marriage and Parenthood Drift Apart, Public Is Concerned about Social Impact." Pew Research Center, July 1, 2007. http://pewresearch.org/assets/social/pdf/Marriage.pdf.

———. "Luxury or Necessity? Things We Can't Live Without: The List Has Grown in the Past Decades." Pew Research Center, December 14, 2006. http://pewsocialtrends.org/assets/pdf/Luxury.pdf.

Thomas, Cal. "Where Are Reagan's Successors?" *Saratogian*, June 9, 2009.

Thompson, Maxine Seaborn, Karl L. Alexander, and Doris R. Entwisle. "Household Composition, Parental Expectations, and School Achievement." *Social Forces* 67, no. 2 (1988): 424–51.

Thompson, Maxine Seaborn, Doris R. Entwisle, Karl L. Alexander, and M. Jane Sundius. "The Influence of Family Composition on Children's Conformity to the Student Role." *American Educational Research Journal* 29, no. 2 (1992): 405–24.

Tiggemann, Marika, and Belinda McGill. "The Role of Social Comparison in the Effect of Magazine Advertisements on Women's Mood and Body Dissatisfaction." *Journal of Social and Clinical Psychology* 23, no. 1 (2004): 23–44.

Tocqueville, Alexis de. *Democracy in America*. New York: Schicken Books, 1970 (1835).

"Trash Mountain." *New York Times*, June 3, 2007.

Trinkaus, John. "Stop Sign Compliance: A Final Look." *Perpetual and Motor Skills* 85, no. 1 (1997): 217–18.

Truss, Lynne. *Talk to the Hand: The Utter Bloody Rudeness of the World Today, or, Six Good Reasons to Stay Home and Bolt the Door*. New York: Gotham Books, 2005.

Tuchman, Gaye. "Pluralism and Disdain: American Culture Today." In *America at Century's End*, edited by Alan Wolfe, 340–58. Berkeley: University of California Press, 1991.

"2001–2002 National Epidemiological Survey on Alcohol and Related Conditions." National Institute on Alcohol Abuse and Alcoholism, 2004. www.beersoaksamerica.org.

"2006 American Community Survey." U.S. Census Bureau, 2007. www.census.gov/acs.

Uchitelle, Louis. *The Disposable American: Layoffs and Their Consequences*. New York: Alfred A. Knopf, 2006.

U.S. Bureau of Justice Statistics. "Key Crimes and Justice Facts at a Glance." U.S. Department of Justice, 2007. www.justice.gov.

U.S. Department of Health and Human Services. *Mental Health: A Report of the Surgeon General—Executive Summary*. Rockville, MD: U.S. Department of Health and Human Services, Substance Abuse and Mental Health Services Administration, Center for Mental Health Services, National Institutes of Health, 1999.

Varon, Jeremy. "Between Revolution 9 and Thesis 11: Or, Will We Learn (Again) to Start Worrying and Change the World?" In *The New Left Revisited*, edited by John McMillian and Paul Buhle, 214–40. Philadelphia: Temple University Press, 2003.

Wade, Erin. "Eight Ways to Avoid 'Helicopter Parenting.'" kvue.com, August 15, 2005.

Wainwright, Martin. "Emails 'Pose Threat to IQ.'" *Guardian*, April 22, 2005.

Waite, Linda J., and Maggie Gallagher. *The Case for Marriage: Why Married People Are Happier, Healthier and Better Off Financially*. New York: Doubleday, 2000.

Wald, Matthew L. "Temper Cited as Cause of 28,000 Road Deaths a Year." *New York Times*, July 18, 1997.

Wallerstein, Immanuel. *The Modern World—System*. Vol. 1. New York: Academic Press, 1974.

Wallis, Claudia. "The Multitasking Generation." *Time*, March 27, 2006, 48–55.

Walsh, Charles. "Civilization Grumpily Faces a Rude Awakening." *Connecticut Post*, December 15, 2005.

Walzer, Michael. "Does the Free Market Corrode Moral Character? Of Course It Does." John Templeton Foundation, 2008. www.templeton.org/market/.

Walzer, Susan. *Thinking about the Baby: Gender and Transitions into Parenthood*. Philadelphia: Temple University Press, 1998.

Warner, Judith. "Kids Gone Wild." *New York Times*, November 27, 2005.

———. "Loosen the Apron Strings." *New York Times*, July 20, 2006.

———. *Perfect Madness: Motherhood in the Age of Anxiety*. New York: Riverhead Books, 2005.

Weber, Max. *The Protestant Ethic and the Spirit of Capitalism*. Translated by Stephen Kalberg. 3rd ed. New York: Oxford University Press, 2002.

Weich, Susan. "Football Dad, Brother Face Charges in Taser Incident." *St. Louis Post-Dispatch*, October 11, 2006.

Wellman, Barry, Anabel Quan Haase, James Witte, and Keith Hampton. "Does the Internet Increase, Decrease or Supplement Social Capital? Social Networks, Participation, and Community Commitment." *American Behavioral Scientist* 45, no. 3 (2001): 436–55.

Wellman, Barry, and Scot Wortley. "Different Strokes from Different Folks: Community Ties and Social Support." *American Journal of Sociology* 96, no. 3 (1990): 558–88.

Whybrow, Peter C. *American Mania: When More Is Not Enough*. New York: W. W. Norton and Company, 2005.

———. *A Mood Apart: Depression, Mania, and Other Afflictions of the Self*. New York: Basic Books, 1997.

Whyte, William H., Jr. *The Organization Man*. New York: Simon and Schuster, 1956.

Williams, Alex. "The Lost Summer: For the College-Bound, the Grind Is Endless." *New York Times*, June 4, 2006.

Wilson, James Q. *The Moral Sense*. New York: Free Press, 1993.

Wilson, William Julius. *The Declining Significance of Race: Blacks and Changing American Institutions*. Chicago: University of Chicago Press, 1978.

———. *The Truly Disadvantaged: The Inner City, the Underclass, and Public Policy*. Chicago: University of Chicago Press, 1987.

———. *When Work Disappears: The World of the New Urban Poor*. New York: Vintage Books, 1996.

Wolf, Naomi. *The Beauty Myth: How Images of Beauty Are Used against Women*. New York: Perennial, 2002.

Wolfe, Alan. *Does American Democracy Still Work?* New Haven, CT: Yale University Press, 2006.

———. *Marginalized in the Middle*. Chicago: University of Chicago Press, 1996.

————. *Moral Freedom: The Search for Virtue in a World of Choice*. New York: W. W. Norton, 2001.

————. *One Nation, After All: What Middle-Class Americans Really Think About: God, Country, Family, Racism, Welfare, Immigration, Homosexuality, Work, the Right, the Left, and Each Other*. New York: Viking, 1998.

————. *The Transformation of American Religion: How We Actually Live Our Faith*. New York: Free Press, 2003.

————. *Whose Keeper? Social Science and Moral Obligation*. Berkeley: University of California Press, 1989.

Wolfe, Douglas A. "Demography, Public Policy, and 'Problem' Families." In *The Future of the Family*, edited by Daniel P. Moynihan, Timothy M. Smeeding, and Lee Rainwater, 171–80. New York: Russell Sage, 2004.

Wolff, Edward N. *Recent Trends in Household Wealth in the United States: Rising Debt and the Middle-Class Squeeze*. New York: The Levy Economics Institute of Bard College, 2007.

Woodward, Bob. "Ten Take Aways from the Bush Years." *Washington Post*, January 18, 2009.

"The World Factbook." Central Intelligence Agency, 2006. www.cia.gov/library/publications/the-world-factbook/index.html.

"The World Factbook." Central Intelligence Agency, 2008. www.cia.gov/library/publications/the-world-factbook/index.html.

Wright, Erik Olin. *Classes*. London: Verso, 1985.

Wuthnow, Robert. *Communities of Discourse: Ideology and Social Structure in the Reformation, the Enlightenment, and European Socialism*. Cambridge, MA: Harvard University Press, 1989.

————. *The Restructuring of American Religion: Society and Faith since World War II*. Princeton, NJ: Princeton University Press, 1988.

————. *Saving America? Faith-Based Services and the Future of Civil Society*. Princeton, NJ: Princeton University Press, 2004.

————. *Sharing the Journey: Support Groups and America's New Quest for Community*. New York: Free Press, 1994.

Zakaria, Fareed. "The Capitalist Manifesto: Greed Is Good (to a Point)." *Newsweek*, June 22, 2009.

Zandi, Mark. *Financial Shock: A 360° Look at the Subprime Mortgage Implosion, and How to Avoid the Next Financial Crisis*. Upper Saddle River, NJ: Financial Times Press, 2009.

Zetter, Kim. "Lori Drew Not Guilty of Felonies in Landmark Cyberbullying Trial." Wired.com, 2008.

Zuckerbrod, Nancy. "House of Representatives Passes Bill to Limit Online Gambling." *Saratogian*, July 12, 2006, 8.

INDEX

ABOUT THE AUTHOR

John Brueggemann is professor of sociology and holds the Quadracci Chair in Social Responsibility at Skidmore College. His writing and teaching focus on issues of class, race, inequality, religion, and social change. He is the coauthor of *Racial Competition and Class Solidarity*. His written work has also appeared in *Social Problems, Work and Occupations, Social Science History*, the *Journal of Contemporary Ethnography, Critical Sociology*, and *Theology Today*. He lives in Saratoga Springs, New York.

Breinigsville, PA USA
05 July 2010
241148BV00003B/2/P

9 781442 200937